THE
VIETNAM
HEARINGS

WITH AN INTRODUCTION BY

J. WILLIAM FULBRIGHT

Chairman, United States Senate Committee on Foreign Relations

VINTAGE BOOKS

A Division of Random House New York

Publisher's Note

Because of the importance of the hearings on the war in Vietnam conducted before the Senate Committee on Foreign Relations, Random House has arranged to bring out this special edition of the proceedings. This volume contains the complete statements of Secretary of State Dean Rusk, Lieutenant General James M. Gavin, former Ambassador George F. Kennan, and General Maxwell D. Taylor. Also included are extensive excerpts from their testimony. The questions put by the members of the Committee, and the responses by the witnesses, have been edited by the publisher to include all significant material bearing directly on the grave political questions raised by American participation in the war in Vietnam. The statement and testimony of David E. Bell, Administrator of the Agency for International Development, who appeared before the Committee on February 4, 1966, have been omitted because they relate primarily to the technical aspects of an Administration request for additional economic aid and deal only peripherally with the political considerations to which the Committee directed itself with the other witnesses. Mr. Bell's testimony as well as the complete report of proceedings are available in a Senate Foreign Relations Committee official document.

The hearings were conducted on January 28, February 4, February 8, February 10, February 17, and February 18, 1966. The members of the Committee participating were: Senators John D. Sparkman (Ala.), Wayne Morse (Ore.), Russell Long (La.), Albert Gore (Tenn.), Frank D. Lausche (Ohio), Frank Church (Idaho), Stuart Symington (Mo.), Thomas E. Dodd (Conn.), Joseph Clark (Pa.), Claiborne Pell (R.I.), Eugene McCarthy (Minn.), Burke Hickenlooper (Iowa), George D. Aiken (Vt.), Frank Carlson (Kans.), John J. Williams (Del.), Karl E. Mundt (S. Dak.), and Clifford P. Case (N.J.); Senator J. William Fulbright (Ark.), Chairman of the Committee, presided.

Contents

Contents

Introduction

In the weeks immediately following six days of public hearings on the situation in Vietnam, the Committee on Foreign Relations received over twenty thousand letters and telegrams from American citizens. None of these communications were the result of organized letter-writing campaigns. A few were scurrilous, but 99 per cent were thoughtful outpourings from every part of America. Some letters supported the position taken by Administration witnesses who sought to justify the involvement of over three hundred thousand Americans on the land and sea and in the air of Vietnam. Others were critical of American involvement in Vietnam. Despite deep differences of opinion on American policy in Vietnam, there was nearly unanimous agreement that the hearings had served the national interest. They seem to have filled a deeply felt need on the part of Americans for an exploration of the reasons why the United States was once again involved in a war thousands of miles from home.

Television coverage of these hearings undoubtedly contributed to public interest. The Committee on Foreign Relations had no control over the extent of such coverage, since public committee hearings are reported by the press, radio, and television at their option, not at the stimulation or invitation of the committee. I believe American news media performed a most worthwhile service in their complete coverage of the testimony of three pro-Administration witnesses (Secretary of State Dean Rusk, AID Administrator David E. Bell, and General Maxwell D. Taylor, Ret.) and two non-Administration witnesses (Lieutenant General James M. Gavin and Dr. George F. Kennan, former U.S. Ambassador to the Soviet Union). Without breaching national security, these witnesses discussed with members of the Committee, and indirectly with the American people, the fundamental foreign policy questions raised by American involvement in Vietnam—a situation which could develop into World War Three.

In the case of a perplexing problem like Vietnam the government can forge ahead on the basis of executive decision, ignoring differences within the body politic or attempting to paper them over, or it can stimulate frank and open discussion. The first course is initially easier, but has within it the seeds of weakness because it ignores differences of view and is founded on an artificial consensus. The second course, the one chosen by the Committee in its hearings, may be initially painful, but it contains elements of strength because it brings differences into the open and initiates a process from which a real consensus may develop.

One can hardly be reminded too often that no policy can be long sustained unless it is supported by a valid consensus. Thus, it can reasonably be argued that even though a consensus does not emerge, the hearings have been useful in demonstrating that one does not exist. The fact that the country is divided over Vietnam policy is not a result of the hearings. The division existed prior to the hearings, and it is better that its extent be known sooner rather than later.

The statements and testimony, which Random House has brought together in this volume, speak for themselves.

They show elected representatives of the American people prodding officials of the Executive branch of our government for answers to difficult questions of national policy. They allow distinguished former government officials with special knowledge and background to present their views and submit them to critical examination. They provide the American people with the raw material upon which they must base their judgment of the efficacy of national policy in serving the national interest. In the British Parliament, the oldest institution of its kind, the ministers are required to respond publicly to questions of the members. The hearings on Vietnam provided a similar opportunity, upon a restricted scale, although some of the principal government witnesses will not appear in public hearings, that is, the Vice-President, the Secretary of Defense, and the Director of the CIA.

Some who watched and attended the hearings and others who will read this volume may believe that there exists a body of secret information which gives officials in the Executive branch of our government special insight which enables them better to determine courses of action which will serve the national interest. This is questionable. I do not deny that there are times when officers of our Departments of State and Defense have in their possession secret information which should not be divulged, information which sometimes may be crucial in deciding upon courses of action. Our growing involvement in Vietnam and the question of whether that involvement serves the interests of the United States is hardly a case to be decided upon the basis of information not available to the conscientious citizen. On national issues of this kind decisions turn not upon available facts but upon judgment. There is no secret information or magical formula which gives Presidential advisors wisdom and judgment on broad policy but which is not available to the intelligent citizen.

Members of Congress and citizens at large do not have the facts or the background to tell the Commander-in-

Chief how to wage war; but they do have the capacity to pass judgment on whether the massive deployment and destruction of their men and their wealth seems to serve their over-all interests as a nation. That is what democratic government is all about. If the American people as a whole, in speaking through their elected representatives, do not have the capacity to know what is good for them in the larger theater of world relationships, then we should abandon the democratic system.

As to the outcome of the war, there is no certainty that a total military victory would serve our national interest; often in the past the results of total victory have been disappointing. The men who wrote our Constitution realized that fact and, being unwilling to rely on the omnipotence of any individual, vested the power to declare war in the Congress, where the national will is most likely to be faithfully reflected, and through which the people can at least share in the responsibility for having declared and approved it.

I believe a reading of these hearings will show that the United States government, because of small steps considered tactical or tentative in nature when they were taken, now finds that to all intents and purposes the nation is at war, without there ever having been a national decision, a national commitment to war. It is for that reason that the nation finds itself, at the time of these hearings, involved in a divisive debate. To the men in the fields, we are at "war." To those who have had their careers interrupted and their hopes blasted, we are at "war." To the budget-makers, the "war" in Vietnam takes priority over all domestic and social activities. But war has not been declared. I know, however, as should all Americans, that the open-endedness of our present involvement is a potentially creeping escalation, which, if continued at the present rate, will engulf the international and domestic life of the nation so completely as to require a national commitment that can be given by a declaration of war.

In *The Mysterious Stranger* Mark Twain wrote the following on war:

> There has never been a just one, never an honorable one, on the part of the instigator of the war. I can see a million years ahead, and this rule will never change in so many as half a dozen. The loud little handful, as usual, will shout for the war. The pulpit will, warily and cautiously, object at first; the great, big, dull bulk of the nation will rub its sleepy eyes and try to make out why there should be a war and will say, earnestly and indignantly, it is unjust and dishonorable and there is no necessity for it. Then the handful will shout louder. A few fair men on the other side will argue and reason against the war with speech in hand and at first will get a hearing and be applauded, but it will not last long. Those others will outshout them, and presently the anti-war audiences will thin out and lose popularity. Before long you will see this curious thing—speakers stoned from the platform and free speech strangled by hordes of furious men who, in their secret hearts, are still at one with those stoned speakers as earlier, but do not dare to say so. And now the whole nation, pulpit and all, will take up the war cry, shout itself hoarse, and mob any honest man who ventures to open his mouth. Presently, such mouths will cease to open. Next, the state will invent cheap lies, putting the blame upon the nation that is attacked, and every man will be glad of those conscience-soothing vanities and will diligently study them and refuse to examine any refutation of them, and thus he will, by and by, convince himself that the war is just and will thank God for the better sleep he enjoys after this process of grotesque self-deception.

Past experience provides little basis for confidence that reason can prevail in an atmosphere of mounting war fever. In a contest between a hawk and a dove the hawk has a great advantage, not because it is a better bird, but because it is a bigger bird with lethal talons and a highly developed will to use them. In China this is the Year of the Horse; in America it appears to be the Year of the Hawk.

Without illusions of the prospect of success, we must try, nonetheless, to bring reason and restraint to the emotionally-charged atmosphere in which the Vietnamese war is now being discussed. Instead of trading epithets about the legitimacy of debate, about who is and is not giving aid and comfort to the enemy, we would do well to focus calmly and deliberately on the issue itself, recognizing that all of us make mistakes and that mistakes can be corrected only if they are acknowledged and discussed, and recognizing further that war is not its own justification, that it can and must be discussed unless we are prepared to sacrifice our traditional democratic processes to a false image of national unanimity.

Our democratic heritage demands that American involvement in Vietnam be discussed before it is too late. These hearings have provided a basis for such discussion.

J. WILLIAM FULBRIGHT
Washington, D. C.
March, 1966

The **Vietnam Hearings**

The Statement and Testimony of

SECRETARY OF STATE

Dean Rusk*

Friday, 28 January 1966

SECRETARY RUSK: . . . I am pleased to be here this morning and I understand very fully the circumstances with regard to our schedule. I am especially glad to have Mr. David Bell, Administrator of AID, with me because among some other things he has spent some time in Southeast Asia, in South Vietnam and in Laos and in Thailand, three countries that make up a very important part of this proposed supplement. But I am pleased to appear before the Committee to support the President's request to authorize appropriation of supplemental funds request, a major portion of this request, $275 million in supporting assistance funds, arises from the continuing and bitter struggle in Vietnam.

In March, 1947, in connection with our then assistance to Greece, which was under guerrilla attack, President Truman stated that, "I believe that it must be the policy of the U.S. to support free peoples who are resisting at-

---

* Secretary of State Rusk was accompanied by David E. Bell (Administrator, Agency for International Development) and Rutherford M. Poats (Assistant Administrator, Far East, Agency for International Development).

tempted subjugation by armed minorities or by outside pressures." That is the policy we are applying in Vietnam in connection with specific commitments which we have taken in connection with that country. The heart of the problem in South Vietnam is the effort of North Vietnam to impose its will by force. For that purpose Hanoi has infiltrated into South Vietnam large quantities of arms and tens of thousands of trained and armed men, including units of the North Vietnamese regular army. It is that external aggression, which the North has repeatedly escalated, that is responsible for the presence of U.S. combat forces.

While assisting the South Vietnamese to repel this aggression, the United States has made persistent efforts to find a peaceful solution. The initiatives for peace undertaken by us and by many other governments during the last five years are almost innumerable. You are familiar with the vigorous and far-reaching peace probes which the United States has made during the past month, which I have had a chance to discuss with the Committee in executive session. None has brought a positive or encouraging response from Hanoi. Indeed, during this period— and while the South Vietnamese and ourselves refrained from bombing North Vietnam—the infiltrations from the North have continued, and the Communists have continued both their military operations and their campaigns of terror in the South. Even during the *Tet* "cease-fire" there were approximately a hundred attacks on South Vietnamese, ROK, and U.S. forces.

The United States has a clear and direct commitment to the security of South Vietnam against external attack. The integrity of our commitments is absolutely essential to the preservation of peace right around the globe. At stake also is the still broader question: whether aggression is to be permitted, once again, to succeed. We know from painful experience that aggression feeds on aggression.

A central issue in the dispute between the two leading Communist powers today is to what extent it is effective—

and prudent—to use force to promote the spread of Communism. If the bellicose doctrines of the Asian Communists should reap a substantial reward, the outlook for peace in this world would be grim indeed. The steady purpose of the United States is to build a world in which all nations—large and small, rich and poor—can progress in peace, secure against external interference. In Vietnam we shall continue to seek a peaceful solution—but we shall do what is necessary to assist the South Vietnamese to repel the aggression against them. As President Johnson put it just last week: "The door of peace must be kept wide open for all who wish to avoid the scourge of war, but the door of aggression must be closed and bolted if man himself is to survive."

The challenge in Vietnam demands the selective application of our U.S. military power in support of the forces of the government of Vietnam. There is no alternative—except defeat and surrender—in the absence of a willingness on the part of the other side to sit down and make a a peace to meet this force with force.

The free Vietnam we seek to preserve through military efforts and sacrifices must not be undermined by economic and social chaos and despair. The expanding scale of Communist aggression and our military response have added new dimensions to the task of AID. Without our AID programs we could win the major military battles in Vietnam and still lose the war and the peace. For this reason I regard our economic assistance programs in Vietnam as equal in importance with our military assistance. We fully intend to reinforce the economic and social progress that South Vietnam has been making during a brutal war and in spite of unremitting destructive efforts by the enemy. We can only help those who wish to defend and strengthen their freedom and to build a better future. The struggle—and the choice—is ultimately theirs to make. The South Vietnamese must believe that they and we are fighting for something worth great sacrifice. It is not enough to fight against something. All the people still able to make this choice in South Vietnam—farmers, school-teachers, merchants, workers, mothers, students, police, soldiers, and government officials—must know that the long struggle is worth their suffering and personal trage-dies. They must know that by this hard course their future will be better than their past.

The first essential, in Vietnam, of course, is security against Viet Cong terror and murder. The second is a unifying spirit or cause to which the people can subscribe, in the hamlets and in the cities. In this spirit the villager and his local leaders and the security forces can cooperate to build ever expanding areas of progress and resistance to Communist appeals and threats. In this spirit the people of the cities can cooperate with their government in devoting their talents and efforts to strengthening the nation against those who would destroy or enslave it. These essential con-ditions of success in Vietnam sound commonplace to Americans. In Vietnam their achievement requires per-formance—now—by government in responding to the needs of the people and creating a partnership with the people. These are basic needs: security, social justice, a chance to grow and market crops at fair prices, protection of the value of incomes, safe water and medical care, and education for the children. With our help and that of other free nations, enlightened elements in South Viet-nam are bringing about this social revolution in the midst of war. The government of Vietnam, in Saigon and in the countryside, is struggling with great handicaps to carry out this constructive effort, which it calls "rural construc-tion." This, coupled with the military defense against the Viet Cong forces, is the heart of our joint strategy.

Without our economic assistance, the entire effort to maintain a sound economy and to build for the future would quickly fail. Destructive inflation would be spawned by the Vietnamese government's necessarily mounting budget and by the wartime dislocations of the economy. Supplies for the rural development program could not be obtained or shipped. Internal transportation, communications, electricity, and other essential services disrupted or overloaded by the war could not be maintained or expanded. A half million refugees could not be sheltered and fed. Millions of Vietnamese would be without any medical attention. Industry would not be able to import the materials and equipment it needs to operate and grow. The development of effective local government, and agricultural and educational institutions, would be handicapped by a lack of expert advisers.

The funds which Congress has appropriated for economic assistance to Vietnam cover less than half the presently estimated requirements for Fiscal Year 1966. There are two principal elements in the request for additional funds. First, to meet the rising and severe threat of inflationary pressures, additional funds are needed to finance imported goods: $175 million are now needed to finance importation for commercial sale of goods such as rice, construction materials, petroleum products, fertilizer, drugs, and many other commodities. In this way we contribute to economic and political stability, by offsetting shortages in local production and maintaining morale essential to the entire effort. Second, $100 million is needed to fund new or expanded activities to strengthen the government of Vietnam's work in contested rural areas. These AID operations include refugee relief; provision of medical teams and individual doctors and nurses; building or repairing of hospitals and veterans' rehabilitation centers; leasing of ships for coastal and ocean supply operations; expanding civil airlift capacity; building of warehouses, bridges, roads; repair of war-damaged rail and other facilities; installation of temporary and permanent electric power services; construction of workers' housing and training centers; police equipment and training—the list grows long. While we look—and work and fight—for the day when South Vietnam will enjoy peace, we must apply our resources and ingenuity to building the foundation for that future.

We are also requesting additional Fiscal Year 1966 funds

to meet other existing or potentially dangerous situations: $7.5 million in supporting assistance is for Thailand and Laos each; $25 million is for the Dominican Republic. In addition, $100 million is required to replenish the AID Contingency Fund, which is already exhausted. Additional funds for Thailand and Laos are necessary to assist these nations in developing and maintaining the economic and political stability to withstand increasingly threatening Communist pressures. These funds are earmarked for non-military security activities and intensified rural development projects in vulnerable areas.

In the Dominican Republic economic and political instability have followed in the wake of last April's revolution. We are determined to help the provisional government create and maintain a stable environment prior to the coming elections in June. It is equally important that we assist the provisional government in meeting its essential current operations so that the new government will not be saddled with a crippling financial crisis, which would threaten its very existence. Additional economic assistance is needed to cover the gap between existing operating and capital budget costs of the government, and tax revenues. These revenues have not increased as quickly as expected because of continued political unrest. We expect these additional funds to alleviate the high level of unemployment, which itself has contributed to Dominican instability.

In addition, the President has requested Congress to provide $100 million in supplemental funds to the AID Contingency Fund. The Fiscal Year 1966 Contingency Fund was small; it is now depleted. It is absolutely necessary that a sufficient amount of Contingency Funds be on hand for the remainder of this fiscal year to permit us to respond immediately and effectively to emergency situations or unforeseen requirements which engage the interests of the U.S.

It might be well, Mr. Chairman, for the Committee in executive session to consider some of those situations which we see potentially on the horizon. I would also like to note that the President's request includes provision for the transfer of funds required for military assistance to South Vietnam from the account of the Military Assistance Program to the account of the Department of Defense. U.S. and other free world military forces have joined in the defense effort in South Vietnam in large numbers. It is more efficient and less cumbersome to program and budget for all U.S. military operations in Vietnam under one unified system. The Military Assistance Program was not created to bear the costs of such combat forces. I commend to the Congress this recommendation. In conclusion, Mr. Chairman, I urge the Committee's support of this urgent request in its entirety, and I welcome any questions or comments which you may have. . . .

SENATOR FULBRIGHT: . . . Could you tell us very briefly, when did we first become involved in Vietnam?

RUSK: I think the first involvement was the assistance that we provided to France during the period of the Marshall Plan at a time when France was faced there with the Viet Minh movement, a very large part of which was nationalist but which also had within it a very strong Communist increment.

FULBRIGHT: What year was that?

RUSK: That began 1949-1950, Mr. Chairman. At that time the attitude of the United States was that it would provide assistance to France in the expectation that France would move promptly to make its own agreement with the nationalist elements in Indochina, and make it clear that the associated states of Indochina—which later became Vietnam (or the two Vietnams) Laos, and Cambodia—would, in effect, be independent. The political movement by the French Government of that day was slower than the United States had hoped for, and the military operations came to the conclusion of the Geneva Conference of 1954. . . .

FULBRIGHT: In what respect were we involved before that [1949-1950]?

RUSK: Well, the discussion of aid to France came up before the spring of 1950, but the policy involvement and the discussions with the French government over it preceded it by some period. I just wanted to point out that spring, 1950, was not our first expression of concern about Indochina.

FULBRIGHT: But it was the first financial commitment, wasn't it?

RUSK: I believe so.

FULBRIGHT: Was France at that time trying to reassert her colonial domination of Vietnam? Was that her objective at that time?

RUSK: I think just at the conclusion of the war, in that part of the world, the first step that was taken was the restoration of the status quo ante bellum in the broadest sense in India, Burma, Malaysia, Indochina, Indonesia, and indeed in part in the Philippines, although the Philippines moved almost immediately for independence. In varying degrees each of these areas become independent from the former colonial country, and in different circumstances.

In the case of France, the first step that was made was to work out something like a commonwealth arrangement, associated states in which France would retain certain authority with respect to defense and foreign affairs. But there was never a firm basis of agreement among most of the Indochinese peoples themselves; and that moved—it proceeded inevitably and I think, properly, toward a more clear independence.

FULBRIGHT: What has puzzled me—and I confess I was scarcely conscious that there was a Vietnam or a movement of any significance because our attention was directed largely to Europe—but what moved the State Department or our government to assist France to retain her control of Vietnam in contrast to our actions in Indonesia, for example?

RUSK: The problem there, sir, was—I am trying my best to remember something which happened quite a few years ago—the problem was not just that, or was not at all that really of assisting France and establishing and reinforcing a colonial position, but to give France a chance to work out its political settlement with these states on the basis of their own independence, and without having Communism as a basic—without giving to the Communists a basic position in Southeast Asia. After the Communists took over authority in Peking, we and the British and the French were consulted on this situation and pretty well agreed that the security of Southeast Asia was of vital interest to the free world, and the joint effort therefore to find an agreement with the nationalists on the one side and to prevent a Communist takeover on the other was a common thread of policy throughout that period.

FULBRIGHT: Do you remember how much aid we gave France in that struggle in Vietnam, between '50 and '54?

RUSK: I think it was approximately $2 billion.

FULBRIGHT: You stated in your original statement that we have a very clear commitment. What is the origin and basis for a clear commitment to the action we are now taking in Vietnam?

RUSK: I think, sir, there are a combination of components in that commitment. We have the Southeast Asian Treaty to which South Vietnam was a protocol state.

FULBRIGHT: What does that commit us to in that regard? This is where there is a good deal of confusion in my mind and I think in the public mind about the nature of that commitment. Does the Southeast Treaty, Southeast Asia Treaty Organization commit us to do what we are now doing in Vietnam?

RUSK: Yes, sir, I have no doubt that it does. A protocol state has a right to call on the members of the organization for assistance. The obligations of that treaty are both joint and several. That is, they are both collective and individual. So that there seems to be no doubt that we are entitled to offer that assistance. But the underlying legal

basis for the assistance is the right of individual and collective self-defense against an aggressor, and there is
clearly an aggression from the North here which has been
persistent and since 1960 has been sharply increased.

FULBRIGHT: You say we are entitled to do this. Are we
obliged to do this under the treaty?

RUSK: I would not want to get into the question of
whether—if we were not interested in the commitments,
policy, and principle under the Southeast Asia Treaty—
of whether we have some legal way in order to avoid those
commitments. I suppose that one could frame some argument which would make that case. But it would seem to
us that the policy, which was discussed and passed upon
by the Executive and the Senate of that day, is that we
are opposed to aggression against these countries in Southeast Asia, the members of the Organization as well as the
protocol states. In addition to that we have bilateral assistance agreements to South Vietnam. We have had several
actions of the Congress. We have had the annual aid appropriations in which the purposes of the aid have been
fully set out before the Congress. We have had special
resolutions such as the one of August, 1964, and we have
had the most important policy declarations by successive
Presidents with respect to the protection of South Vietnam
against Communist aggression. . . .

FULBRIGHT: . . . How did you foresee the end of this
struggle? I mean do you think we are likely to be there
five, ten, or twenty years? What do you foresee the outcome of this even if we are successful in the military
activities? . . .

RUSK: To put it in its simplest terms, Mr. Chairman, we
believe that the South Vietnamese are entitled to a chance
to make their own decisions about their own affairs and
their own future course of policy. That they are entitled
to make these decisions without having them imposed on
them by force from North Vietnam or from the outside.
We have—we are perfectly prepared to rely upon the
South Vietnamese themselves to make that judgment by

elections through their own government, by whatever way is suitable for them to make that decision. Now, we have indicated a good many points which have a bearing on this matter. We are not, for example, trying to acquire a new ally. If South Vietnam and the South Vietnamese people wish to pursue a nonaligned course by their own option, that is an option which is open to them. If they wish to join in the regional activities in the area such as Mekong River development and projects of that sort, that is open to them but we do believe they are entitled not to have these answers decided for them on the basis of military force organized from Hanoi, initiated from Hanoi, in the leadership of a front which was organized in Hanoi in 1960 for the purpose of taking over South Vietnam by force.

FULBRIGHT: Do you think they can be a completely free agent with our occupation of the land with two hundred or four hundred thousand men?

RUSK: If the infiltration of men and arms from the North were not in the picture, these troops of ours could come home; we have said that repeatedly. They went in there, the combat troops went in there because of infiltration of men and arms from the North, and that is the simple and elementary basis for the presence of American combat forces. . . .

SENATOR MORSE: Mr. Chairman, I am not going to ask the Secretary any questions this morning for the reason that I now state: I disagree with practically every major premise not only contained in his prepared statement but in his discussion in the last few minutes. I completely disagree with his interpretation of the SEATO Treaty. I do not think the SEATO Treaty justifies in any way the unilateral American action in South Vietnam based on the SEATO Treaty. But what I do propose to do, Mr. Chairman, to, at the first executive session of this Committee, to move that this Committee proceed with hearings in depth on the Vietnam crisis. If the Committee does not see fit to do that, I shall introduce a resolution with some co-sponsors in the Senate, calling for an investigation and hearing on our policy in Vietnam for the American people; they are entitled to it. . . . I only want the record to show that I completely disagree with the Administration's policies in Vietnam from the aspect of international law or treaty obligations and sound foreign policy, and I think that point of view is prairie-firing across the country, and this Committee, in my opinion, has the clear duty to proceed at once with prolonged hearings in depth on the Vietnam crisis. Therefore, I will defer my questions until such a hearing is held. . . .

SENATOR GORE: . . . As the Chairman has said, your pending request is too pertinent to the issue which troubles most of our citizenry, that this would seem an appropriate time to begin an examination of our undertaking in Southeast Asia. I suppose you and I, like most men, are victims of our past pronouncements. I would like to—just as a preface to my question—to draw a fine line between support and approval. I have not approved of our policy in Southeast Asia from 1954 until now. I have supported and expect to support funds sufficient to give weapons, ammunition, matériel to our armed forces who are there, not at their choice but at the orders of their government. Whether you have been correct in advocating our escalated involvement there over the years, or whether I have been correct in disapproval is really beside the point now. We are there, committed, likely to be there a long time. So, with that brief preface, I would like to first refer to your own statement this morning . . . when you say of the South Vietnamese people, "They must know that the struggle is worth their suffering and personal tragedies." . . .

I think when you apply that to the American people, you come to the heart of one of the excruciating difficulties of our democratic society today. Many people do not believe, many members of Congress do not believe, that the costs, the risk of a nuclear war, the dangers of a war with China or perhaps with both China and Russia, are worth the endeavor. I would like to pause and, in fairness, give you a chance to comment upon that.

RUSK: Thank you, Senator. First I would like to say that although I welcome the continuing examination of this very great matter of public policy by the Congress, I would point out that this is not a beginning. I know of no subject in the past five years which has been discussed—that is, since I have been directly and intimately involved with it —which has been discussed more frequently, in greater depth, month in and month out over a period of time, with the Congress than has Vietnam. More time has been spent on it than any single subject so far as our foreign policy is concerned. Nevertheless, it should continue, and with greater depth and with greater extent. Senator, it is tragic that in the year 1966 we should be called upon to use force to deal with armed aggression after all that has happened since 1945.

At the end of World War Two this country demobilized so rapidly that by 1946 we were told by our military that we did not have a single division ready for combat nor a single air group ready for combat. Our defense budget came down to within reach of $10 million, say, in 1947 and 1948. We tried to get rid of the nuclear bomb for everybody, including the United States, in the Baruch proposals. As soon as the war was over we went into the commitment of large resources for binding up the wounds of war and helping the reconstruction of that war-torn world. But then we found that there was such a thing as aggression in the world, that there were those who were prepared to use force contrary to the elementary purposes of the United Nations Charter, to upset the kind of world that was anticipated in the United Nations Charter. We have had a series of pressures by force in Iran, in Greece, in Berlin and in Korea, and in other places.

One would suppose that it is too late in history for that kind of technique to be used any more. But if it is to be used, then we have the most searching question to answer and that it, whether we shall get out of the way of those who are prepared to seize their neighbors by force, particularly those to whom we have commitments, or whether we should let them succeed and come to the conclusion that force is profitable, that their brand of world revolution can succeed on the basis of militancy and armed action, and that there is, therefore, no reasonable prospect of the kind of world that we tried to write in the United Nations Charter—coexist or not survive.

Now, in this process in this postwar period the American people have taken over 165,000 casualties in a combination of crises. Others have taken more. It is tragic that this problem could arise. It could end literally in twenty-four hours, Senator, if these people in Hanoi should come to the conclusion that they are not going to try to seize Vietnam and Laos by force. If they are determined to try to do so, then we and others have some very fundamental decisions to make, and in making them, it seems to me, sir, that we have to reflect upon how one builds a peace. Do we build it by standing aside when aggression occurs or do we build it by meeting our commitments?

Now, a human being can't be absolutely certain what the right answer in these things is to be. We who are older have the problem of deciding what it is we ought to forget. Those who are young have the problem of discovering the reality in those things they have had no chance to remember. So these are difficult questions, Senator, and we hope that we can find the right answer.

GORE: I certainly concur that they are very difficult. . . . Accepting the fact that we are there, rightly or wrongly, where are we and where do we go and what do we do and what are the risks? These are—and where do we arrive?—these are questions which the Committee will seek in the days and weeks ahead. I was not too favorably impressed in the last few days with the statements by Administration leaders, including yourself this morning, that during the bombing pause infiltration had continued from the North. Has it not continued also from the South, and did you expect—

RUSK: Senator, there is a fundamental difference—

GORE: Was there any agreement, did you honestly expect that because there was a cessation of bombing of North Vietnam that they would ipso facto stop all their military movements? The question I am trying to pose is, is this a realistic approach or is this a propagandistic approach?

RUSK: No, Senator, I think it would be a great mistake to put those two forces on the same footing, and not just on the basis that we are on our side. The North Vietnamese armed forces have no right whatever to move from North Vietnam into South Vietnam to seize South Vietnam. That is aggression. It is contrary to the military clauses of the 1954 [Geneva] Agreement, contrary to the general principles of international law, contrary to general standards set forth in such documents as the United Nations Charter.

We have joined in supporting South Vietnam as a part of their right of individual and collective self-defense. I have related it to a treaty as far as the United States is concerned. It has been approved also by legislation. The point is that there could be peace if North Vietnam would give up its illegal and aggressive efforts to take over South Vietnam by force. Of course, we used an airlift to supply Berlin when it was blockaded, but no one suggested that that airlift was illegal. Of course, we aided Greece when the guerrillas were moving in Yugoslavia and Bulgaria, but nobody suggested that was illegal, but was in pursuit of peace.

We have probed every conceivable—maybe there are some we have not been able to imagine—but we have probed every possibility of bringing this matter off the battlefield to the conference table, and we had hoped—we didn't know what the chances were, they appeared to be somewhat small, I must admit—but we had hoped on the basis of what a good many governments had told us, including some Communist governments, that if the bombing were suspended, that there might be a chance to bring this matter to the conference table. Now, the infiltration continued and no signs from the other side that they were going to give up their effort. Obviously we can't stop our reinforcements of our own men and can't stop urging others to do the same. . . .

SENATOR CHURCH: You have often said, Mr. Secretary, that—and I believe you said again this morning—that the United States doesn't want, that our national interests don't require, the establishment of any permanent American military base in South Vietnam.

RUSK: That is correct, sir.

CHURCH: Does our national interest require and is it our intention to retain a permanent American military base in South Korea?

RUSK: We have no present plans to withdraw our forces from there. This has to be judged on the basis of the total situation in the Far East. Senator, let me say that the doctrines and the policies espoused by Peking today constitute perhaps the most important single problem of peace. I have had a foreign minister on the other side of the curtain, I prefer not to name him, say that moving Peking to peaceful coexistence is the number-one problem in the world today. We would like to reduce our military commitments abroad, if we can do so consistent with our commitments and the maintenance of peace.

CHURCH: How many American combat troops are now stationed in South Korea?

RUSK: In South Korea, I think it is approximately fifty-five thousand.

CHURCH: It has been twelve years now roughly since the truce, is that correct?

RUSK: Yes, sir, that is correct.

CHURCH: How many Chinese combat troops are stationed in North Korea?

RUSK: I think there are no Chinese there at the present.

CHURCH: There are none?

RUSK: Not in significant numbers.

CHURCH: For how long have there been none?

RUSK: Since about 1954 or '55, I believe, sir.

CHURCH: Haven't we spent a great deal of money over the years in building up a very large and efficient South Korean Army?

RUSK: That is correct, sir.

CHURCH: Do you regard that army as adequate to protect South Korea against any threat that might be posed by North Korea?

RUSK: That would be a close question. I think it is not—

CHURCH: But a division of that army has been removed from South Korea to Vietnam, isn't that correct?

RUSK: That is correct, and the South Korean forces are effective, and well trained, and have a fine combat capability. The difficulty is that just across the Yalu River are very, very large forces indeed.

CHURCH: In China itself?

RUSK: That is correct, sir.

CHURCH: Well, that difficulty is likely to continue as long as China is there.

RUSK: That is right, sir.

CHURCH: Very well. We presently have two hundred thousand American troops in South Vietnam. Indications are that the buildup is going to continue. I notice Senator Stennis, who has often been right in predicting the course of events in Vietnam, indicated yesterday his belief that it might require as many as six hundred thousand American troops. I know Hanson Baldwin, the military commentator of the *New York Times,* has indicated it might require a million. Supposing that whatever the requirement may turn out to be, our military concentration, our American buildup of military forces in South Vietnam, is finally sufficient to suppress the Viet Cong, and to pacify South Vietnam. Would you then think that it is likely to be any easier for us to withdraw from South Vietnam than it has been for us to withdraw from South Korea?

RUSK: Well, we have stated, Senator, in good faith and

sincerity, that we do not wish to retain our own forces in South Vietnam. . . . Indeed the only reason for their presence is the infiltration of men and arms from North Vietnam. So the answer to your question would turn on what North Vietnam's conduct and attitude is.

CHURCH: But North Korea hasn't been engaging in that kind of activity in South Korea for many years, has it?

RUSK: No, sir, but you will recall—

CHURCH: But our troops are still in South Korea.

RUSK: You will recall that in the case of Korea, there was considerable discussion before the outbreak of the fighting in Korea about whether we should keep our troops in Korea following the war. There were some on the military side who wished to withdraw them completely, because our forces were rather thin in relation to their commitments all over the world. There are—were—those on the political side who doubted that that was a wise course in 1948-49 and urged we keep at least some force behind in Korea. The decision was finally made that we would withdraw them, and then a year later the attack occurred. There have been indications that the withdrawal of those forces in 1948 and 1949 contributed to a miscalculation on the other side as to what the situation would be in Korea. We would hope there wouldn't be such a miscalculation again. I don't know what the future will hold on this particular point. It would depend a good deal on the general orientation, attitude, and posture of Peking. . . .

SENATOR SYMINGTON: Don't you think that if more frankness was expressed by the Administration with respect to the growing problem incident to the Chinese becoming a nuclear power, and the relation of that fact, plus their current political intransigence, if that was interpreted more into the South Vietnam problem and publicly, at least reasonably comparable to the way that we hear about it in executive, military, and other briefings, don't you think that would help clarify the Vietnamese problem before the American people and perhaps reduce some of the criticisms that come from various sources about what is going on today?

RUSK: Senator, we have tried to expose fully to the public, subject to a very limited number of security problems, the elements in this situation. We have talked a great deal. People don't remember things that are said very long. At the end of 1965 I drew together what was already on the public record, the things which have been said about the content of a possible peace in Vietnam; these so-called fourteen points were looked upon as something quite new. We do talk a great deal; there are those who think I talk too much. It is hard for the news media to get the space or the time or the attention of their readers and listeners for background and context. I think this is one of our problems of public exposition. I think this is something in which not only the Executive Branch but members of the Senate and House can help us with as they talk about these things with their people back home.

We have tried to make it clear over and over again that although Hanoi is the prime actor in this situation, that it is the policy of Peking that has greatly stimulated Hanoi and has apparently blocked the path toward a conference. For example, a few months ago Hanoi had a delegation in Moscow. In their joint communiqué they made a statement which seemed to refer with approval to the idea of a conference on Cambodia and Laos. We would be glad to be present at such a conference and so indicated. It was our information that Peking moved in on Hanoi, possibly on Cambodia, to block the prospect of such a conference. I think there is no doubt about the militancy and the aggressiveness of Peking's policy. Indeed it has caused great problems inside the Communist world, quite apart from the problems it has caused in the free world. . . .

SENATOR CLARK: Mr. Secretary, as you know, I have become progressively more in disagreement with your and the Administration's policy in Vietnam as the war there continues to accelerate. I regret that very much. I think you know my very high personal regard and respect and indeed affection for you, and it makes me very unhappy that we are not in accord.

President Kennedy, in a CBS television interview on September 2, 1963, said, and I quote: "In the final analysis it is their war. They are the ones who have to win it or lose it. We can help them, we can give them equipment, we can send our men out there as advisers but they have to win it, the people of Vietnam against the Communists." Why have we turned this into what is becoming more and more every day an American war? In your opinion is this essential to the security of the United States?

RUSK: Senator, I think that—I welcome this question because I think that there is a substantial misunderstanding about what is happening in South Vietnam on this very point. The fact that we have a large number of U.S. combat forces there causes our own press to concentrate very heavily on the activities of U.S. forces. The truth is that the South Vietnamese continue to carry the great bulk of the struggle there. On any given day there might be, say, two, three or four U.S. battalions in operation, say one Korean battalion, but fifteen to twenty South Vietnamese battalions. The hundreds of incidents that occur every week and are maintained at a high level have their major impact upon the South Vietnamese. The fifty-five thousand South Vietnamese forces are taking the heaviest casualties. They are the ones who are out over the countryside every day in large numbers, and in not only substantial numbers of large unit actions but hundreds of small unit actions around the country, looking for the guerrillas, trying to find them and trying to deal with them. . . .

CLARK: Well, I am prepared to leave the whole subject with the observation that I would hope very much that we are going to stop escalating this war any further. I think is was about a year ago that you told me—and I don't think I am revealing any confidences because I think you have said it publicly—that we have lots of wiggle room. I think we are running out of wiggle room. I think we are coming pretty close to the point of no return, and personally I am scared to death we are on our way to nuclear World War Three. . . .

RUSK: Senator, first on this matter of escalation, I did indicate to the Committee the other day that we would try to provide a chronology of this Vietnam affair, because it does show that escalation has been escalation by the North. For four years there was infiltration from the North before there was any bombing of North Vietnam; the 325th North Vietnamese Division moved from North Vietnam through Laos to South Vietnam before there was bombing of North Vietnam. If other sides would de-escalate and get these infiltrators home, things could move very fast here, sir. They could move very fast.

CLARK: Well, since the bombing of North Vietnam began last February and ended in December, it did not prevent the infiltration and buildup of regular troops of the North Vietnamese Army in South Vietnam in addition to substantial equipment and supplies. What reason is there to think that a resumption of bombing would do what wasn't done when we bombed before?

RUSK: Well, these strikes have undoubtedly made infiltration more difficult, more costly, and have imposed some limits on the scale which was available. Certainly no bombing, non-bombing, did not prevent the infiltration of regular units of the North Vietnamese forces into South Vietnam. . . . I don't want to speculate on problems that are before us at the moment, but when a truck goes forty-five miles in five days because of its procedures that are directly related to the danger of air attack, I should think that it is of some advantage that it takes that truck five days to move those forty-five miles than five hours. . . .

SENATOR PELL: . . . First, what percentage of the Viet Cong forces are basically not South Vietnamese, natives born in South Vietnam? As I understand, there are about a quarter of a million Viet Cong. What portion of those would be from North Vietnam?

RUSK: I think there are a good many South Vietnamese ethnic people who were sent down by North Vietnam, so I would include those as North Vietnamese for the purpose of deciding where the aggression lies. They were armed and trained and sent down as—to provide the cadre and the bands and the terrorists in South Vietnam. I would suppose that that would be comparable to, say, the Federal Republic of Germany organizing people who used to live in East Germany into similar bands to be sent into East Germany. I would suppose that 80 per cent of those who are called Viet Cong are or have been Southerners. . . . And that North Vietnamese ethnic people might be in the percentage of about 20, although they play a very important role and they are there now as organized elements of the North Vietnamese Army.

PELL: But then I realize that one can't play with figures, but it would be a fact that the United States forces in South Vietnam would be about four times the number of those born in North Vietnam who are with the Viet Cong and there would be no Chinese in South Vietnam.

RUSK: We have not seen Chinese in South Vietnam. There have been occasional rumors to that effect, but whenever we have checked them out, so we don't find Chinese taking part in the Viet Cong operations.

PELL: This question of whether it is a Vietnamese war or an American war is one that concerns us here because we see so many signs of South Vietnamese or Vietnamese concern. The more you read it, the more you realize it is really one country, one people, one basic language with various divisions; if there were any ethnic divisions, it would be the Montagnards, I guess, so we have to determine how much of this is a civil war and how much is not. Your view is, I know, that the major portion of the aggression originates in the North, would that be correct.

RUSK: That is correct, sir. It was the—the present effort

was decided upon in 1959 in Hanoi. It was publicly organized and announced in Hanoi during 1960 and it has been followed up ever since. Then there is, Senator, I think, a very special case here in these divided countries. We can't accept the fact that because West Germans and East Germans are both Germans, that if they can go after each other that this is simply an indigenous affair. I can assure you the Russians wouldn't accept it on that basis.

When the North Koreans went after the South Koreans with many organized divisions, we couldn't accept that as an indigenous affair, a civil war among Koreans. There have been agreements, there have been settlements, there have been demarcation lines that are as important as frontiers, and if we are going to organize the peace we had better insist, in the case of these divided countries, if there are any problems those problems should be settled by peaceful means and not by force; otherwise this world is going to go up in smoke.

PELL: Wasn't there a question in the Korean War, most of the North Koreans were South Koreans?

RUSK: Millions of North Vietnamese left Hanoi in 1964 to live in the South because they did not wish to live under the Communist regime. I am sure you would discourage us from the idea of organizing those millions of North Vietnamese now in South Vietnam and sending them to the North.

PELL: Not at all. Maybe it would be an excellent idea and then it would have been a Vietnamese war.

RUSK: I had thought you were concerned about escalation, Senator. That would be a major escalation. . . .

PELL: Another point here, on the problem as I see it, we were out there several years ago and the military told us with a little more force and with a little more effort the war could be won, they could see light at the end of the road. I know how you must be concerned with hearing these statements from your military colleagues year after year, and yet each year we do what the military asks us, and we give them what they want. I don't think any of

their requests for money or matériel have been turned
down and we seem no nearer the end of the road now
than we were then.

The alternatives as I see them are both unacceptable:
to have an Algerian kind of withdrawal, or, on the other
hand, a general escalation into World War Three. I am
trying to figure out what cost is acceptable in between,
and I wonder why you find the Gavin theory wrong. I
have read Gavin's theory, putting our troops in enclaves,
and trying to de-escalate. Why is it not the best approach
to that? Where do you think General Gavin is incorrect?

RUSK: First, let me say I am grateful to you for raising
the issue of alternatives. I mean it is easy to worry about
the problems we have on our present course of action. All
of us can worry about them. But we have to choose among
the courses of action that are available, and I think that
there have been a good many people who have concen-
trated on worrying about the problems we see in front of
us without grappling with the choices that have to be
made among alternatives. . . .

Now, some aspects of the Gavin doctrine I think we
can talk about much more frankly in executive session,
but we see no sign that the other side is de-escalating, we
see no sign that they are prepared to stop doing what they
are doing. Now, to use a rather vernacular expression, I
don't believe myself that we can ask our men in uniform
just to put themselves into half a dozen or a dozen Guan-
tanamos and then hunker down and let the other side pick
the time and the place and the weapon and the buildup
of forces and take them on one enclave at a time. There
are people who are shooting at you, and I am inclined
to think that unless they stop, you have to shoot back,
and that the initiative in that sense should not be left to
those who are marauding through the countryside there.

Now, if the other side had any interest in de-escalating,
there are many ways in which that could be registered
and that it is, would be, a pretty important step toward
peace, but that is, the word we have had from them is just

the opposite, it is just the opposite. There are specific military aspects to it that I would prefer not to get to in open hearing. But I would want to be sure this is not simply a next step to withdrawal. Suppose we had those enclaves. Then the Viet Cong could organize the rest of the country and organize people who don't want the Viet Cong, the Buddhists and the Catholics and the others have made it clear they don't want what the Viet Cong is offering, and forces then would be holding certain small cells there and I just don't see any future outcome to that except failure.

PELL: But, Mr. Secretary, as you pointed out, the question here is alternatives and many of us have wrestled with it and have tried to come up with alternative approaches; they all seem equally unpleasant. But don't you see the end of the road we are following now? After we have erased Hanoi and Haiphong, which we could do in a couple of hours, and after we have chewed up their army of three hundred thousand, as Senator Mansfield in his report points out, in an open-ended situation it would be filled in by the Chinese forces.

RUSK: I don't see the future in as precise terms as that. I think when we look back over the crises we have had since 1945, one cannot spell them out that clearly and that far into the future. I think the other side has some problems. They have got to be looking at alternatives. If they have some elements of rationality, as we think they must have despite some of the difficulty in getting across to them in communications, then they have some serious problems just as we do, and a number of these postwar situations that has led to the possibility of peace.

PELL: In conclusion then, Mr. Secretary, would you not think that the course we have followed so far and the expansion so far has resulted in little expense and no real loss to China—has really gone along with the Chinese national interests.

RUSK: Well, I think what China considers to be a national interest of theirs is very much engaged here and that is the application of the technique of militant—of a militant war or liberation as they call it. I don't believe myself that Peking welcomes us in Southeast Asia. But I don't subscribe to the view that I have heard expressed by some, that the Soviet Union is very glad that we are all mixed up in this problem and that China is very glad to see us all mixed up in this problem. I think that they would prefer that we not come there at all. They would prefer to have seen their world revolution move ahead. I don't think that they are getting what they want in this present situation nor are we yet. We have got to have more than we have at the present time if we are going to have peace. . . .

SENATOR MC CARTHY: I would like to raise a question, pursuing a question Senator Pell just raised a little farther. He asked why it was that there was no countermove in North Vietnam by land forces either under orders or South Vietnamese who might do it on their own. You said, well, this is escalation in a sense and you asked if he was against escalation and you don't think that was a good policy. I don't think that is a good answer. What is the difference between that and bombing North Vietnam? Is there a diplomatic or a military reason that doesn't apply to one and does to the other?

RUSK: The South Vietnamese forces have had their hands pretty full with the task in front of them. I really feel I would rather get into this—I ought to get into this in executive session rather than open hearings. This gets us into some difficult problems. . . .

MC CARTHY: I think we accepted for five or six years the ideas expressed by General MacArthur, General Eisenhower, General Gavin, and General Ridgway, and others that a land war in Asia was invisible. Is that theoretical position still held or do we have among the military figures in America today a changed point of view?

RUSK: Senator, the nature of a struggle of this sort where the initiative is not ours, where we did not start it and where we didn't want it to begin with and where the aggression comes from the other side is, of course, substantially determined by the other side. At the present time the situation in South Vietnam does not take the form of armies, land armies, locked in combat with each other; it continues to be basically a guerrilla operation. The overwhelming part of the problem is terror and sabotage. The fixed units that the other side might have, battalions or regiments, occasionally engage in combat, as the kind of regiment. But the great mass of the problem is the guerrilla action by smaller groups intimidating villages, blowing up highways or bridges, assassinations and kidnappings and techniques of that sort.

One cannot say with complete confidence what the future will hold, but I would just point out that at this stage, in this situation, the other side has been pursuing this on a typically guerrilla basis. They are doing so both as a matter of practice and apparently also as a matter of doctrine.

MC CARTHY: I know that to be the case.

RUSK: The fire power that is available to the government and allied forces out there is very large indeed, and the other side has found it very difficult to sustain battalions or regiments in camp for any protracted period.

MC CARTHY: Well, I don't think that quite answers my question.

RUSK: I know it didn't, sir. . . .

SENATOR AIKEN: Just one question. I was interested in the questions Senator McCarthy asked of the Secretary. I understood the Secretary to say that the other side would determine whether the United States becomes locked in a land war in Asia or not. Did I hear that correctly?

RUSK: In the sense, sir, that just as the other side moved large numbers of organized divisions across the parallel in Korea, we had to face the question as to whether we would leave them alone, get out of the way, let them have it, or whether we would hit them.

AIKEN: They will determine then whether we send four

hundred thousand or two million men into Southeast Asia?

RUSK: I think, Senator, that—

AIKEN: Don't you suppose they will be making other decisions for us, perhaps, if we agree that they have this one to make?

RUSK: Well, it is almost in the nature of aggression, Senator, that the initiative lies with the aggressor. If it would be left up to us, there wouldn't be any shooting out there at all. We wouldn't have been there with troops. We want peace in the area and we have wanted it for the past, entire postwar period. Now, when somebody else starts shooting, then decisions have to be made as to what is done about that and by whom and what the responsibilities of the United States might be in that situation.

AIKEN: That would apply to any part of the world.

RUSK: It would apply particularly to those countries with whom we have commitments. I indicated earlier this morning we don't look upon ourselves as the gendarmes of the universe and we are not trying to establish a Pax Americana right around the globe, many others carry responsibilities and many other types of aggressions and fighting have been dealt with or resolved without the participation of the United States.

AIKEN: Did I hear the radio report correctly this morning which indicated that the United Kingdom says that her contributions to our trouble in Vietnam will consist of not calling on us for greater contributions to protect her resources in different parts of the world? Would that be a real contribution? . . .

RUSK: No, Britain has had a direct responsibility in Southeast Asia because of the problem between Indonesia and Malaysia, and they have had a fairly substantial portion of their defense budget committed in Southeast Asia. So that problem is not resolved, and there has been fighting there in Malaysia and in Borneo, with infiltration elements. No, I would think that radio report was rather missing the point.

AIKEN: I think I have got the situation as clear as I might, Mr. Chairman. . . .

SENATOR WILLIAMS: Speaking of the contribution Britain has made, why is it that they have not stopped their ships from sending supplies to Vietnam?

RUSK: We are at the present time in closest touch with Britain about that matter, as with one or two other governments. The free world shipping has been substantially reduced. I think the average monthly rate now is about thirteen. Most of those are small ships operating out of Hong Kong. About half of those that do come in, come in in ballast, take out coal to Japan and some fresh fruits and vegetables to Hong Kong or eastern Siberia. We do not like that free world shipping going into Haiphong, and we have been working on that with governments and have succeeded in reducing it very sharply. But we are not yet at a point with which we are satisfied, and we continue to work on it.

WILLIAMS: Did Great Britain ask us for our cooperation in her efforts to blockade Rhodesia? Couldn't we have asked her to take the same prompt steps she is asking us to take?

RUSK: This was not just a bilateral matter between us and Britain. This was part of a general worldwide attitude with respect to the Rhodesian problem, and it also engaged some direct specific interests of the United States in Africa, so that this was, this is, relevant, but it is not the decisive point in this question of the Haiphong shipping.

WILLIAMS: As I understand it, some of our other so-called allies are likewise supplying North Vietnam with shipping?

RUSK: I think, sir, in the first place, no strategic goods of any sort are supplied by free world shipping, and certainly none by our allies. The shipping has been reduced now to basically the Hong Kong shipping. There are occasional ships from other states in there, but the governments of those countries have been able to deal with it to a very considerable extent. We have some hopeful prospect that this matter be resolved.

WILLIAMS: Do they furnish us with a manifest of their cargo?

RUSK: We have ways of knowing what is on board, yes, sir.

WILLIAMS: Is it not true that in times of war all types of supplies to a certain extent are war materials, even food?

RUSK: Well, I would think that would be true in a most general sense. Certainly those ships coming in ballast to take things out would not be in that category. But some things are much more war material than others. . . . Mr. Chairman, may I inject one remark, because there might have been some misunderstanding? When Senator McCarthy, and I regretted he had to leave, when he asked his question, the point that I was reluctant to comment on as to what the shape of this matter might be in Asia, on a particular matter as to whether our senior commanders or military advisers are advising against what we are doing, because of the problem of a land war in Asia, the answer to that question is no, and I will so inform Senator McCarthy. I did not want to avoid that part of his question. It was the projection into the future that I was somewhat diffident about. . . .

FULBRIGHT: Mr. Secretary, as you know, I have been in the Senate and the Congress quite a long time, and ever since I have been here I do not recall any issue about which there is so much apprehension about a military involvement, and this is a reason, I think, why some public discussion of it at this time is appropriate. . . . You said there had been great discussion in depth about Vietnam. I would submit, in all honesty, that the discussion was rather superficial. We had a relatively small commitment even as late as the time of the Bay of Tonkin affair, and I personally did not feel that we had undertaken a course of action that could well lead to a world war. I certainly was rather taken aback by the statement in the morning paper by Senator Stennis—who, as you know, is chairman of the Preparedness Subcommittee, and has the most intimate relations with the Joint Chiefs of Staff—in which he speaks quite firmly and provocatively about the use of nuclear weapons, about the Chinese coolies, which is not a very complimentary term, as you know. I would consider that it has changed a lot, and we did not discuss this in my presence with the same feeling about it that we now have, that we are now engaged in a very serious undertaking. I think it is a lack of understanding that accounts for this apprehension, and there is some ambivalence in some of the statement. . . . I believe that one of the reasons for this concern and apprehension is a feeling on the part of some people, at least, that I have read in the press, very reputable scholars and others, that we have inadvertently, perhaps, for irrelevant reasons, stepped into a colonial war in 1950 on the wrong side. Whether or not we did is one of the questions at issue.

Something, it seems to me, is wrong or there would not be such a great dissent, that is evidenced by teach-ins and articles and speeches by various responsible people. I do not regard all of the people who have raised these questions as irresponsible. I think it is our duty, the duty of the Committee and the Administration and others to try to clarify the nature of our involvement there and what it is likely to lead to and whether or not the ultimate objective justifies the enormous sacrifice in lives and treasure. I think, in all honesty, that is why there is such interest in this matter. It is very difficult to deal with. I have never encountered such a complex situation. It is not clear-cut, like Korea or like the Second World War. You state very positively this is aggression by the other side. But this is not quite as convincing under the circumstances as it was in North Korea, for example. There was an overt aggression. This is a subtle thing. This is not comparable to the bombing of Pearl Harbor. There was no doubt—I do not know of anyone who said, "Well, that is not an engagement for an all-out commitment." This is subtle. Perhaps this is new, as you say; it is different, but it needs to be understood if we are to approve of it in the sense of voting these very large sums which everyone believes if we pursue this policy, and in connection with the resumption of bombing, that we are then committed, that we have passed the Rubicon, and I think that is what justifies some discussion of this.

I do not like to delay you from your work and to keep you here, but I think I am expressing my own feeling—not only my own feelings, but the feelings of some of my colleagues, and I know of some of my constituents. So all I am trying to do is to clarify what we really are about. I suspect sometimes that there has been a change in policy from that which we disavowed after the Spanish-American War. You deny that there is a Pax Americana, but the fact is we have troops in Europe, very large numbers, in Korea, Vietnam, the Dominican Republic. We have military missions in half the nations of the world, probably more. I don't know what this means. It has all come about gradually and in connection with an aid program. The aid program has been one element in this. I confess I have supported it all the time. I am having very grave reservations about whether that was wise.

I am perfectly willing if, at the proper time, I so conclude, to admit I made a mistake. Perhaps it is impossible for a great nation to do that. I do not know. But I think there have been examples of that, where great nations have drawn back from some commitments which they felt were wrong. I am not ready to say at the moment that I am positive that this was wrong, but I certainly am anxious to have greater enlightenment about just what we are about and what is our ultimate objective.

This is why I asked you in the very beginning if you could formulate for me more clearly just what is our objective. That is why I referred to this question of the Britisher. He tried to simplify it by saying, "Well, now, let's put aside all this talk about democracy in South Vietnam." You know that is unrealistic. There are no institutions there, and never have been, of democracy. This is an ancient kingdom and with no established institutions, and he put it aside, and says what you are doing is—you do not like that word, I do not either—imperialism; but it is a word, I do not know a better word now. And what we are doing is saving the free world from Communist encroachment, and we are going to do it everywhere. This was expressed rather clearly in the time of the Truman Doctrine, and we followed that in that instance and in some others.

Is this still that commitment, that wherever there is a possibility or probability of an expansion in the future of a Communist state that we are going to meet it and stop it? Is that a right way to describe it or not? All I am asking for is clarification of what our objective is in this struggle.

RUSK: Well, Senator, let me comment, if I may, on the broader aspect of your very thoughtful statement. When I said we are not embarked upon a Pax Americana, I was thinking specifically of the fact that our obligations run to forty-two allies. Those are allies because of action taken by the Executive branch and the Senate in combination. All of those are allies under treaties ratified by the Senate by an overwhelming vote. In the case of Southeast Asia I think there were what, one or two votes in the Senate against that treaty. There was no reservation on that treaty that, of course, this does not apply if things get tough. . . .

FULBRIGHT: In the Southeast Asia Treaty, it seems to me, as I read it, the obligation is to consult with our allies in the case of these non-overt aggressions. We have no unilateral obligation to do what we are doing. Now, you say we are entitled to do it. That is different from saying we have an obligation under this SEATO Treaty. I mean, we are entitled, I suppose, as a great power to do nearly anything we want to. We are entitled to move in the Dominican Republic, because we have the power to do it. I did not believe you had any treaty authorization to do it, but I do not want to quibble about that. But in this case, do you maintain that we had an obligation under the Southeast Asia Treaty to come to the assistance, all-out assistance, of South Vietnam? Is that very clear?

RUSK: It seems clear to me, sir, that this was an obligation—

FULBRIGHT: Unilateral.

RUSK: —an obligation of policy. It is rooted in the policy of the Treaty. I am not now saying if we had decided we would not lift a finger about Southeast Asia that we could be sued in a court and be convicted of breaking a treaty. This is not the point I want to talk about.

FULBRIGHT: Mrs. Neuberger brought up a question very well that is the type of thing that comes to mind. She said the day before yesterday, "President Johnson and his advisers made it quite clear that in their judgment the Vietnam war is a clear and documented case of aggression by North Vietnam against South Vietnam. This policy recognizes the de facto existence of two independent sovereign nations, the capitals of which are Hanoi and Saigon. The President also said in his State of the Union Message that we 'stand by the Geneva Agreements of 1954.' The public is aware of very little of the detail of that historic agreement, but one feature they are likely to remember. The 17th Parallel was provisional and was 'not in any way to be interpreted as constituting a political or territorial boundary.' On the basis of it the United States is saying both that it stands on the principle that there is no political or territorial boundary separating North and South Vietnam and that we must stand and fight in South Vietnam because that nation has been attacked by its aggressor neighbor of the north. When Americans scratch their head over this logic they are not excusing Communist aggression nor saying that the U.S. ought not to be in Vietnam. It is simply a puzzle over why our stated reason for being there and our stated terms for withdrawing seem to cancel out each other."

This is the type of puzzlement that afflicts us poor laymen who are not in on all of the real secrets of diplomacy. It does puzzle me.

RUSK: Well, Senator, in the case of divided states, there were original agreements in the case of Germany, Korea, and Vietnam anticipating the unification of those states.

FULBRIGHT: What agreements are you referring to? Not 1954?

RUSK: Oh, yes. I think the 1954 Agreement anticipated the prospect of a unification of North and South Vietnam.

FULBRIGHT: Well, it specifically says not to be.

GORE: . . . This is the Final declaration of Geneva Conference, July 21, 1954, Point 6: "The Conference recognizes that the essential purpose of the agreement relating to Viet-Nam is to settle military questions with a view to ending hostilities and that the military demarcation line is provisional and should not in any way be interpreted as constituting a political or territorial boundary."

RUSK: That is correct. Now, in the case of Germany and Korea, as well as Vietnam: those were divided by demarcation lines, and in the background were agreements anticipating the unification of those divided countries. In the process, time, and development of events, however, Germany has been recognized by some countries, West Germany by the overwhelming majority; North Korea has been recognized by some, South Korea by the overwhelming majority; the same with the two Vietnams. Now, the problem is whether those issues that exist in these divided countries are to be settled by force or are to be settled by peaceful means. We believe they should be settled by peaceful means. If there are differences and difficulties, they can be brought to the conference table and talked about. But if efforts are made in any of these three divided countries to settle the question of unification by force, then I think we are in a very, very grave and dangerous situation throughout the world. . . .

CHURCH: If this is the philosophy underlying our policy, Mr. Secretary, I should have thought that it would have been difficult to have ever fought a civil war in this country, had the same principles obtained a century ago. At that time, I suppose, the Southerners felt there had been an invasion of the South from the North; and had England, which favored the South, adhered to the same principle that now seems to govern American policy, and had sent troops in the name of self-determination into the Confederacy, I think they would have been hard put to convince Abraham Lincoln that there should have been an election to determine the ultimate outcome of the war. I mean, I think without in any way suggesting that the situation was an exact parallel, I think these principles upon which we rest our policy are subject to very serious question. . . . Now, in Vietnam you can look at the war in Vietnam as a covert invasion of the South by the North or you can look at it as some other scholars do, as basically an indigenous war to which the North has given a growing measure of aid and abetment; but either way you look at it, it is a war between Vietnamese to determine what ·the ultimate kind of government is going to be for Vietnam. When I went to school, that was a civil war. I am told these days it is not a civil war any more.

RUSK: Well, Senator, I do not follow that point at all because whatever you call it there is aggression from North Vietnam against South Vietnam across that demarcation line contrary to the military clauses of that 1954 commitment, and in the case of that commitment known to North Vietnam before they started against South Vietnam.

CHURCH: Have all the provisions of the 1954 Agreement been adhered to on either side?

RUSK: No, they have not.

CHURCH: Were the elections which were called for generally anticipated at the time that Agreement was made? Were they held?

RUSK: Neither in North or South Vietnam.

CHURCH: Right. So it cannot be said that violations of

the Agreement have been all one-sided, and certainly our case does not rest upon that kind of reasoning.

RUSK: That is correct. The case—the basic fact is that large numbers of armed men and large quantities of arms have been sent illegally from North Vietnam into South Vietnam to try to take over South Vietnam by force.

FULBRIGHT: May I ask in that connection, what is the explanation of why in 1956, in pursuance of the terms of the Geneva Accords, elections were not held? . . . We backed Diem, did we not? Didn't we have much to do with putting him in power?

RUSK: Well, we supported him.

FULBRIGHT: That is what I mean.

RUSK: That is correct.

FULBRIGHT: And he was—to an extent had—a certain dependence upon us, did he not?

RUSK: We were giving him very considerable aid, Mr. Chairman.

FULBRIGHT: . . . In accordance with the Treaty he was requested to consult about elections, and he refused to do so, is that correct?

RUSK: Well, neither his government nor the government of the United States signed that Agreement.

FULBRIGHT: But isn't it correct? We will come to that as a separate point. But it is correct he refused to consult, is that correct?

RUSK: I think that is correct, sir.

FULBRIGHT: Now we will come to this business of our signing. Why, in your opinion, didn't we sign it? There were nine members there, and eight signed it. We refused. Why didn't we sign it?

RUSK: I have tried to find in the record a full discussion of that subject. Quite frankly, I have not been able to. I think—my general impression is that the United States was at that time not persuaded that this was the best way to settle this affair, and did not want to be responsible for all of the elements of the Agreement. They did say that they would give it—that they would acknowledge it . . . and would consider any attempt to upset it by force as a threat to the peace.

FULBRIGHT: Not having signed it, what business was it of ours for intervening and encouraging one of the signatories not to follow it, specifically Diem?

RUSK: Well, the prospect of free elections in North and South Vietnam was very poor at that time.

FULBRIGHT: Now, they have always been poor, and will be for a hundred years, won't they? That was not news to you. I mean, this was a device to get around the settlement, was it not?

RUSK: No, no, Mr. Chairman. I do not believe the prospect of free elections in South Vietnam anyhow are all that dim.

FULBRIGHT: Have they ever had them in two thousand years of history?

RUSK: They have had some free elections in the provinces and municipalities in May of this year.

FULBRIGHT: Under our control and direction.

RUSK: Not under our control and direction; no, sir.

FULBRIGHT: Who supervised them?

RUSK: Multiple candidates, with 70 per cent of the registered voters voting, and with results which indicate that people in these local communities elected the people that you would expect them to elect in terms of the natural leaders of the community. . . .

AIKEN: Are the successful candidates still living now?

RUSK: Well, they are as far as the government is concerned. The Viet Cong continue to kill them, assassinate, kidnap them.

AIKEN: Knock them off.

RUSK: I am sure those who were elected are not in office.

AIKEN: That discourages candidacies.

RUSK: Yes, it does.

FULBRIGHT: Well, there are a lot here that discourage candidacies, too. It is not a very easy life any way you take it. It is just a matter of degree, I think. Coming back to 1954, because the President in his State of the Union Message said, I quoted it, I do not need to quote it again, he stands, he is ready to negotiate, I guess, to settle on 1954. We did not sign it, we did make a unilateral declaration. Bedell Smith, who was Under Secretary of State. . . .

FULBRIGHT: Do you recall what he said? . . .

RUSK: Well, he said that we would accept—in effect we would accept the settlement and consider any attempt to upset it by force as a threat to the peace.

FULBRIGHT: Then, for the next four years there was, according to what you have said—we can go into that, perhaps, later—but aggression, as you call it, did not start until 1960. The next four years the carrying out of the Agreement was really abandoned by way of elections, was it not, and we did not allow them or did not encourage them to have it, and apparently the North Vietnamese did not do anything either very substantial, did they? I do not know. I am asking you really.

RUSK: Senator, I regret that I did not, in the words of the House of Commons, have notice of this particular questioning on this particular period. I would need to review the record and be much more briefed and detailed on it.

FULBRIGHT: I won't pursue it at this time.

RUSK: But I will be glad to return to the Committee and pursue this line of questioning.

FULBRIGHT: I do it for this reason that I tried to state: that I think there is some feeling that, perhaps, we have intervened, as [Senator Church] indicated a moment ago. that we have intervened in a family quarrel here, and that we may not be justified on the grounds here presented, which leads me again to come back to this question a moment ago raised by the Englishman, which, in all frankness, is a more understandable and a simpler and, perhaps, more justifiable reason if you are willing to rely on that, that this is such a danger to the free world and to our own security, even the possibility or probability—possibility, I reverse those—either the probability or possibility of Chinese Communist imperialism, that is of their expanding physically, I presume in this area, I think that is traditional, at least it is understandable to me. If that is the ground, it is more understandable, whether justified or not, I do not know, but it is more understandable. Are you unwilling to put it on that ground?

RUSK: Well, I am unwilling to cast the United States in the role of a policeman of the universe or one who is disposed to committing on the world a Pax Americana in every possible situation.

FULBRIGHT: I do not mean every possible—

RUSK: Rather than on the specific commitments undertaken by this government and by this nation by action both of the Executive and the Legislative branches.

FULBRIGHT: This is what needs discussion. I do not see the specific commitment. I do not see the Southeast Asia Treaty. I think it might be worthwhile for you—to ask if you would care to—to give us maybe in writing something to clarify this even further, with specific reference to that part of the Treaty and the provisions which require it because I am not convinced of it, I am not sure about it. I am not any better briefed on this than you are. None of us are very well briefed on this area because, frankly, I did not anticipate at this period that this was a serious matter, I mean anything like it is. I thought it was just one other country among many to whom we were giving aid, and I really never became concerned about this matter until about the time of the Bay of Tonkin, and I paid no particular attention to it, and that is why, I think, there is this unhappiness, as evidenced by—well, you saw in this morning's paper fifteen of the members, many of them the younger members, newer members, of the Senate, who seem to be unhappy about the expansion of this war. I do not think they made up their minds that they are dead set against what your purpose is. I think they are not quite clear what the purpose is, and would like an opportunity to examine it further before they have to vote on commitments which are irrevocable. . . .

GORE: . . . In preparation I have looked up some of the documents. I have here the SEATO Treaty to which you refer and to which, let me remind you, Mr. Secretary, South Vietnam is not a signatory.

RUSK: It is a protocol state.

GORE: It is a protocol state, that is correct. But insofar as its being a specific commitment, here is the specific language: "If, in the opinion of any of the parties the inviolability or the integrity of the territory or the sovereignty or political independence of any party in the treaty area or of any other state or territory to which the provisions of paragraph 1 of this Article from time to time apply, is threatened in any way other than by an armed attack or is affected or threatened by any fact or situation which might endanger the peace of the area"—here is the commitment—"the parties shall consult immediately in order to agree on the measures which should be taken for the common defense."

RUSK: That is—

GORE: If that is a specific commitment to wage war in Southeast Asia, I do not understand it. . . .

RUSK: Paragraph one of Article IV says: "Each party recognizes that aggression by means of armed attack in the treaty area against any of the Parties or against State or Territory which the parties by unanimous agreement may hereafter designate"—and that means the protocol states which they unanimously designated—"would endanger its own peace and safety, and agrees that it will in that event act to meet the common danger in accordance with its constitutional processes."

I think part of the confusion here is over the question as to whether this is, in fact, an aggression by the use of arms against South Vietnam. The Chairman referred to the fact that people are not as clear about this as they were in

Korea because divisions moved across. In the case of South Vietnam they moved, in the first instance, by stealth, they moved through the jungle. But, nevertheless, they were armed men and in substantial numbers.

From November of 1964 until January of 1965 they moved the 325th Division of the North Vietnamese Army down to South Vietnam. There was no bombing going on at that time. Now, this in an aggression by means of an armed attack.

GORE: Was that before or after we moved forces into South Vietnam?

RUSK: Well, the division moved after we had put—had reinforced our own forces there. But nevertheless, we did not have our own combat personnel in South Vietnam for a period of some years during which there was steady infiltration of armed men and armed supplies from the North.

GORE: . . . Going back to the SEATO Treaty, where are the constitutional processes with respect to the United States that we agreed to follow in SEATO?

RUSK: The processes which have been determined through consultation between the President and the leadership, for example, such processes as the resolution of the Congress of August, 1964.

GORE: Was that a constitutional process?

RUSK: I would think so, sir. That was a joint resolution of the Congress, signed by the President, which can be repealed by a concurring resolution which would not need the signature of the President.

GORE: Is a declaration of war a constitutional process?

RUSK: It would be one. It would be a constitutional process, but it is not the only constitutional process.

GORE: I voted for this resolution following the attack upon our ships off Tonkin Bay. I interpreted that resolution as proving the specific and appropriate response to this attack, and the chairman of this Committee, in presenting such a resolution, stated to the Senate that this was his interpretation. I certainly want to disassociate myself [from] any interpretation that this was a declaration of war. . . . Or that it authorized the Administration to take any and all steps toward an all-out war. I specifically interpreted that as an attack which we had experienced as a specific and limited response thereto.

RUSK: Mr. Chairman, may I just read that resolution? It is very short.

FULBRIGHT: Yes.

RUSK: It says: "That the Congress approves and supports the determination of the President, as Commander-in-Chief, to take all necessary measures to repel any armed attack against the forces of the United States and to prevent further aggression.

"The United States regards as vital to its national interest and to world peace the maintenance of international peace and security in Southeast Asia. Consonant with the Constitution of the United States and the Charter of the United Nations and in accordance with its obligations under the Southeast Asia Collective Defense Treaty, the United States is, therefore, prepared, as the President determines, to take all necessary steps, including the use of armed force, to assist any member or protocol state of the Southeast Asia Collective Defense Treaty requesting assistance in defense of its freedom."

There was a legislative interpretation of the Southeast Asia Collective Defense Treaty, and this resolution can be amended, can be repealed, by a concurring resolution of the Congress which would not require the approval of the President, by its terms.

FULBRIGHT: I was just reviewing what I said in that debate. Senator Nelson, in August 6, 1964, addressed this question to me. I may say, I do not remember the origin of this resolution. Did it come to the House first or to us first?

RUSK: It is a House resolution, Mr. Chairman.

FULBRIGHT: As I recall it, it was acted on very quickly, and it was under the impression that there had been a violent armed attack upon our ships, is that correct?

RUSK: That is correct, sir.

FULBRIGHT: As I recall it, it was acted on very quickly. Mr. Nelson, Senator Nelson, asked me, he said: "I have a couple of additional questions. But first I wish to say I did not suggest that by the use of hindsight I would now conclude that the intervention in 1954 was wrong. I do not know. I understand the neccessity for the United States, since it is the leader of the free world, to do all it can in furtherance of the protection of the idea of freedom and independence, and to do so we must take gambles. We shall lose some, we shall win some. I believe the public is slow to recognize that we have vast responsibilities, and they can expect us to win every gamble that we take. I do not expect that. I do not now rise here to criticize the original decision. But I am concerned about the Congress appearing to tell the Executive branch or the public that we would endorse a complete change in our mission. That would concern me."

This was addressed to me. And I responded: "I do not interpret the joint resolution that way at all. It strikes me, as I understand it, that the joint resolution is quite consistent with our existing mission and our understanding of what we have been doing in South Vietnam for the last ten years."

"Mr. Nelson: "Did I correctly understand the Senator from Arkansas to say a while ago that the language of the resolution was aimed at the problem of further aggression against our ships and our Naval facilities?"

"Mr. Fulbright: I think that is a logical way to interpret the language."

Of course, I was doing this under the belief that really expressed the statements made by the Senator from Tennessee. . . .

I think this point is that I, along with most of us, certainly did not at that time visualize or contemplate that this was going to take the turn that it now appears about to take. I do not know whether it is or not, by resuming bombing, resulting in escalation, and in accordance with such statements as in this morning's paper by the chairman of the Subcommittee on Preparedness, that this could well be heading toward a nuclear war. I think that is a mission quite different from what I had in mind at that time.

RUSK: I think, Senator, it is entirely fair to say that the exact shape of the situation as it has developed was not known in August of 1964, and that the exact measures which might have to be taken to give effect to the policy could not then be known and completely clarified, because so much of this turns upon what the other side has been doing all this period. But the policy of the Southeast Asia Treaty and the policy of the resolution has been long known to be the policy of the United States as expressed both by the Executive and the Legislative branches.

FULBRIGHT: Wouldn't you agree though in light of that, that that should not be interpreted as an authorization or approval of an unlimited expansion of the war?

RUSK: Well, we are not in a position of an unlimited expansion of the war. The steps that have been taken have been taken over a period of time with considerable caution and restraint, while every possibility of peace was being explored, and on these matters there has been frequent consultation with the various committees and the leadership of the Congress as the situation has developed. . . . We did not lose contact with the Congress in August, 1964. Both sides have been in business, and we have been discussing this matter in great detail since then.

FULBRIGHT: But Senator Mansfield certainly thinks there is a prospect, a possibility, of what he calls an open-ended conflict, which is a euphonious way to say all-out war, and Senator Stennis' statements certainly indicated that he is contemplating the possibility of that or he would not have made such a statement as he made yesterday.

RUSK: There are some dangers, of course, Mr. Chairman, in any of the situations, and that problem has been with us in each one of the principal crises we have been faced with since 1945.

FULBRIGHT: . . . Don't you think we ought to understand what we are in for, and that the Congress should give its further approval of this changed situation?

RUSK: Well, that question as to whether the Congress would wish to take up special action beyond that of August or in connection with the proposal which is before the Committee today, is one which is a matter for consideration between the Executive and the Legislative branches, and I would not have a . . . recommendation on that particular point this morning, sir. . . .

FULBRIGHT: I was going to say in view of that, would the approval of this very large increase in authorization be interpreted as an approval of our policy, as indicated it may be by Senator Stennis and others?

RUSK: You mean the $12 billion military supplement and this?

FULBRIGHT: Is this to be taken as an approval of an unlimited expansion of the war?

RUSK: You are not being asked, Mr. Chairman, for an unlimited expansion of the war.

FULBRIGHT: I know . . . but I am talking about the interpretation of it to be put upon it. In fact, I think I saw in the newspaper an article, I do not wish to put too much credence in that, but I think it said this would be interpreted as an approval of an all-out war. Would you think it should be interpreted that way?

RUSK: I think the Executive and Congress must at all times move together on these matters as they have in the past. I think these additional funds, both on the military and economic side—

FULBRIGHT: I do not think that is responsive. You do not have to answer if you do not like. You can say that is not anticipated. It is not responsive. But do you or don't you think it should be interpreted that way? You do not have to answer it, but the other is not responsive. I do not wish to—

RUSK: I will have to take it under advisement.

FULBRIGHT: That is all right if you do not wish to answer it, that is quite all right at this time. I do think before we act it ought to be answered. . . .

MUNDT: In that connection, Mr. Secretary, do you think that we have reached a juncture in this era of uncertainty and indecisiveness where, perhaps, the Administration should send some statement down which we could approve or disapprove or amend?

RUSK: Well, as I say, that is a matter that has been under advisement. The Congress has before it two very important pieces of legislation which have to do with a very large supplement to the defense budget, and a very substantial increase in the aid appropriation. That is against the background and in the light of events which have developed since the August, 1964, resolution was passed, and I would suppose that in the course of this discussion the Congress would have a chance to discuss among itself and to pass judgment upon the situation as we see it at the present time.

MUNDT: Did the President send down a message in conjunction with this other resolution you are talking about?

RUSK: Yes, there is—

MUNDT: I wonder if there is anything in that message which makes it clear whether or not this was an approval of policy.

RUSK: In the August, 1964, resolution—I would have to check that, sir. There was, as you know, a very extensive—

MUNDT: Will you check it and put in the record any clarifying statement which might have been included if there was one at that time?

RUSK: There was, as you know, very full consultation.

MUNDT: It seems to me there was a paragraph there that was very pertinent to this discussion this morning.

RUSK: There was a full discussion of this with the leadership before this matter was taken up here in the Congress, as you will recall.

MUNDT: Yes. But that was off the record.

RUSK: Yes. Yes, it is on page 122 of the book of documents here. There was a message to Congress on August 5, 1964, a rather short message. There he refers in his message transmitting this on this occasion, he refers to four simple propositions that he made on June second. First, America keeps her word. Here as elsewhere, we must and shall honor our commitments. Secondly, the issue is the future of Southeast Asia as a whole. A threat to any nation in that region is a threat to all, and a threat to us. Three, our purpose is peace. We have no military, political, or territorial ambitions in the area. Four, this is not just a jungle war, but a struggle for freedom on every front of human activity. It seems quite clear the way this matter was discussed at the time, it was not related solely to the attack on a ship in the Gulf of Tonkin. . . .

CHURCH: Mr. Chairman, in connection with other countries, it seems to me that you have tried very hard to enlist the support of other countries in ways that are open to you as the Secretary of State. If other countries have not responded, I think it is not due to any mistake in tactics on your part, but because those countries, for their own reasons, either see the war differently than we do and do not think their vital interests require them to participate, or feel that we will take care of the war for them, and thus that they need not participate. Whatever the reasons, I do not think it is due to any failure on your part to indicate the American interest in getting further participation in the Vietnamese war.

But you have said . . . two or three times here this morning that you are distressed that concern should be shown suddenly when the going gets tough. I simply want to say for the record that I have shown concern about our policies for the past two years. I have spoken out in every way I know. I have written articles. I have talked on the Senate floor long before the going got tough because it seemed to me that our policy was heading us into the predicament in which we now find ourselves. That predicament, I think, has little to do with past resolutions of the Congress or the legality of the present situation in the light of American treaty commitments.

I do not think that in the face of the actuality of war Congress is going to repeal the law, and there is very little to do but support the American boys who are committed there with such funds as may be required. The real question, it seems to me, gets down to a closer examination of our policy and where it is leading us in the world. From what you have said this morning, it seems to me that you draw no significant distinction between the kind of threat we faced in Korea and the kind of guerrilla war situation that now confronts us in Vietnam. In either case you have indicated that this is Communist aggression. In the former case it is overt, in the latter case covert, but nonetheless the kind of Communist aggression that requires us to intervene with large American forces to draw the line, so to speak, in Asia as we drew it in earlier years in Europe. Is that a fair statement of your position?

RUSK: With respect to those situations where we have a particular commitment, not as a matter of general philosophy. But, Senator, let me make a comment on this brief question of predicament. I think one would not understand this situation at all unless one were to call it for what it is, namely, Ho Chi Minh's war. It is not McNamara's war; it is not the United State's war. It is Ho Chi Minh's war. Maybe it is Mao Tse-tung's war in terms of the support that he has given to Ho Chi Minh, and the roadblocks he has thrown against any possibilities of peace.

We made a major effort since the spring of 1961 to find a peaceful solution to this problem of Southeast Asia. Mr. Kennedy, Mr. Khrushchev talked about it in Vienna in June, 1961. They agreed that everybody ought to leave Laos alone. That led to the Geneva Conference on Laos and the agreement on Laos. That was a good agreement. It did not work because Hanoi did not for a day take its men out of Laos as it was supposed to, and did not for a day stop its infiltration of North Vietnamese into South

Vietnam by the Ho Chi Minh Trail through Laos specifically contrary to that agreement.

Nevertheless, there have literally been hundreds of discussions with other governments, including governments on the other side, in the intervening period, trying to probe the possibilities of a peaceful settlement. During 1965 alone I myself had more than a hundred and twenty discussions with the highest officers of other governments all over the world on just this point, on just this point. During the past thirty-five days there has been a major new effort to enlist the assistance of other governments, including Communist governments, to bring this matter to a peaceful conclusion. Those efforts have been harshly and peremptorily rejected by the other side. The infiltration continues. This is Ho Chi Minh's war.

CHURCH: Mr. Secretary, if I may interrupt there?

RUSK: Yes, sir; please.

CHURCH: I have never called this war McNamara's war.

RUSK: I understand, and I am not arguing with you, Senator. I just wanted to make it clear on the predicament.

CHURCH: If it is Ho Chi Minh's war, is not it true that Ho Chi Minh was the chief architect in securing Vietnamese independence against the French?

RUSK: He was the leader of a nationalist movement that had in it many elements: and many of the elements of that nationalist movement are now in South Vietnam supporting and trying to build a system in South Vietnam that is not Communist.

CHURCH: Is it not true that at the time that the war was fought and the French were driven out, that Ho Chi Minh was generally regarded as the leader of the revolutionary effort?

RUSK: That is correct, sir.

CHURCH: So this now is Ho Chi Minh's war; that may be one of the reasons why so many Vietnamese are willing to die. . . . It seems to me that there is a difference between guerrilla war and revolution, the kind of aggression that we faced in Korea and in Europe, and further that the underdeveloped world is going to be beset with guerrilla wars regardless of the outcome in Vietnam, and we will have to live in a world afflicted with revolutions for a long time to come. That is why it is so important to try to determine what our basic foreign policy is going to be as it grapples with these revolutionary wars in many parts of the underdeveloped world in the future; and, as I have listened to your explanations this morning, I gather that wherever a revolution occurs against an established government, and that revolution, as most will doubtlessly be, will be infiltrated with Communists, that the United States regards it in its interest to prevent the success of Communist uprising. This, at least, has been the policy we followed in the Dominican Republic and in Vietnam. I wonder whether this is going to continue to be the policy as we face new guerrilla wars in the future?

RUSK: Senator, I think it is very important that the different kinds of revolutions be distinguished. We are in no sense committed against change. As a matter of fact, we are stimulating ourselves very sweeping revolutions in a good many places. The whole weight and effort of the Alliance for Progress is to bring about far-reaching social, economic changes.

CHURCH: That is change, Mr. Secretary, without violence. History shows the most significant change has been accompanied by violence. Do you think that with the foreign aid program we are going to be able to—with our money—to avert serious uprisings in many of these destitute countries in future years?

RUSK: Not necessarily avert all of them, but I do believe there is a fundamental difference between the kind of revolution which the Communists call their wars of national liberation, and the kind of revolution which is congenial to our own experience, and fits into the aspirations of ordinary men and women right around the world. There is nothing liberal about that revolution that they are trying to push from Peiping. This is a harsh, totalitarian regime. It has nothing in common with the great

American revolutionary tradition, nothing in common with it.

CHURCH: The objectives of the Communist revolution are very different indeed from the objectives of our own. But objectives of revolutions have varied through the centuries. The question that I think faces this country is, how we can best cope with the phenomena of revolt in the underdeveloped world in the years ahead? And I have very serious doubts that American intervention with military power will often be the proper decision, and that too much intervention may well spread Communism throughout this part of the world rather than thwart it.

The distinction that you draw between the Communist type of guerrilla war and other kinds of revolution, if I have understood it correctly, has been based upon the premise that in Vietnam the North Vietnamese have been meddling in the revolution in the South and, therefore, it is a form of aggression on the part of the North against the South.

But I cannot remember many revolutions that have been fought in splendid isolation. There were as many Frenchmen at Yorktown when Cornwallis surrendered as there were American Continentals. Senator Pell tells me more. I accept the correction. In any case, it seems to me that the Communists have not changed the rules of revolution by meddling in them, and the question is not whether we approve or disapprove of their goals. When we were an infant nation we stood up for the right of revolution, and I am afraid . . . what I am worried about, Mr. Secretary, is this: That where we, if we, intervene too much in wars of this type, our policy may well turn out to be self-defeating. . . . I think that the significant thing about the underdeveloped countries in recent years is the conspicuous lack of progress that the Communists have made in taking it over, and where they have had success it has been in cases where Communism has been able to catch hold of nationalist aspirations, as in Vietnam, where the Communist leader was the authentic architect of Vietnamese independence, and where it has been carried on the momentum of nationalist aspirations. . . .

I think that in these areas where the sensitivity toward Western imperialism, borne of three centuries of colonialism, is so very great, that Mao Tse-tung might want us to move in massively with the import of Western troops from the opposite side of the world, believing that this intervention serves the larger interests of China in Asia, and tends to spread Communism by identifying Communism with nationalism, and our own policy with the hated Western imperialism. This is not how we regard the policy nor how we define our objectives. But the important thing may be how Asians feel about it, and in that respect Mao Tse-tung may have a better basis for judgment than do we.

RUSK: Senator, I cannot for a moment find a way to identify the purposes of the Liberation Front organized in Hanoi in 1960 with the purposes of the American Revolution or the purposes of the national revolution which we associate with decolonization. We are prepared, and have said so over and over again publicly and privately, to let the South Vietnamese themselves decide that question. The other side is not willing to do that. They are not prepared to let the South Vietnamese choose their government. They said as late as this morning, Hanoi broadcast, that—or at least in a letter to the chiefs of the other Communist countries—that the Liberation Front must be accepted as the sole spokesman for the South Vietnamese people.

Now, we know very well from our many, many contacts with the South Vietnamese people and their leaders, and not just those in government but outside, that that is exactly what the South Vietnamese people do not want. But this can be tested in a free election. This can be tested in a free election. The 325th Division that moved from North Vietnam to South Vietnam did not come in there to provide the South Vietnamese with a liberal, democratic revolution in keeping with the modern trend of the sort of revolutions that we should welcome, not at all.

CHURCH: Couldn't this question have been tested by a free election in 1956 in South Vietnam? Aren't we all these years late?

RUSK: And in North Vietnam.

CHURCH: And blood and treasure later coming back and asserting what we might have done then without all of the agony?

RUSK: Well, this was not tested in North Vietnam or in South Vietnam in 1955 or 1966, and I know very well that the South Vietnamese are not going to be the first people in history free to elect a Communist regime. I do not know what the people in North Vietnam would do if they had a chance to vote and have a free election. . . .

GORE: Mr. Secretary, I think you may observe from the number of questions this morning that there is some need to spell out in detail to the American people the validity of our position in South Vietnam. I am willing to accept, as I indicated earlier, the fact that we are there, misguidedly or wisely. In this exchange of views, which I hope may result in some benefit, I would like to submit to you that Vietnam is not the big factor here. The big factor is the equation between the Big Three powers involved there.

I was impressed that you quoted—impressed with the statement which you quoted of a minister, a foreign minister of an Iron Curtain country, which he made to you, to wit, that the biggest problem in the world today was to bring the Red Chinese to the acceptance of the principle of peaceful coexistence. I do not recall whether you quoted him as saying it was the biggest problem or one of the biggest problems.

RUSK: I think he said the biggest problem.

GORE: I would agree that is one of the biggest problems. I am not sure it is not the biggest problem, viewed in the long run. What is your reflection upon this statement of this foreign minister?

RUSK: I think that the doctrine of an unlimited world revolution by militant means in a doctrine that is so incompatible with the peace of the world and the system of international society that we are trying to build on the United Nations Charter, that it is certainly one of the largest questions, if not the largest question.

GORE: I agree. Now, if that be the case, whether there are factors which I do not now foresee as a strong possibility, but as I see them, the equation between the three big powers, the United States, Russia, and China, is the important element involved in this predicament, as Senator Church described it. In the formulation of policy, I would urge you to urge upon the President the prime consideration of those factors rather than the loss of face or other factors that might be involved with respect to Vietnam proper. This, it seems to me, is where the danger of a nuclear war rests. I would be most reluctant to see this country play brinksmanship with nuclear war. I would not wish to approve such a policy.

RUSK: Senator, those are matters that are taken fully and earnestly into account. I do not think that I would agree, and I do not think you were saying, that the shape of the world should be determined by these three great powers at the expense of the interests and the rights of the other nations.

GORE: No, I did not say that.

RUSK: No, you did not say that. But the issues that you mentioned are fully taken into account in all of our considerations.

GORE: You recognize then that the equation between the three large powers involved here will determine whether or not there is to be a global war?

RUSK: I would not limit it to that equation. I think that the problem of general war is somewhat more complicated than that. But this is a very important part of the problem.

GORE: A war between the United States and North Viet-

nam is not a global war. We are having that one now. . . .
So if it is to be escalated into a world conflagration, it is
not within the power of Vietnam so to escalate it. Such
an escalation would either have to come from us through
an attack upon or confrontation with or hostilities with a
world power or an action on their part to engage us in
hostilities.

RUSK: Yes, I was not thinking specifically of Vietnam.
I was just reluctant, as a general matter, to say that the
problem of a general war is solely that among those three
that you mentioned. . . .

The Statement and Testimony of

LIEUTENANT GENERAL

James M. Gavin

Tuesday, 8 February 1966

GENERAL GAVIN: May I say once again, it is a great privilege for me to appear before this distinguished Committee. I look upon this as a public service where it is a privilege to be given a citizen to perform. Secondly, I particularly appreciate the opportunity to appear in an open hearing because I feel strongly these issues are of the utmost importance to our people. They should hear the differing views, and out of this discourse will come, hopefully, a coalesced and consolidated national will to get on with the work at hand.

May I say, sir, at the outset, that in the background of my point of view that I have arrived at and expressed in that communication to *Harper's* magazine went two years of service with the Philippine Scouts in the late 1930s, and since that time considerable interest in the affairs of Southeast Asia.

At the time of the fall of Dienbienphu, at the direction of the Chief of Staff, I visited Korea, Formosa, Saigon, talked to Diem, talked to General Ely there, General Collins, General Daniels, and others about the problems; went on to Thailand and talked to Mr. Sarit. Among other things at that time I recommended the construction of a highway from Bangkok to Mekong, feeling that Thailand was a very sensitive spot and very likely might become a very deeply involved part of the Southeast Asia, deeply involved in our own strategy and affairs.

Since then, perhaps one of the most interesting experiences I have had was with Mr. Kennedy. About a month after [I went] to the post in Paris he asked me to return to talk about the problems of Laos. He was confronted with a very difficult situation, and I speak from memory now. We were supporting Phoumi [Nosavan], a rightist, and the question confronting President Kennedy was to what extent should we become involved in land warfare in Laos. I do not know, but I would suspect if he had sought the advice of the Pentagon, we no doubt would have committed forces and ultimately more divisions and more divisions. But to Mr. Kennedy this made little sense and, indeed, the more we talked about it, the more I agreed with him; a landlocked country, remote from the immediate application of sea power and somewhat less of air power seemed to offer a hopeless situation to us.

He asked me, therefore, to go to Paris, upon my return, and enter into discussions with Souvanna Phouma to see if we could not convince that gentleman that we were interested in a "free, neutral, independent Laos." This I undertook to do. Admittedly it was with some misgivings at the outset because Souvanna Phouma had a reputation of being then very close to the Communists, and I was not at all sure of how our negotiations would come out. Mr. Harriman very ably conducted negotiations in Geneva in parallel with my own discussions in Paris. After about six or eight meetings, and very fruitful and fascinating meetings they were for me, we did arrive indeed at a treaty that, hopefully, guaranteed the freedom, neutrality, and independence of Laos.

I was aware then, as I am now, that what our President sought to achieve was a political settlement to what appeared to be a potentially serious military problem. He was absolutely right. He was absolutely right, and we did arrive at that solution. Since then I have continued to devote a great deal of my time to matters of global strategy in our commitments.

Last summer I was asked—late last spring I was asked by the *New York Times* to do an article on the meaning of the atomic bomb twenty years later. This was for the early-August edition of the *New York Times Magazine*. I had given a great deal of attention to the bombing in 1940, and even then came to the conclusion that urban bombing lacked credibility for a number of reasons perhaps not worthwhile going into here, and I wrote an article that I was denied publication at that time. I felt that the problems of the bomb were quite different than simply escalating World War Two experience into more and more and more applied power.

As the summer came to an end, my thinking on this matter got into [the] real meaning of the changes in global strategy that in my opinion have taken place in the last twenty years, and I did an article on this; and in the midst of this I was exchanging correspondence with Mr. Fisher, talking about strike cavalry which was a postulation advanced in early 1950s, considered far too radical for acceptance at the time, now has valid and accepted battlefield application. So I, at that time and late in the summer —early fall, decided that in the view of our total spectrum of global commitments and the changing nature of global strategy, we had better look hard at our Vietnamese commitment. It was becoming alarmingly out of balance and this was the basis for the letter I wrote which I will be very happy to come back to later.

I might say that all I said in that letter was, let's look at (a) where we are today, what our commitments are, what it is costing, and what we do; (b) what the alternatives are, what these costs might be, and having done this, let's make up our mind what we are going to do. My feeling was that we were being escalated at the will of opponents rather than at our own judgment, and I based this as much upon the statement of many officials who have been to that war-torn country and who returned with optimistic statements only to find they have had to change them successively thereafter, which suggested to me that in the very beginning they didn't understand what the requirements were and thus couldn't estimate accurately what the needs might be to meet those requirements.

In that letter I, too, in passing made reference to Hanoi and Peking and the futility of bombing, pointing out that just more of this would cause more problems, create more problems than it would solve. I referred specifically to "urban bombing." I would like to make that clear. . . .

FULBRIGHT: I just wanted to place this in time. Was this in '62?

GAVIN: No, this was late last year . . . and *Harper's* came out about my thinking of the strategy which I would like to talk about briefly. At the moment I am, in passing, touching upon the letter. I have a feeling as our bombing went on beyond what were obviously military targets, such as ammunition dumps, tank cars, or concentrations of trucks and military targets, to power plants and such as that, we were slowly creeping to urban bombing. I wanted to lay this at rest for once and for all time. Just bombing a city per se, for psychological reasons, achieves little in the way of military effect and, in fact, today in the court of world opinion could be extremely damaging and we would have nothing to show for it, and I want to be sure I have that off—that in my own opinion just bombing Peking wouldn't serve anything.

Now, sir, if I may talk a little about the matter of global strategy into which I would like to fit Vietnam. Two of the most significant things that have happened in our time certainly have been the bomb and the space exploration, both of which have tremendous military significance. The bomb is a very interesting case in point. The first question we asked ourselves was the meaning of the bomb. Was the bomb the beginning of a new age, in which the atom would solve our military problems that we have been unable to solve in the past by other means, or was it indeed the end?

I suspected at first that it was the end, although this was a very minority opinion, and now I am absolutely satisfied. As man has sought to impose his will on an opponent from the beginning of recorded history, he has sought to use energy in every form that he could get it— bludgeon, metallic penetrating instruments, metallic pellets fired by chemical charges, to the explosion of the fission of the atom and fusion of the atom itself. He finally has suggested bringing down to the earth the very explosions that take place on the surface of the sun: fission. He has brought the energy of the cosmos itself to the earth. He no longer can use it because it could destroy a major segment of the human race. He is at the end of the search for energy with which to impose his will on fellow men, he is at the end, that search has terminated. Now he must find more discreet means, more discriminating means. He must find greater mobility, rapid data transmission, he must keep this under control. He must know what is going on everywhere as quickly as he can find out so as to keep under control local conflagrations and thus avoid the major catastrophe that might occur if, thoughtlessly, nuclear weapons were used.

If this is so, and it is purely a concept in which I do not ask you to share agreement but I am grateful for the opportunity of expressing it, if this is so, then for the first time in human history something very unusual is happening in warfare, and I believe indeed it has.

Strategy has to do with those measures which, taken short of war, make absolute victory certain. If war occurs inadvertently, you are sure to win. It seems to me the best analysis I have been able to make—

SENATOR SYMINGTON: Excuse me, what was that, if war occurs inadvertently? I didn't understand.

GAVIN: If a war occurs inadvertently, if your strategy is right you are going to win. And I will give you an example of that, Mr. Symington. I might say, if I may, that

I have given a great deal of thought and done some writiny on the subject; I taught political science at the University of California, four weeks in 1946 on' a sabbatical, and I haven't come to these conclusions rather casually. They represent for me, at least, considerable effort and thought. It seems to me, therefore, that our strategy today should be based upon, first of all, a dynamic and viable prospering economy, an economy that can export entrepreneurial skills, managerial techniques, dollars for acquisition, ventures abroad, to help other people. We have developed a way of life that provides an abundance of means for our people, and we should continue to export this just as aggressively as we can to help other people. I am not talking about economic colonialism, for the enlightened businessman working abroad today is trying to help other people help themselves. People are not born equal nor indeed are nations born equal, and they need help to achieve a place for their people. They need help of many kinds. We have been doing extremely well in this respect.

While I am talking in this context of strategy, it seems to me, for example, . . . if fifteen decisive battles from the beginning of history to Waterloo were to be rewritten today, it would include the demise of Mr. Khrushchev, who sought to coexist with his own totalitarian system organized on the basis of planning and not on market demand, who failed because he simply couldn't get the grain grown, he didn't have fertilizer and his economy just simply couldn't produce; and characteristically, as happens in a failing strategy, he sought the tactical gambit to recoup. He went to Cuba in a great adventure that, thanks to our great President, and our Secretary of Defense, he was defeated in. I would say that his demise is one of the decisive setbacks in all history, and I think now . . . that our efforts to work closely with the Soviet people should be rewarding; in fact I believe that in the President's State of the Union Message the reference to making changes in our tariff laws to encourage trade is a very good thing.

We have done a great deal exporting professors, enter-
tainers, and scientists; now export businessmen and their
techniques. I think we can go a long way together. There
was a turning point and it was the demise of Mr. Khrushchev.

Well now, I would say further that strategy today is in
the realm of science and technology. Out of science and
an adequate research program we are producing an abundance of new knowledge that will energize our economy
and keep it moving and, very briefly, I think that in the
court of world opinion, world opinion itself, we have the
area that will have a very great deal to do with what we
may do. I would draw a parallel of the use of energy
and power through the many, many centuries of human
existence when people were restrained by their fellow
men in what they could do. They may have wanted to
do many things. Even cities, states, restrain what their
armed forces could do, and this nation has shrunk, . . .
this world has shrunk to the point today where we simply
can't do all the things we would like to do.

I have always felt that one of our greatest captains of
all time was General MacArthur, and yet even he had to
come to realize and learn the hard way that the use of a
nuclear bomb, because we had them in our arsenal, did
not permit him under his mandate from the United Nations to use it. It was simply an intolerable thing.

I have touched on three areas of strategy that I believe
are of overriding importance. My concern, therefore, for
Vietnam first became aroused when I found us cutting
back in our global commitments in the realm of economics, for I began to suspect that the escalation in Southeast Asia would begin to hurt our strategy position. If
this has significance now, it may have tremendous significance in the long run. When we begin to turn back
on what we are doing in world affairs through our economic endeavors to support a tactical confrontation that
appears to be escalating at the will of an enemy, we are
in very dangerous territory in my opinion, and for this

reason what we are doing there deserves looking at.

There are several areas where confrontations occur tactically. I mentioned Cuba. Europe is one today, in my opinion. Our commitments in Europe are far in excess of our needs, not only troop commitments but logistical support to back up those commitments. To get to Asia, the Korean commitment is one we must maintain, and we are maintaining it. The support of Chiang Kai-shek, Taiwan, the offshore islands of Quemoy and Matsu likewise. Southeast Asia is a very volatile, dynamic area of operation. Vietnam is not alone. Thailand I look upon as a very, very dangerous area and one that we should regard most seriously at this time.

Therefore, in looking at it, I raise some questions. First of all, what do we have today and what can they do? And I simply stated today we have sufficient forces in South Vietnam to hold areas along the coast, where sea and air power can be made fully effective, and then we can use this power as we see fit to do so. I then suggested that we might look at the alternatives very realistically.

Are we really trying to seal off Vietnam entirely, extend the 17th Parallel all across—all the way across to the Mekong River? This has been considered. One could put a *cordon sanitaire* across there at considerable cost. It would still be open-ended a bit at the end but it is possible. One could extend the security down to the Cambodian border. But to me these appear to be terribly costly in manpower and our national wealth, and I use the word "wealth" to include material resources.

So I finally came to the conclusion—and I think this is very important in view of the charges that have been made about what I have said—and I quote, "We must do the best we can with the forces we have deployed in Vietnam now." Nothing more than that. I did not say withdraw, retreat, go ahead, attack, do anything else. We must do the best we can with what we have in hand, keeping in mind the true meaning of global strategy in world affairs today.

Economics, science and technology, and world opinion will in the long run serve our strategic interests well if we handle our national resources wisely. On the other hand, tactical mistakes that are allowed to escalate at the initiative of an enemy could be disastrously costly. Since the advent of the space age there has been a revolution in the nature of global conflict. The confrontation in Vietnam is the first test of our understanding of such change or lack of it. The measures that we now take in Southeast Asia must stem from sagacity and thoughtfulness, restraint and an awareness of the nature of strategy in this very rapidly shrinking world, and that is right from the letter I wrote to *Harper's*.

Now, Mr. Chairman, perhaps at this point, I might say nothing further and I would be very pleased to have an opportunity to answer any questions that may be addressed to me.

SENATOR FULBRIGHT: Well, thank you very much, General. I think your review of the over-all strategy is very useful. Speaking for myself, not being a military man, it has great appeal, but I won't wish to pass judgment on it further than that. I believe, General, you had something to do with the study of Indochina about 1954 when you were working with General Ridgway.

GAVIN: Yes, sir, I was the Chief of Plans and Development beginning in early '54 and I stayed in that position and then in research for several years.

FULBRIGHT: Did you participate in the study that General Ridgway ordered relative to the feasibility of at that time entering into Indochina?

GAVIN: Yes, Mr. Chairman. We considered the advisability of entering the Hanoi delta, and as I recall, to be precise, we talked about the need for some eight divisions, plus some thirty-five engineer battalions; we anticipated the supply would be very great, medical and so on, and there was some significance of Hainan Island if we were going to go into the delta and so on. We gave it quite thorough consideration.

FULBRIGHT: In General Ridgway's book *Soldier,* on page 276, he said this, and I would read it and see if you would comment on this, General Ridgway's statement: "I felt it was essential therefore that all who had any influence in making the decision on this grave matter should be fully aware of all the factors involved. To get these facts I sent out to Indochina an Army team of experts in every field, engineers, signal, communication specialists, medical officers and experienced combat leaders who knew how to evaluate terrain in terms of battle tactics. The area they found was practically devoid of those facilities which modern forces such as ours find essential to the waging of war. Its telecommunications, highways, railways, all the things that make possible the operation of a modern combat force on land, were almost nonexistent. Its port facilities and airfields were totally inadequate. To provide the facilities we would need would require tremendous engineering and logistical efforts."

On page 277 he writes: "We could afford an Indochina, we could have one, if we had been willing to pay the tremendous cost in men and money that such intervention would have required, a cost that, in my opinion, would have eventually been as great as or greater than that we paid in Korea. In Korea we had learned that air and naval power alone could not win a war and that inadequate ground forces cannot win one either.

"It was incredible to me that we had forgotten the bitter lesson so soon. We were on the verge of making that same tragic error. That error, thank God, was not repeated. As soon as the full report was in I lost no time in having it passed on up the chain of command. It reached President Eisenhower. To a man of his military experience its implications were immediately clear. The idea of intervention was abandoned and it is my belief that the analysis which the Army made and presented to higher authority played a considerable, perhaps a decisive, part in persuading our government not to embark on that tragic adventure."

Well, General, so far as now are the conditions in Indochina any different today than they were at that time?

GAVIN: There is one basic difference, sir. He was talking about going into the Hanoi delta and going right to the Chinese frontier, which certainly meant the immediate intervention of Chinese opposition. Now we are considerably farther south, we are talking about the 17th Parallel on down. Other than that, I would say conditions are not essentially different, although this is a very important point, too. I should say, too, in the way of background there is more than just a cold piece of paper in this type of planning. We spent a lot of time worrying about it; certainly I did.

I had considerable combat experience in Europe from Africa to Berlin, and I knew that I would be responsible for planning the conduct of operations, and I devoted a great deal of talk about it with colleagues who had considerable experience in Southeast Asia and China. We finally decided, when we were all through, what we were talking about doing was going to war with Red China under conditions that were appallingly disadvantageous. We were talking about going to war with her thousands and thousands of miles from the heart of our warmaking capacity, and it frankly made little sense to a man who had to go do the fighting. So I was more than pleased to see General Ridgway take the initiative, and it took more courage to do it as he did and say, "let's take a look at this. It makes little sense to do it."

FULBRIGHT: Do you think the conditions in South Vietnam, the conditions mentioned in this statement, are any more favorable to the conduct of war than in North Vietnam? Is the terrain more favorable, are the conditions of health more favorable?

GAVIN: No. . . .

FULBRIGHT: So your conclusion was that, as I say, it might probably lead to a confrontation with China, and I would take it you felt and General Ridgway felt this was not a wise thing to undertake then. Do you see any reason why it would be any wiser to do today?

GAVIN: No, I don't. I must say, though, I think the initiative is perhaps that of the Chinese. It is indeed that of the Chinese.

FULBRIGHT: What do you mean by that?

GAVIN: I think that the confrontation will occur when and where they choose to make it occur. For this reason—

SENATOR GORE: Mr. Chairman, I didn't understand it. Did he say the initiative was with the Chinese now?

SYMINGTON: Will you repeat the question, Mr. Chairman?

FULBRIGHT: He did say the initiative is now with the Chinese; did you not?

GAVIN: I feel in Vietnam, yes, this is what I said a moment ago, and this is what makes me uneasy. The escalation is not occurring at our will as much as it is in response to an escalation of an opponent who is supported by the Chinese. There may be variations of nuance to this but I feel the confrontation with the Red Chinese is a real compelling fact of life today, and for this reason I am quite uneasy about an overresponse in Vietnam. We could get ourselves so deeply involved in Vietnam as to seriously lack the capability we should have if Korea were to reopen; in Thailand if it became very, very serious. And then fitting this into the spectrum of global commitments, then I am concerned because our international strategic position is being eroded badly. So the choice is not whether we will be in Vietnam—we are there—but to use with judgment and discretion what we do there. That is what I maintain we should do.

FULBRIGHT: It is a little subtle there about the initiative being in the hands of the Chinese. If our escalation is confined or if it doesn't take place in North Vietnam, it certainly would minimize the risk of Chinese entry. The

Chinese are not now presently engaged in this war directly.

GAVIN: No, not directly, except through logistical support. I would be happy if the initiative were entirely ours, and we could do just as we pleased and increase our cutback just as we see fit.

FULBRIGHT: Why can't we?

GAVIN: Well, I think we tried to and we have successively escalated and increased our commitments for reasons that seem to be beyond our control.

FULBRIGHT: I don't understand. What are the reasons that make it beyond our control?

GAVIN: . . . I think that our Secretary of Defense should be quite prepared to answer a question of that sort. We first sent trainees and then we felt we had to send combat advisors. This seemed to be adequate at one time. Then we had to send troops to protect our bases—

FULBRIGHT: Why did we have to do this? You say we had to do all this. What was the force, the irresistible force, that made us to do this?

GAVIN: . . . It was the judgment of our Secretary of Defense this had to be done, and I am not questioning why he exercised that judgment. I just know it is a historical fact it has been done.

FULBRIGHT: The fact it has been done doesn't necessarily mean that we had no choice in the matter.

GAVIN: No, quite true, this is quite true.

FULBRIGHT: It seems to me in several instances there was a freedom of choice. This is rather a strong country and I think we could have some control over whether we proceed or not proceed in this area.

GAVIN: Yes, I would say so.

FULBRIGHT: So this is where it loses me that we had to do this. There is an inevitability about it apparently from your statement that I have not been able to see.

GAVIN: Yes, perhaps we didn't have to. We could have stopped at any point along the way, as you know.

FULBRIGHT: If I understood General Ridgway's state-

ment, he said we could do this, we could win . . . but
that the cost was out of proportion to what we could gain
by doing it. . . . Would you agree with that?

GAVIN: Yes, I would indeed. . . .

FULBRIGHT: I don't see any great change in the circumstances between 1954 and the present that would warrant
any different conclusion from the study you made.

GAVIN: No. As I pointed out, in the theater, to a man
doing the fighting, there is a little difference there but it
is not of great national significance so far as our commitment goes. . . .

SPARKMAN: [You say, in your article in *Harper's,*] "On
the other hand, if we should maintain enclaves on the
coast, desist in our bombing attacks in North Vietnam and
seek to find a solution through the United Nations. . . ."
Was that to be taken as meaning that you simply meant
to pause in the bombing until you had a chance to take
it to the United Nations?

GAVIN: Yes. I would point out, sir, this letter was written in late November, and I have the letter accompanying
it, the letter which went in on November 30, and it
seemed far remote from this hearing. At that time it
seemed to me first of all I wanted to head off any idea
that urban bombing was the answer to our problem. That
is why I made specific reference to Hanoi and Peking.
Then I said desist. I didn't say stop. I didn't say cease it,
I didn't say give it up. I said, Let's slow down and take a
look at this situation. This is what I meant. . . .

I would be happy to talk about bombing, and I feel this
way about it: if General Westmoreland has a mission to
carry out, I see no reason for restricting his military targets, combat forces, combat weapons coming into the
area. Our young men deserve this support. I don't see
why he has to go to anyone else to make a decision to
deal with this type target. I began to be very uneasy in
late November when we were bombing public utilities,
power plants, and I could see us beginning to bomb cities
or women and children and noncombatants who might

lose their lives in great numbers, and we began slowly to creep into urban bombing. This is why I said, Let's desist now in our bombing and take a look at this whole situation, what our commitment is, perhaps we can find an approach through the United Nations or Geneva. I didn't know, nor does anyone else know. This is what I mean by that. . . .

SPARKMAN: I am glad to hear you answer with reference to bombing military objectives, in fact I was going to ask you that question. Would you include the harbor of Haiphong on that?

GAVIN: I really don't know enough about it, sitting here in this hearing. I would have to know more about the actual conditions of the harbor. I would presume it could be mined or it could otherwise be blockaded. I wouldn't know enough about it.

SPARKMAN: I mean action against it in any way, not necessarily from the air.

GAVIN: Yes, I would say its utility value should just be done away with since it is a major port of entry for military supplies. . . .

SPARKMAN: . . . I think that is a very clear statement and I think certainly it is a very good statement. Now, you do say that, "In the meantime we must do the best we can with the forces we have deployed in Vietnam, keeping in mind the true meaning of strategy and global affairs." . . . In other words, you are advocating maintaining the force at its present level?

GAVIN: That is exactly what I said, yes sir. . . . May I elaborate on this? I was startled to find in the budget request figures for '67, fiscal year '67, we are going into $10.5 billion into Vietnam, and this is why as a citizen who has devoted a lifetime almost to the study of our global position and the nature of global conflict, this is what worries me quite a bit. Is Vietnam at this point worth this investment of our national resources, with all the other commitments we have worldwide? Are we not becoming too mesmerized with this? Are we not losing sight of the total global picture? So I recommend therefore that we make do with what we have. Now I was very happy to have an opportunity to go over to the Pentagon and talk to Mr. McNamara and Mr. Vance about this very thing. Could we do better with what we have, for example, and I really don't know. I don't believe he is sure at the moment either. We have many commitments in many areas along the coast and inland, and it might be possible, in a purely military sense of gaining an advantage, to redeploy our resources. I don't know. It would be certainly unwise in any combat to maintain a status quo, just sit there and do nothing. So I think we should not only do the best with what we have but look at how we might do better with what we have.

SPARKMAN: General Gavin, I remember that in the MacArthur hearings General Bradley one time used the expression with reference to a land war in Asia, particularly in China, in which he said, it would be the wrong war in the wrong place at the wrong time. You hold somewhat to that view, I take it?

GAVIN: Well, I—may I speak for myself, sir. I think he was referring to a war— . . . combat in Korea and Manchuria. Unfortunately we are in—we are involved in Southeast Asia—our young men are doing a splendid job there. I don't think the armed forces have done a better job right from the outside of the word "go" in combat. They have done a fine job and we must give them the best support we can, keeping in mind the nation's total commitments. So I couldn't quite agree with that as General Bradley once expressed it.

SPARKMAN: You do point out in your article, though, if we are going to have a war with Red China, it ought to be in the Manchurian area rather than in the southern area.

GAVIN: To be very objective in a military sense about this as an advisor, . . . I would say if China brings upon herself a global war, the place to fight her is not in Southeast Asia. The place to fight her is where you can take away the real heart of her warmaking capacity, the Ruhr of China, and this is the Manchurian area. . . .

SENATOR HICKENLOOPER: . . . Do I understand that you advocate that we hold what we have? That is a rather broad statement, but is it in essence that we hold what we have and we not attempt to extend or expand our physical control of the area in South Vietnam except by, let's say, peaceful means?

GAVIN: Yes, sir.

There is a not too subtle point involved in the use of language here. When I wrote that we were then apparently escalating at a rather steady rate, we were up around two hundred thousand men. Some writers were saying we may need to double this to five hundred thousand. There was even talk about a million men, I understand, by some military columnists. I felt that the time had come to take a reappraisal of where we were, feeling we were being initiated not at our own will and judgment but at the initiative of the opponent, and therefore I did say, Let's take a look at what we now have there, what we can do with what we have, and see if we can't find another solution to this problem, because the alternative is quite clear; we can go ahead and go to half a million men or three quarters of a million men but if we do this, we must understand that these are all the implications. . . .

HICKENLOOPER: General Gavin, regardless of what your own personal desires or program would be, what do you conceive to be the objective of our country and whatever allies we have in the activities in South Vietnam today? . . . What is your conception, how do you understand it?

GAVIN: Yes, this is the impression I get from reading about it. No one has told me that.

We are seeking to establish a government, that is, a democratic government, a government chosen by the people of South Vietnam and that can operate freely without interference by the Viet Cong, that is all. We haven't a desire for bases, we haven't a desire to stay there. We want them to have a good government of their choosing.

HICKENLOOPER: Under the history of the last two or three years, do you believe that that would have any possibility of being accomplished by holding what we have now and not attempting to escalate in any way, . . . that is, in any material substantial way?

GAVIN: I am really not sure. I was led to believe a year or two ago, that, yes, this was quite possible. We were saying that we could, by merely providing trainees and instructors. So I don't know. I have decided I had better worry a little bit more about this now. I would like to know what the alternatives are, and there is much talk about. . . . I would like to know where we are going, this related to the total commitment this country has, whether it would be a sound investment.

HICKENLOOPER: Do you consider this to be primarily a military operation in South Vietnam or is it basically a political operation in South Vietnam?

GAVIN: Well, certainly, its character has become military in its entirety now. It was originally political. When we were just providing advisors—a handful, I believe it was—it was really a political problem. But the commitments of military forces on both sides have made it overwhelmingly a military problem we seem to be trying to solve by military means. I guess this relates to what I said about Laos and the late President Kennedy's solution to the Laotian problem. It was, in prospect, a foreboding military problem. We found an adequate political solution to it. If we can solve political problems in Vietnam, the military problem would disappear. It may be far too late for that now.

HICKENLOOPER: At the present time the evidence seems to indicate that the Viet Cong control more than 50 per cent of the land in South Vietnam. . . . I don't know what the percentage is. We get various estimates. . . . Let's say two thirds. If we followed the policy of—let's say, to use your word—desisting on our military activities or standing fast or holding, what would keep the Viet Cong from running riot over the rest of . . . South Vietnam?

GAVIN: . . . I said desisting in the application of bombing. The use of the land forces in any way we can use them effectively I think should be carried out.

HICKENLOOPER: Well, that reverts under the circumstances there mostly to jungle fighting, would it not?

GAVIN: Yes, that is what it is today.

HICKENLOOPER: I am interested in your comments upon bombing military objectives, military targets. . . . It is my understanding that one of the ultimate actions of a war on either side, if they can't win quick victory right in the field, is to attack the enemy's, wherever they can, to attack the enemy's basis of strength, his production facilities, the things that feed the war machine, which certainly . . . I would think would include power plants, I would think it would include canals, I would think it would include railroads, and all manner of things, factories that produce the sinews of war for his armies. . . . So I don't understand why power plants should be excluded.

GAVIN: Sir, I must say I look upon this as one of the great illusions of all time, that through air power you can really win this way. I think the results of the Strategic Bombing Survey will show that as our bombing was increased, German production went up until we overran facilities. I don't think you can hold them by bombing it nor really win by bombing.

HICKENLOOPER: That has been pretty much of an undisputed military theory for a long, long time. . . . We used to say, before the airplane came into such great prominence, that you could take ground with artillery but you couldn't hold it unless you put men on the ground that you temporarily captured with artillery fire.

GAVIN: Yes, the airplane to me is transportation, and the use of the airplane in Vietnam today is sensationally attractive, the big helicopter, the Hercules, and the role the Air Force is playing in this respect is absolutely indispensable. But this isn't bombing, bombing is another matter.

HICKENLOOPER: Now, I don't like to get into professional arguments here . . . But I presume you have read the report, at least, of General Maxwell Taylor's speech in New York somewhere around the first of this month.

GAVIN: Yes, I have, sir. . . .

HICKENLOOPER: He is quoted as saying, in effect, at least that he knew of no officer with "current" responsibility who shared the enclave theory. They go on and refer to your—I assume that was referring to your article in the February issue of *Harper's* magazine—and then he comments in this speech that if we don't succeed in South Vietnam, the efficacy of a war of liberation will be established and proved, and that—I take it that it would follow that we could expect more attempts at wars of liberation around over the world in various places if this succeeded in South Vietnam.

And I will read this paragraph. This is allegedly a direct quote from the speech: "General Taylor says this country cannot escape its destiny as the champion of the free world. There is no running away from it. The impulse to withdraw our troops into safe enclaves in South Vietnam has much in common with the yearning for safety beyond defenses at our coastlines, and is equally illusory." I assume you are thoroughly familiar with this speech as it was reported?

GAVIN: I have, I guess, a copy of it in front of me, purported to be a copy in the *Washington Post*.

HICKENLOOPER: Yes, probably the same that I have. Now it seems to me that regardless of how or when that got us into this situation in South Vietnam, it seems to me that our presence there as the most formidable part of the free world may go far beyond the question of, let's say, winning a battle. It is an ideological struggle that we are facing at that point. Would you agree that there is an ideological factor here?

GAVIN: Oh, sure, no question about it.

HICKENLOOPER: And if we don't win that ideological battle, then what do you think will happen to American prestige in Africa and South Asia and Indonesia and the Philippines and Formosa, Japan? . . .

GAVIN: Yes, would you include Cuba in that?

HICKENLOOPER: Well, it looks to me like Cuba has been pretty well conceded to the Communists already.

GAVIN: Straining, we go halfway around the world to worry about them so much when we leave Cuba being ninety miles from the shore.

HICKENLOOPER: Well, I agree with some criticism on that, but we are not in there now. I am talking about the old Communist philosophy from Moscow, that the way to Paris is by way of Peking, and the encirclement policy of capturing first South Asia, moving through South Asia, moving on into Africa or portions of it, and the Mediterranean and so on under that long-range theory.

GAVIN: Yes, sir, I assume you base your question upon the statements made by General Taylor, Senator, and these I find deeply disturbing. I am not sure he read what I wrote but he has these things to say. He attributes to me a holding strategy, a permanent cessation of bombing, a halt to further United States reinforcements, a withdrawal of United States ground forces, which would lead to a crushing defeat, a capitulation, abandonment of many people, a retreat. He refers to it as a retreat which would be disastrous and a great defeat and so on. I don't understand this. This to me is a technique that I found so very distressing, that all these things are attributed to someone, and then you are asked why you feel like this, and why did you say these things, and you find yourself defending what you didn't say. I don't think he read what I wrote. . . .

HICKENLOOPER: One of the purposes of this is to clarify the situation because there is a great deal of confusion. . . .

GAVIN: Yes. On matters of wars of liberation, the serious

import of these. . . . Yet I worry that since the initiative may be that of the Chinese, let's say, we feel that we must rise to each confrontation with every national resource, and defeat this then and there with all that we have. I have no doubt in the long run that our system will triumph vis-à-vis that of the Chinese Communists, no question in my mind about it. What I want is to see my nation . . . show restraint and act wisely and be well around the periphery with each confrontation. I think we are doing quite well in Vietnam. I worry about going further. Whether or not we win a so-called war of liberation vis-à-vis the Chinese doesn't worry me half as much as all the other things that could happen with us. I think we are doing quite well in total confrontation. . . .

SENATOR MORSE: My first question will deal with a concern that you have expressed throughout your testimony at various times this morning and I would put it this way. It seems to me you are concerned about where may we end up . . . in this war in Southeast Asia vis-à-vis China, and we have got to face that general question of policy. We can't stick our heads in the sand and say there is no danger of a war with China. I hope they will have sense enough not to involve themselves in a nuclear war, but who knows.

So my first question is, suppose they do, suppose they decide to move on the ground; suppose we get into a war with them and we do the bombing and we knock out their cities and their nuclear installations and their industrial complex but they still carry on on the ground. What is your estimate of how many American troops we will have to send over in the early stages of that war?

GAVIN: That is quite a complex question, Mr. Senator, and I would like to be fully responsive to it. Much would depend on the theater, much would depend on where they would have to go. I sometimes wonder what the theater slice is for Vietnam because to maintain a division must take four to five times that many people really behind the slice to keep them there. If the major confrontation were to occur as I would hope it would in northern China, in the Manchurian area, operating out of Korea we could probably do quite well with perhaps double the forces we had in Korea and when we were involved there, when General Ridgway was in command. I would like to be specific but the question does not lend itself to specific answers.

MORSE: I understand. I don't see how you can be specific but I think it is important, however, in this public hearing that the question be raised. . . . To elict from you . . . a response as to whether or not you could do it with the number of men that we now have in Southeast Asia or double that or triple that. Is it not true, judging from what other military leaders have said in the past, that it would take a good many hundreds of thousands of men to fight Red China on the ground, whether you do it in Manchuria or whether you move up from South Korea to the border of China?

GAVIN: Yes, If the commitment began with Chinese volunteers, followed by some semblance of semi-regular forces, I would say our commitment would escalate very rapidly to double and double again the force we have in Southeast Asia, just to save themselves and save their own resources and bases.

MORSE: And when we got through forcing her to her knees, and I am satisfied we could, at a horrible cost but that we could—final surrender—does that end our occupation in China?

GAVIN: No. I have a feeling that at this point, if you got that far down the road in total conflict, you would involve the USSR in some role or another, and whether they would seek to enter the vacuum in Mongolia in China I don't know, but I suspect they would and there would be real problems in further confrontations in the successive— following the defeat of China.

MORSE: Assuming Russia doesn't come in and it is the United States versus China, after we force her to surrender, there is still going to be a China devastated. As she is, would it be possible for us to just automatically withdraw our troops and go home or would we have a policing job to do for a long time thereafter?

GAVIN: Well, there is no doubt that there would be hundreds of millions of Chinese left who would be in dire, dire straits, many of them very ill from the effects of the use of nuclear weapons; the whole base of food production, food availability, the economy, the agriculture would be laid flat; and I would assume we would take some responsibility for trying to get the situation straightened out. . . . It would be an appalling problem to deal with, I would think.

MORSE: Would that not be also an appalling drain on the economic resources as well as the manpower of our country?

GAVIN: Yes, it would, no question about it.

MORSE: Now let's take the possibility of Red Russia getting involved. I am surprised at the number of people who seem to want to say, "Oh, Russia wouldn't want to come in." But we have a duty of giving some thought to the problem, if she does come in, what our position will be then. If Russia should come in on the basis of the fact that she has a security pact with China or for any other reason, do you think Russia would fight us in China or would she fight us in New York City, in Chicago, and Washington as we fought her in Moscow and Stalingrad?

GAVIN: Well, Russia will always fight where it is to her advantage to do so. I think the policies of Stalin of aggrandizement still are present, perhaps latent, but there. And I would think if she saw clearly an opportunity to achieve greater control of greater amounts of territory she would go ahead and seek to her advantage wherever it would take her, northern China or wherever it would be. If this involved a confrontation with us, I don't know. This is another matter. I think she has great respect for our nuclear weapons. . . .

MORSE: Mr. Chairman, let me ask one more question.

You spoke in response to a question by Senator Hickenlooper about what we might do if we escalated the war into Hanoi and into the harbor, and you said we might either mine it or blockade it or I assume both. Have you given any thought, General, as to what the position of noncombatant countries in respect to their flags would be if we blockaded the harbor? Would you name for us the neutral or noncombatant nations that would lower their flag to that blockade, including the Union Jack?

GAVIN: No, I think we would be in very serious trouble with our allies. . . .

MORSE: And that blockade would be no better than its enforceability.

GAVIN: That is right.

MORSE: Do you know of any time in the history of the British Empire when that Union Jack has ever been lowered to a blockade that the British Empire was not a party to?

GAVIN: No, I know of none and this matter has come up in the past . . . when we were dealing about some problems with China. I know this is a very difficult thing to deal with and probably it would be impossible to enforce. Blockade it alone.

MORSE: Do you think the Russian flag would be lowered to that blockade?

GAVIN: I don't know. I doubt it.

MORSE: When we sank the first Russian ship when it wasn't lowered to that blockade, do you think they would send us a valentine in February or send us a bomb?

GAVIN: I suppose they would be inclined to bomb.

MORSE: I much prefer valentines. . . .

SENATOR AIKEN: General Gavin, as I understand from newspaper reports that you favor holding what bases we now have, whether inland or on the coast, is that correct?

GAVIN: Again, where we stand today?

AIKEN: Right where we are now, and not any ground forces. Just what is a state of siege? I am asking that question because all the fighting seems to be taking place on the perimeters of our bases, whether inland or on the coast. . . . I realize there are different kinds of sieges, perhaps, but all the fighting seems to be taking place on the perimeter of our bases.

GAVIN: Yes. First of all, I might say that I was not more specific on what we have there because I, indeed, do not know. I do not have any access to classified information, and I just know from what I read in the newspapers, and I do know we have established air and sea bases along the coasts in several areas, and also we have pushed our units into the interior in a seek-and-destroy operation. They appear at the moment to be doing quite well, and again I can only say from what I read in the press. There was an interesting column yesterday by Mr. Alsop in which he speculated about the possible use of less force if one pursues this tactic, than in holding up and digging in in some sort of a periphery around the coast, which I did not have in mind. But I do not know. I do not think that there is a state of siege at all. Far from it. They seem to be doing quite well with what they have.

AIKEN: Assuming that we hold the bases which we now have and perhaps increase our force to the numbers indicated by—which may be indicated by General Westmoreland, how long a job do you suppose it would be to restore a reasonable degree of security to the people of South Vietnam?

GAVIN: I really do not know, sir. I do not know that anyone does. If we were to add another hundred thousand men, I would expect that this would be matched by commitment from the Viet Cong and possibly begin to see a commitment of Chinese support.

AIKEN: You do not think it would take as long as it took in the Philippines?

GAVIN: Oh, that went on for many, many years. The pacification was not completed until we had been in there, oh, twenty years at least. This is a very rough guess. But I would expect that we may be involved in Southeast Asia for many, many, many years. Perhaps not that long, but a long time.

AIKEN: There are other reports which are rather puzzling in a way. Every little while we read that a large body of allied troops, maybe as many as ten or fifteen thousand, surrounded a lesser body of Viet Cong troops, possibly of regimental strength, and are drawing a net on them; and then a few days later, when the net has been drawn tight, we find that there are only a few of the Viet Cong caught in it. What becomes of them? Where do they go? Would you have any guess as to what becomes of them?

GAVIN: Sir, my guess is hardly a bit better than yours. I do know from having served in the Island of Luzon and out on Bataan, and spent quite a bit of time with Filipinos, the Filipinos themselves, in a military operation you deal with a language problem, and the problem of security; I think in many cases that they are probably well informed about what we are doing, and we find difficulty knowing what they are doing. The environmental conditions are such that we probably have a difficult time adapting to them compared to the natives we are dealing with, and the sum total of all of this is that despite our courage and our equipment and the gallantry of our troops, we just have a very tough problem to handle. It is a little beyond our resources at times.

AIKEN: Yes. I noticed that you said that we might not now be in a position to determine the degree of escalation, that China might determine that for us. Where does Russia come into this picture? I had not seen any outward indications that Russia was at all displeased with our getting more seriously involved in that part of the world.

GAVIN: Well, if one were to judge from what one reads in the press, the Russians and the Chinese have a very serious difference of view about support to Hanoi any way. The Russians have presumably provided surface-to-air missiles, which are of a dubious performance so far. They are apparently getting these through China by rail

to Hanoi. I think Russia would like to be identified with
Ho Chi Minh's mind as the real supporter and savior of
the North Vietnamese people. On the other hand, I do
not think the Chinese are going to stand for this for a
moment. If there is any identification it will be the Chinese Reds. Personally, I would think that Ho Chi Minh
would like to stand between the two and not be identified
with either.

AIKEN: He seems to have indicated that himself from
time to time. I suppose Russia could not only deliver surface-to-air missiles; they could deliver most any kind of
missiles to North Vietnam if they thought the occasion
required it.

GAVIN: Yes. They would be quite sensitive about the
classified material of a very sophisticated nature going
in there, I am sure, and for this reason they would be
restrained in what they did. If they were likely to be overrun, they would be very, very touchy about that because
missiles and their associated guidance equipment are still
quite highly classified in that type of sophisticated
armor. . . .

SENATOR CARLSON: . . . I gathered from one of your
statements that we might have to put troops in Thailand.
Would you discuss that a little bit? Did you not make
that statement?

GAVIN: Yes, yes. Of course, I do not have access to the
actual troop dispositions or deployments there, but as I
understand it from the sources I have, and mostly newspapers, the Pathet Lao are still aggressive in Laos. The
Viet Cong are beginning to show up in Laos. I would expect them to give Souvanna Phouma a very difficult time
and be in the Mekong [basin in] no time at all, indeed if
some forces are not there already. We now have logistical
deployments in Thailand in anticipation of troubles there
of a very serious order of magnitude, harbors, bridges,
highways, which are almost the forerunner of a proper and
efficient deployment of troops . . . but these things are

taken as a matter of caution, so I would think that the Viet Cong would go ahead with the urging and support of the Chinese and engage us and engage the Thais— Laotians and then the Thais and involve ourselves.

CARLSON: General, just following that same line of thinking, isn't the question going to be why should we not at least remain and prosecute the war in Vietnam with a hope that it would not expand into other areas of Southeast Asia?

GAVIN: Yes, absolutely. I think this is a very proper question, and the answer might be, indeed, yes. In fact, if we were going to fight in Thailand, I am not concerned about if we fail in Vietnam; Thailand is coming, Thailand is coming anyway. I am concerned about the requirements for both. If it is $10.5 billion in Fiscal 1967 for Vietnam, what is it going to be in 1968 or 1969 for Thailand, too, because we have both. It is not either one. We have both, and it may well be to our advantage, I rather think tactically it is, although I am not on the ground. I am speaking in a rather different environment here. I would think it would be well to hold a major area of Vietnam if we were going to get involved in Thailand, because this would put us in position of being not far from the communications of the Chinese supply forces that would have to supply down into Thailand.

CARLSON: I believe you stated, in response to a question, that you were not opposed to the bombing of military objectives in North Vietnam.

GAVIN: That is right, sir.

CARLSON: That is one of the issues that is confronting our people. I receive much mail on it, and I am sure everyone in the country has, of the various different viewpoints as to whether we should bomb or should not bomb. . . . I have before me a release of General Wheeler's statement which was taken before the Senate Armed Services Committee and released. I am going to quote just one paragraph, and in it he discusses the three blue chips that we have when we come into negotiation . . . : "One of them is the bombing of North Vietnam; the second is the deployment of United States and third country forces into South Vietnam; and the third is the prospective withdrawal, under appropriate circumstances, of our forces and third country forces." It was his contention, if we stopped bombing North Vietnam, we would lose a great advantage when we come to negotiations, and I would assume you would agree with most of us that we would settle this some day by negotiation.

GAVIN: I would hope so. I read General Wheeler's statement with a great deal of interest. I have a tremendous admiration for him. He is unquestionably the best man we have in the armed forces today. I had an uneasy feeling that somehow we were not talking about the same thing. Actually, of course, the bombing is a blue chip that we have. I would like to make it quite clear that one thing I wanted to head off was any extrapolation of the immediate World War—post-World War Two thinking that you can bomb cities and gain military results of any impressive sort whatsoever. Today, with the weapons we have, taking out complete cities will unquestionably create more problems than they will solve for us. One may go all the way back down the road, where you are just giving vital bomber support to a platoon out in the middle of, well, of the highlands, let us say. It is a very difficult line to draw.

I personally cannot imagine, with my military background, having our young men out there committed to battle, where their very lives depend on using every resource they have, to allow military dangers to arise in front of them, and then to ignore them; and the front may be a hundred miles away, and it may be a tank column or a flight of bombers or any such military target as that. But I would not just extrapolate this on to bombing the North, let us say. Somewhere in between you have to draw the line. . . .

SENATOR MUNDT: General, you have a statement in your

article in *Harper's* that sort of predicts a pretty dim future for the world, and I would like to have you talk about it a little bit. I quote it to you. It is on page eighteen, which says: "If the Chinese Communists continue on their present course of aggression and, at the same time, continue to develop more devastating weapons—and I refer to nuclear weapons—the time may come when China will bring upon herself a nuclear war. But that time is not here yet." What can we do to avert that kind of catastrophe? Because China is not going to bring upon herself a nuclear war without probably attacking us. . . .

GAVIN: I mean every bit of that. . . . I rather suspect that basic to the Chinese problem is the problem of isolation in the affairs of the world. It seems to me, sooner or later we are going to have to find a way to bring China into the councils, and I speak of the United Nations, the councils of the world. We have got to get these people into the society of people to talk about these problems.

Now, I think they will go ahead on an aggressive course, that is the course they are now on, and will develop nuclear weapons, fission weapons and fusion weapons, hopefully they will learn the appalling and shocking casualties that these weapons can inflict both directly and indirectly, and hopefully that their adjustment to the problems of the world, their acceptance into the family of nations, their education as a result of their own technical developments may bring about a point of view on their part such as we can live together and coexist together and trade together. But this is not in prospect now.

The way things are now going I think they will continue on an aggressive course, they will continue to be aggressive in Southeast Asia, they will continue to export their brand of totalitarian Communism in Africa, in South America, and wherever they can find a foothold, pleading the cause they peculiarly plead that "it is us, the colored people against the other people, we understand your problem, and these other people do not, the Soviets or the United States or the Europeans." I think they will

continue on this course for some time, and I can foresee
the possibility of them initiating a war that will end up
in a nuclear holocaust. I can see this possibility happening. I hope it could be avoided. . . .

MUNDT: Have you any suggestions to make as to specific steps that American military or diplomatic policies
we might take to avert this awful calamity that you allude
to?

GAVIN: Yes, sir. I sure have. . . . I think we ought to
mind our business and get on to developing a strategy
that we have in recent years that is totally successful. I
left the service in 1958, honestly concerned about the
strategy we were then embarking upon. It was one of
massive retaliation, the time and place of our choosing,
and we are just beginning to suspect that [at] that time
we needed a change. I felt it was totally wrong. I felt
the problems we were going to live with were not total
war but limited war all around the periphery. I was then
concerned with the success of the Soviet system as I saw,
from a scientific principle, they were doing extremely
well. I am not satisfied in the last eight years we have
definitely demonstrated to them that our system is far
more productive not only of material goods and comforts
for our people, but of weapons as well, and they are now
seeking to find some accommodations in the world of eco-
comic competition. . . . I believe in dealing with the
Chinese problem. If we keep in mind our total global
strategic commitments and take care of those and conduct
ourselves well, dealing with the confrontations the Chinese give us on this very abrasive interface with ourselves
in China as best we can, discreetly and with some wisdom,
to overcommit ourselves in Southeast Asia or anyplace
else, for that matter, Thailand, could be a very serious
mistake in case of our total equipment.

MUNDT: Do you think success or failure, either alternative, is going to have any impact on this problem of
whether the Chinese develop a system of nuclear weapons?

GAVIN: No, no. I think they will go on with that as fast as they can.

MUNDT: Do you think it will make any difference in the over-all picture whether we lose or win in Vietnam?

GAVIN: Oh, I think—I think regardless of the outcome of the Vietnamese confrontation, and I cannot conceive of us really losing there with the resources we have, I think that they will get on with their nuclear weapons program. It is a matter of the highest priority. . . .

SENATOR CHURCH: . . . I understand that back in 1954 when, following the French defeat at Dienbienphu, the question was posed as to whether the United States should intervene militarily . . . in Indochina, that you and General Ridgway, who played a very prominent role in Korea . . . were of the opinion that this ought not to be done. Is that correct?

GAVIN: Yes, true. I was his Chief of Plans and Operations and he was Chief of Staff.

CHURCH: From a military standpoint then, you must have thought that the vital security interests of the United States did not require the deployment of American troops in Indochina. Is that correct?

GAVIN: True. That is right.

CHURCH: Now, if we had not intervened in the interim since . . . and if we had not made the pledges that have been made to the Saigon government, and committed American presence and prestige there, in other words, if you were again faced with the same question without what has happened in the intervening period, would you still be of the same opinion that the vital security interests of the United States from a military standpoint do not require the deployment of American troops in Indochina?

GAVIN: Yes, sir. I would say so. "Vital" is a key word there.

CHURCH: I wanted to get that on the record, General,

because there has been so much discussion of withdrawal, and I do not know anyone around this table, certainly no member of the Foreign Relations Committee, that has advocated a withdrawal . . . under the present circumstances . . . in Vietnam. But we have to draw a clear distinction between a military assessment of our vital interests and the situation in which we now find ourselves when we have made a very great commitment of American prestige and a very solemn political commitment that has to be thrown into the balance in determining now what is best to do. . . .

Now, if the war continues to spread northward and westward toward the Chinese frontiers, and if the Chinese intervene and come down into Vietnam, as they did in Korea, in your opinion, General, could we then stop the Chinese from the air, that is to say, by deploying our naval and aerial power, and stop them through bombing?

GAVIN: No, they could not be stopped from the air. Incidentally, you could not do that in North Korea either.

CHURCH: That is right. If they were stopped at all, they would have to be stopped on the ground.

GAVIN: In my opinion, yes, sir.

CHURCH: Now, with respect to China itself, should we find ourselves locked in a war with China, is it your opinion, General, that we could subdue China by an all-out bombing attack against them?

GAVIN: Nuclear bombing.

CHURCH: Well, let us say, first of all, conventional bombing.

GAVIN: In my opinion, it would take nuclear bombs anyway, and there is no question about it: if we were to elect to use nuclear weapons the devastation would be incredible that we could inflict on any nation. Our stockpile is tremendous, and the devastation would be beyond understanding. . . .

CHURCH: But even if we were to spread such an incredible desolation through the employment of nuclear weapons, do you think it would require a physical occupation of China by American land forces to effect a conquest of China itself?

GAVIN: If you seek conquest, yes. Certainly not of all of the real estate, but of all of the key areas.

CHURCH: How many American troops, in your judgment, would that require?

GAVIN: Gee, I do not know, sir. I am sorry, I would be guessing.

CHURCH: But it would require, even according to the most conservative guess, many million, would it not?

GAVIN: Yes. You are dealing here with something that would be an awful thing, because we have global commitments that would require us to meet NATO and SEATO and many bilaterals, and this would be an exceedingly difficult thing to do.

CHURCH: At the time that General Ridgway, fresh from his Korean experience, advised strongly against intervention in Indochina, he considered, you will remember, the possibility of a war with China itself. . . . And I think in that respect it might be profitable to read one paragraph that Ridgway wrote. It reads as follows: "But I challenge any thesis that destroying the military might of Red China would be in our own long-range interest. We would create there by military means a great power vacuum. Then we would have to go in there with hundreds of thousands of men to try and fill that vacuum, which would bring us face to face with Russia along its seven thousand mile frontier. If we failed to go in, then Russia herself would fill it and the threat to our own security would not have been abated one iota." Are you in general agreement . . . or in disagreement with that?

GAVIN: I would be in agreement with that. . . .

SENATOR CASE: . . . We have often heard it stated, in guerrilla war you need a ratio of friendly forces to guerrilla forces of about ten-to-one. I do not know whether this is correct or not. But let us say five or ten. . . . We have a couple of hundred thousand troops in Vietnam now, and the Vietnamese forces have about 560,000 a total of 760,000. According to Defense Department figures that the staff has given us, there were 236,000 North Vietnamese in there at the end of the year.

GAVIN: Yes.

CASE: That ratio was not proper for what we were trying to do even now.

GAVIN: Yes.

CASE: I understand the South Vietnamese are urging us to put in additional troops to put the ratio up to six-to-one. That would make something like 656,000 American men.

GAVIN: Yes.

CASE: Only about fifty-six thousand more than the number suggested by Senator Stennis in a recent speech.

GAVIN: Yes.

CASE: I take it you are not in favor of this kind of increase in the size of our forces in Vietnam? . . .

GAVIN: I am not in favor of it as an automatic proposition that we must go to a ratio of five-to-one, eight-to-one, seven-to-one, ten-to-one, any figure whatsoever. I think you can—by the innovation of such things as Sky Cavalry we can make one man equal to one guerrilla any time, and it is not just a matter of adding manpower.

CASE: Well, have you any ideas as to the size, as to the increase, which you would approve or would disapprove?

GAVIN: No, I do not. I do not.

CASE: You do not rule out five hundred thousand, six hundred thousand, seven hundred thousand men?

GAVIN: At this point I must say that I would become quite concerned. What we would be talking about then, sir, is a budget of $20 billion, $25 billion. In terms of our strategic commitments worldwide, I would be very seriously concerned. I would think three quarters of a million men—if we get that involved, the Chinese surely would open up Korea. I think we are getting onto another magnitude-type confrontation once we double and triple what we have there, and this is just an opinion, I must admit.

On the ground General Westmoreland may have different ideas entirely. . . .

CASE: You would regard any such escalation, such as two or three times the number we have now, as serious and undesirable?

GAVIN: Yes, indeed I would. . . .

SENATOR CLARK: General, I would like to associate myself with the many nice things that have been said about you here today. I think you have shown a great deal of courage, and have made a very real contribution to this problem. You have said several times this morning that you thought that we ought to make do with what we have. I think I took down accurately the statement, "We can't afford to pull out. We should not escalate." Is that a fair statement of what you have said?

GAVIN: Yes. As I expressed it in that article. Let's stay where we are, [see] what we can do with what we have.

CLARK: What concerns me, and a lot of the rest of us, is whether, if we make do with what we have, we aren't going to get chased out. What is your view on that? My point being, the other side has escalated, as that great military strategist Joseph Alsop has written about the buildup of the North Vietnamese Army, and an indication that because they have escalated to such an extent, we must escalate too, or else we will be chased out. What is your view on that?

GAVIN: Yes. Specifically about that article, it is a strange article.

CLARK: It is indeed.

GAVIN: I suspect what he is going to say next is we should probably double our strength there. I think this is what he is leading to.

CLARK: I have no doubt. I suspect, and I have no reason to say this other than that I know Joe Alsop pretty well, he would be dropping bombs on China pretty soon. But let's get back to the main problem here.

GAVIN: Yes, sure.

CLARK: Can we afford to do with what we have got, or are we going to have to put more troops in because we can't hold what we have got with what is there now?

GAVIN: I don't know, and of course this is very much up to the Viet Cong and the Chinese backing them. To the extent they want to commit their own resources, they are tough decisions we have to face up to. But I hope that we will make the decisions ourselves, and not be forced to make them to match what the other side does. This is my point of view at the moment.

CLARK: What bothers me is that we may have passed the point where we can make the decision. I assume that you would not want to go on record as to what you think are the capabilities of our present two hundred thousand men there now, without knowing a lot better than I do, maybe a lot better than you do, as to what we are up against.

GAVIN: I couldn't give you anything more. It would be quite improper for me to second-guess what General Westmoreland can do with what he has. I do know we had certain resources there not long that were looked upon as quite adequate. We are doing quite well with them today. I would hesitate to speculate beyond that. I would be loath to see us escalate indefinitely, and double and double again what we have.

CLARK: In other words, you would go pretty slow on escalation in terms of both men and material? . . .

GAVIN: Oh, indeed, absolutely.

CLARK: Now it was in September, 1963, that President Kennedy said, and I think I quote fairly accurately, that this is their war. We can help as advisors, we can help with money, but they have to either lose it or win it. In your opinion are we over that point now? And unless we put substantial additional American forces into that war, are we going to be chased out?

GAVIN: Yes, I certainly think we are beyond that point. I base this upon my conversations with Mr. McNamara about a week or so ago . . . the limitations now and the availablity of certain Vietnamese manpower are very, very severe. They can't do much more.

CLARK: Do you think the South Vietnamese—I don't want to overstate it—you don't think they can do much more?

GAVIN: Not an awful lot more. This I believe now.

CLARK: So then it is really an American war, isn't it?

GAVIN: It is certainly becoming that.

CLARK: Now have you been able to make any estimate, or on the basis of your military experience is it possible to make an estimate of the costs in terms of men and money of (a) staying where we are, and (b) retaining substantial parts of the territory we have lost? Would not the latter be much more expensive, both in terms of casualties and money?

GAVIN: Well, I would think so, yes. I would think so despite the opening paragraphs of Mr. Alsop's article, whereby by falling back to the areas you hold, you can reduce your casualties and do more with less troops. No, I would think the logic would be that if you were going to extend your search and destroy effort, you have to have more manpower.

CLARK: And if you extend your search and destroy efforts, are you not inevitably going to run up casualties?

GAVIN: Oh, I would think so, sure.

CLARK: In your concept is it possible by holding the territory we now have, minimizing the search and destroy, which at least to a layman reading the newspapers does not seem to have very useful long-range effects, you will minimize casualties?

GAVIN: Well, are you saying just stop where we are and really cut back on any further forays?

CLARK: Offensive operations. That doesn't mean a sally-forth from a strong point . . . but as opposed to these amphibious landings on the coast well north of where the people and the rice are.

GAVIN: Yes.

CLARK: Could we not, in your phrase, make do with

what we have a good deal better if we weren't engaged in offensive jungle operations with amphibious landings and similar types of offensive missions?

GAVIN: Oh, I am not sure that I am in a position to answer that. I think we can continue to do very well with what we have for quite some period of time. We seem to be doing quite well now, using the air mobility we have, the helicopters we have, the sea mobility that we have. I think we can continue to do quite well.

CLARK: Mr. Alsop's theory, which I want to emphasize I do not agree with, is that if we were to withdraw to these enclaves—and I think he misquoted you in this article—

GAVIN: I think he did, too. I am glad you noticed that.

CLARK: In terms of holding these strongpoints, his theory would be that unless we can continue to destroy out in the elements of the grass and the jungle with substantial American casualties, we are in the end going to be cut off or chased out, and the costs will be even higher if we adopt the present somewhat offensive attitude of trying to dig them out of the jungle and kill them.

GAVIN: Yes, that is the way I understood his article.

CLARK: You don't agree with that?

GAVIN: I don't agree that by continuing to be aggressive in our explorations out of the areas we now hold, that we can hold our casualties down and reduce the forces we need by one third, which is the figure he used. He said if we did not do this, we would have to have three times as many troops. I don't understand that calculation.

CLARK: I don't either. . . .

SENATOR PELL: . . . General Gavin, I much admired your article when it came out and inserted it in the [*Congressional*] *Record* on January 27, so that it could stand on its own merits and not just the press reports of it. I wanted to ask you two questions, one of a military nature and one general. First, the military side, I was wondering what your view was of the effectiveness of the bombings, because my own thought is that in guerrilla warfare, bombing may well prove counterproductive.

We recently heard that 70 per cent of the casualties in the Vietnamese hospitals came from the effects of our bombing there. The Administration will be giving us figures of these casualties which the committee is awaiting now. It seems to me to be counterproductive in that it creates enemies, particularly among the civilian population in the North, and that it can harden the will of the North Vietnamese. In this connection in your article I noticed you used the phrase "to increase the bombing or to bomb Hanoi or even Peking will add to our problems rather than detract from them, and it will not stop the penetration of North Vietnamese troops into the South."

You I know are familiar with the Rand Report on the Malaysian experience, where it showed what happened in their campaign, where they used less bombs in ten years than we use in one month. They had a steady policy of never using napalm. . . . Finally, today the newspapers I noticed said in the headlines, "BOMBING CANNOT END WAR." Bearing these facts or these opinions in mind, and speaking from the military viewpoint, what is your view as to the effectiveness, from the viewpoint of containing these guerrilla aggressions, of our present bombings in North and South Vietnam?

GAVIN: I don't think that I am in a position to give you a quantitative answer to that, Senator. Bombing is an extension of the arm of the man fighting on the ground, when he is dealing with problems . . . immediately near him to the front or the rear, depending on the circumstances, and I don't think he should be denied this immediate support. . . .

When we get beyond this and go to our rather speculative targets, targets that involve areas of high-density civilian occupation, then I very seriously question the value of it. It does tend to harden the resistance. It is difficult to see the results. And I would be delighted to see and welcome an opportunity to see statistics on what the exact results of the bombings have been. For example, the long-range bombings by the B-52s from Guam I understand. But again to get to the end spectrum where bombing to me is undesirable, I refer to Peking and Hanoi; just to take those cities out for psychological reasons wouldn't help a bit in solving the problems of dealing with the guerrillas in Southern Vietnam. I don't think so at all.

PELL. In specific military terms, though, the present saturation bombings of areas in South Vietnam with napalm, not necessarily in support of troop operations but what you call area bombing, is this effective in your view or not?

GAVIN: I don't know about specific bombing operations that they have undertaken like that. I might say in World War Two we used saturation bombing with heavy bombers, carpet bombing in front of the infantry. This is a rather stabilized situation, where you knew where your enemy was, knew what your objective was, and you could lay it in the right place and go after them. It was useful there. Any specific situations you have in Vietnam, I am not sure that I could comment on those because I honestly don't know.

PELL: Thank you. Another more general question, from my information as to history, I was wondering where you think we should come out in the end? What should we do now? I have listened to the questioning all morning, and I am still a little confused in my own mind as to what your recommendations would be, not the alternatives you offer but what you would do, bearing in mind what General Wheeler said in commenting on your article that: "This must primarily of course be a Vietnamese operation." If that quotation is correct, that means we can't continuously escalate our commitment of troops. Yet I see no other alternatives. What do you see?

GAVIN: Yes. I don't know, and I don't know what is happening at Honolulu or what has happened there in the last couple of days, but I would hope that we could prevail upon the Saigon government to consider ways and means of establishing a government that would be satisfactory to them, and perhaps ultimately a relationship with the Hanoi government, but we can't just continue to escalate our manpower while this deadlock goes on and on.

I would say stop right where we are, with a minimum of any buildup beyond this. We will always have to replace casualties as long as people are there. They don't have to fight to have a high casualty list. So we will have continue to send men there even with what we have. With what we have we should try to find some way— a political solution to the problem. . . .

MUNDT: . . . If you were making the decision in the command position for all America, what specific changes would you bring about compared with the present strategy we are employing in Vietnam?

GAVIN: First of all, I would cease the escalation until I had a better look at what we are now doing. By this I mean—

MUNDT: Do you mean cease sending in extra troops?

GAVIN: We have to send replacements for what we have. Cease expanding the commitment there.

MUNDT: You say you would cease the escalation. What do you mean by that?

GAVIN: Stop expanding the forces we have there.

MUNDT: Stop expanding it?

GAVIN: That is right.

MUNDT: What else?

GAVIN: Now beyond that, I think we have got to have flexibility in what we are doing. I am not quite sure if the present deployments are the best deployments. I have talked to the Secretary of Defense about this. It may be that he may in the long run, if he does not expand his force, have to make changes. I do not know. This is a matter for him to decide. It would be most presumptuous for me to sit here and say what he and General Westmoreland should do.

But the point I want to make is that with the conditions now confronting us, we can take what we have and how we are now deployed, and see what we can do with it, or just go ahead and escalate apparently at the will of an opponent as we have in the past, and how far we will want to escalate, consider the alternative missions that might be open to us, to go ahead and try to seal off South Vietnam, seal it off by extending the 17th Parallel with a *cordon sanitaire* all the way over to the Mekong.

This has been considered in the Pentagon as one possible solution. This would involve a tremendous number of men, and you would still have the Cambodian border open. But if this is the ultimate, then I am trying in a rather scientific way to say we have condition A, condition B, take our choice, let us decide what we want to do, rather than drift in between, because someone says there is another raid by the Viet Cong, we need another hundred thousand men and another hundred thousand men, and with each return of a responsible official from Vietnam, we receive optimistic statements about, "Well, at last the situation is in hand. We may not be winning but we are not losing either."

Now last fall I thought the time had come to say, Let us put a stop to this. Let us see where we are. What can we do with what we have? Having done this, I consider the alternatives and decide whether we want to undertake them. This is all it amounts to.

MUNDT: One final question. The main argument as I have listened to Secretary McNamara and Secretary Rusk, and many, many times off-the-record discussions and in public discussions, and the President, I understand the overwhelming reason why we are continuing the war in Vietnam, and it is for two reasons, and they both have considerable appeal to me. One is that we must avoid being defeated by the Communists in a battle confrontation; and two, we must avoid giving them any rewards in that area for their aggression, and that failure in either of those two areas is more likely to produce a global war, and if we can succeed in stopping either one of those two eventualities or both—will you agree with that general description?

GAVIN: No, sir, I would not agree with that.

MUNDT: If not, can you phrase it in your words?

GAVIN: No, sir, I do not agree with that. If we are just simply going to set out to avoid defeat and avoid rewarding the Communists for their aggression, and we therefore decide in doing this that we have to match every commitment he makes, every man he sends, we will send manpower, and we finally get our involvement so out of balance with all of our other global commitments we are losing, we are in a very dangerous condition in our whole global commitment, and in fact we could lose seriously by doing too much in this particular confrontation, to try to achieve these very things.

MUNDT: If we are not trying to achieve these two things, what are we trying to achieve?

GAVIN: I think we are trying to set up a government for South Vietnam that is acceptable to the people, and once this is established, we are willing to pull out. . . .

CLARK: General, I have come to three tentative conclusions as the result of my study of this problem, aided substantially by your testimony here today. I am going to read them to you and then ask you to comment. My first conclusion is this: Viewing Vietnam in the light of our global commitments, and our national capability, the military realities there today are such that the cost in casualties and money of crushing the enemy, retaking our lost real estate, and pacifying the country are too high to be acceptable.

GAVIN: They reached the point of doubtful acceptability.

CLARK: You would change it to, "reached the point of doubtful acceptability"?

GAVIN: Yes, sir.

CLARK: My second tentative conclusion is that the real problem is how to make a truce which is consistent with the military realities. Some would say that by more and bigger bombing, and by a big buildup of troops, we shall be able to change the military realities in our favor. Experience and history of this wretched war are against that hope, for the forces against us can be increased indefinitely, and the notion of a decisive military superiority over the land powers of Asia is a dangerous fancy. That is Walter Lippmann, incidentally, which I concur in.

GAVIN: "Hopelessly against us" is strong language. "Makes success minimal," I would say. I would generally go along that "hopeless" is a pretty strong word there.

CLARK: Let us take a couple of purple adjectives out and come to the same conclusion. . . . That the real problem is how to make a truce consistent with military effort.

GAVIN: Yes, sir.

CLARK: My third point is, while we are waiting for that truce, while we are working for that truce, in the meanwhile we should stay where we are with what we have got, increasing our forces and our money commitment only to the extent necessary to hold our present position.

GAVIN: That is right, exactly. I would add, may I say, that once you have flexibility and according to your resources there, while you do not escalate the total, you retain the flexibility position.

CLARK: For every conceivable kind of tactic which holds any kind of success.

GAVIN: That is right. . . .

PELL: General Gavin, to return for a moment to this point about bombing, as I understand your thinking, am I correct in saying that in guerrilla warfare, bombing other than direct military targets or indirect military support, as you said earlier, that that kind of bombing is productive, but more generalized bombing is counterproductive? Would that be a correct statement?

GAVIN: I would say that is a correct statement, yes.

PELL: Thank you. And finally, where you could look ahead as a historian in reverse, in the future, see us twenty years from now, at which point presumably all these unified countries would be unified, Germany would be unified, Korea would be unified, Vietnam would be unified, what kind of solution do you see in the screen, on the side that we would be coming out with?

GAVIN: Solution to what?

PELL: Solution to the general situation. Do you see a unified Vietnam in line with Yugoslavia, a national but not expansive state? Do you see South Vietnam eventually taking over North Vietnam? Do you have any thoughts as to where we will be in 1986?

GAVIN: Well, I must say for twenty years my crystal ball is pretty clouded.

PELL: So are we all, but we ought to have a grand design. The thing I admire about General de Gaulle, whom you know so well, is that he had a grand design. I am not sure that we have a grand design.

GAVIN: You raise a very interesting question that has not come up in this discussion, and that is whether or not a Tito-type government can be formed. I have good reason to believe that Ho Chi Minh would resist the Chinese as much as he resists the Russians. And the present Chairman of the Joint Chiefs of Staff was a colonel commanding the troops in Trieste when we were having serious trouble there. I was Chief of Staff at Naples at the time. We had a plane shot down. Our outposts were being attacked. The man we supported in World War Two was court-martialed and assassinated by Tito, and people were up in arms wanting to attack Tito.

I think the best thing we ever did was allow that government to come into being and demonstrate this man could bring in being an independent government of his own, free of Stalin and defying him. I am not at all satisfied that Ho Chi Minh might [have] a good government. No one has demonstrated to me that this is not so.

PELL: I thank you for that answer very much indeed, because in the long haul it seems to me that the virulence of Communism itself will recede.

GAVIN: Yes.

PELL: We will be faced with other totalitarian forces and other imperialistic nations, and our problem is to hold the line and contain it while it is in the acute stage.

GAVIN: Yes. I would like to have given that answer. I am sorry. . . .

The Statement and Testimony of

THE HONORABLE

George F. Kennan

Thursday, 10 February 1966

MR. KENNAN: Mr. Chairman, and distinguished members of the Foreign Relations Committee. The subject on which I am invited to give my views this morning is, as I understand it, the complex of problems connected with our present involvement in Vietnam. I would like to explain, in undertaking to speak to this subject, that Southeast Asia is a part of the world for which I can claim no specialized knowledge. I am not familiar with the official rationale of our policy there except as it has been revealed in the press. I cannot recall that I have ever, either during my official service in government or subsequently, been drawn by the Executive branch of our government into consultation on the problem of our policy in Southeast Asia, or even been made privy to the official discussions by which that policy was decided.

I am sure that there are many data that are relevant to any thoroughly founded judgment on these matters which are not available to me, and this being the case, I have tried in recent weeks and months not to jump to final conclusions even in my own thoughts, to remain sympathetically receptive. both to our government's explanations of the very real difficulties it has faced and to the doubts and questions of its serious critics.

I have not been anxious to press my views on the public but I gladly give them to you for whatever they are worth, claiming no particular merit for them except perhaps that they flow from experience with Communist affairs that runs back now for some thirty-eight years, and also from the deepest and most troubled sort of concern that we should find the proper course, the right course, at this truly crucial moment.

The first point I would like to make is that if we were not already involved as we are today in Vietnam, I would know of no reason why we should wish to become so involved, and I could think of several reasons why we should wish not to. Vietnam is not a region of major military, industrial importance. It is difficult to believe that any decisive developments of the world situation would be determined in normal circumstances by what happens on that territory. If it were not for the considerations of prestige that arise precisely out of our present involvement, even a situation in which South Vietnam was controlled exclusively by the Viet Cong, while regrettable, and no doubt morally unwarranted, would not, in my opinion, present dangers great enough to justify our direct military intervention.

Given the situation that exists today in the relations among the leading Communist powers, and by that I have, of course, in mind primarily the Soviet-Chinese conflict, there is every likelihood that a Communist regime in South Vietnam would follow a fairly independent course. There is no reason to suspect that such a regime would find it either necessary or desirable in present circumstances to function simply as a passive puppet and instrument of Chinese power. And as for the danger that its establishment there would unleash similar tendencies in neighboring countries, this, I think, would depend largely on the manner in which it came into power.

In the light of what has recently happened in Indo-

nesia, and on the Indian subcontinent, the danger of the
so-called domino effect, that is the effect that would be
produced by a limited Communist success in South Vietnam, seem to me to be considerably less than it was when
the main decisions were taken that have led to our present
involvement. Let me stress, I do not say that that danger
does not exist. I say that it is less than it was a year or two
ago when we got into this involvement. From the long-
term standpoint, therefore, and on principle, I think our
military involvement in Vietnam has to be recognized as
unfortunate, as something we would not choose deliberately, if the choice were ours to make all over again today,
and by the same token, I think it should be our government's aim to liquidate this involvement just as soon as
this can be done without inordinate damage to our own
prestige or to the stability of conditions in that area.

It is obvious, on the other hand, that this involvement is
today a fact. It creates a new situation. It raises new questions ulterior to the long-term problems which have to be
taken into account; a precipitate and disorderly withdrawal
could represent in present circumstances a disservice to
our own interests and even to world peace greater than
any that might have been involved by our failure to engage ourselves there in the first place. This is a reality
which, if there is to be any peaceful resolution of this
conflict, is going to have to be recognized both by the more
critical of our friends and by our adversaries.

But at the same time, I have great misgivings about any
deliberate expansion of hostilities on our part directed to
the achievement of something called "victory," if by the
use of that term we envisage the complete disappearance
of the recalcitrance with which we are now faced, the
formal submission by the adversary to our will, and the
complete realization of our present stated political aims.
I doubt that these things can be achieved even by the most
formidable military successes.

There seems to be an impression that if we bring sufficient military pressure to bear, there will occur at some

point something in the nature of a political capitulation on the other side. I think this is a most dangerous assumption. I don't say that it is absolutely impossible, but it is a dangerous assumption in the light of the experience we have had with Communist elements in the past. The North Vietnamese and the Viet Cong have, between them, a great deal of space and manpower to give up if they have to, and the Chinese can give them more if they need it. Fidelity to the Communist tradition would dictate that if really pressed to extremity on the military level, these people should disappear entirely from the open scene and fall back exclusively on an underground political and military existence rather than to accept terms that would be openly humiliating and would represent in their eyes the betrayal of the future political prospects of the cause to which they are dedicated.

Any total rooting-out of the Viet Cong from the territory of South Vietnam could be achieved, if it could be achieved at all, only at the cost of a degree of damage to civilian life and of civilian suffering, generally, for which I would not like to see this country responsible. And to attempt to crush North Vietnamese strength to a point where Hanoi could no longer give any support for Viet Cong political activity in the South would almost certainly, it seems to me, have the effect of bringing in Chinese forces at some point, whether formally or in the guise of volunteers, thus involving us in a military conflict with Communist China on one of the most unfavorable theaters of hostility that we could possibly choose.

This is not the only reason why I think we should do everything possible to avoid the escalation of this conflict. There is another one which is no less weighty, and this is the effect the conflict is already having on our policies and interests further afield. This involvement seems to me to represent a grievous misplacement of emphasis on our foreign policies as a whole. Not only are great and potentially more important questions of world affairs not receiving, as a consequence of our involvement in Vietnam, the attention they should be receiving, but in some instances assets we already enjoy and hopefully possibilities we should be developing, are being sacrificed to this unpromising involvement in a remote and secondary theater. Our relations with the Soviet Union have suffered grievously, as was to be expected, and this at a time when far more important things were involved in those relations than what is ultimately involved in Vietnam and when we had special reason, I think, to cultivate those relations. And more unfortunate still, in my opinion, is the damage being done to the feelings entertained for us by the Japanese people; the confidence and the good disposition of the Japanese is the greatest asset we have had and the greatest asset we could have in East Asia. As the greatest industrial complex in the entire Far East, and the only place where the sinews of modern war can be produced on a formidable scale there, Japan is of vital importance to us and indeed to the prospects generally of peace and stability in East Asia.

There is no success we could have in Vietnam that would conceivably warrant, in my opinion, the sacrifice by us of the confidence and good will of the Japanese people.

Yet, I fear that we abuse that confidence and good will in the most serious way when we press the military struggle in Vietnam, and particularly when we press it by means of strategic bombing, a process to which the Japanese for historical reasons are peculiarly sensitive and averse. I mention Japan particularly because it is an outstanding example, both in importance and in the intensity of the feelings aroused, of the psychological damage that is being done in many parts of the world by the prosecution of this conflict, and that will be done in even greater measure if the hostilities become still more bloody and tragic as a result of our deliberate effort.

It is clear that however justified our action may be in our own eyes, it has failed to win either enthusiasm or confidence even among peoples normally friendly to us.

Our motives are widely misinterpreted, and the spectacle
—the spectacle emphasized and reproduced in thousands
of press photographs and stories that appear in the press
of the world, the spectacle of Americans inflicting grievous
injury on the lives of a poor and helpless people, and particularly a people of different race and color, no matter
how warranted by military necessity or by the excesses of
the adversary our operations may seem to us to be or may
genuinely be—this spectacle produces reactions among
millions of people throughout the world profoundly detri-
mental to the image we would like them to hold of this
country. I am not saying that this is just or right. I am saying that this is so, and that it is bound in the circumstances
to be so, and a victory purchased at the price of further
such damage would be a hollow one in terms of our world
interests, no matter what advantages it might hold from
the standpoint of developments on the local scene.

Now, these are the reasons, gentlemen, why I hope that
our government will restrict our military operations in
Vietnam to the minimum necessary to assure the security
of our forces, and to maintain our military presence there
until we can achieve a satisfactory peaceful resolution of
the conflict, and these are the reasons why I hope that we
will continue to pursue vigorously, and I may say consist-
ently, the question—the quest for such a peaceful resolution of the conflict, even if this involves some moderation
of our stated objectives, and even if the resulting settlement appears to us as something less than ideal.

I cannot, of course, judge the military necessities of our
situation. But everything that I can learn about its political aspects suggests to me that General Gavin is on the
right track in his suggestions that we should, if I understood him correctly, decide what limited areas we can
safely police and defend, and restrict ourselves largely to
the maintenance of our position there. I have listened with
interest to the arguments that have been brought forward
in opposition to his views, and I must say that I have not
been much impressed with some of them. When I am told

that it would be difficult to defend such enclaves, it is hard for me to understand why it would be easier to defend the far greater areas to which presumably a successful escalation of our military activity would bring us.

I also find it difficult, for reasons that I won't take time to go into here, to believe that our allies, and particularly our Western European allies, most of whom themselves have given up great territories within recent years, and sometimes in a very statesmanlike way, I find it hard to believe that we would be subject to great reproach or loss of confidence at their hands simply because we followed a defensive rather than an offensive strategy in Vietnam at this time.

In matters such as this it is not, in my experience, what you do that is mainly decisive. It is how you do it. And I would submit that there is more respect to be won in the opinion of this world by a resolute and courageous liquidation of unsound positions than by the most stubborn pursuit of extravagant or unpromising objectives.

And finally, when I hear it said that to adopt a defensive strategy in South Vietnam would be to rat on our commitment to the government of that territory, I am a little bewildered. I would like to know what that commitment really consists of, and how and when it was incurred. What seems to be involved here is an obligation on our part not only to defend the frontiers of a certain political entity against outside attack, but to assure the internal security of its government in circumstances where that government is unable to assure that security by its own means. Now, any such obligation is won that goes obviously considerably further in its implications than the normal obligations of a military alliance. If we did not incur such an obligation in any formal way, then I think we should not be inventing it for ourselves and assuring ourselves that we are bound by it today. But if we did incur it, then I do fail to understand how it was possible to enter into any such commitment otherwise than through the constitutional processes which were meant to come into play when even commitments of lesser import than this were undertaken.

Now, just two concluding observations. I would like it understood that what I have said here implies nothing but the highest respect and admiration for the fighting qualities of our forces in the field. I have the greatest confidence in them, men and commanders alike. I have no doubt, in fact, that they can and will, if duty requires, produce before this thing is over military results that will surprise both our skeptical friends and our arrogant adversaries. It is not their fighting qualities. It is the purpose to which they are being employed that evokes my skepticism.

Secondly, I would like to say I am trying to look at this whole problem not from the moral standpoint but from the practical one. I see in the Viet Cong a band of ruthless fanatics, partly misled, perhaps by the propaganda that has been drummed into them, but cruel in their purposes, dictatorial, and oppressive in their aims. I am not conscious of having any sympathy for them. I think their claim to represent the people of South Vietnam is unfounded and arrogant and outrageous. A country which fell under this exclusive power would have my deepest sympathy, and I would hope that this eventuality at any rate would be avoided by a restrained and moderate policy on our part in South Vietnam. But, our country should not be asked, and should not ask of itself, to shoulder the main burden of determining the political realities in any other country, and particularly not in one remote from our shores, from our culture, and from the experience of our people.

This is not only not our business, but I don't think we can do it successfully. In saying this, I am only paraphrasing, and very poorly, the words once uttered by one who had at one time been a member of the United States Senate, and who, had a Foreign Relations Committee existed in his day, would unquestionably have been a member of it. This was John Quincy Adams, and I would like your permission to recall, before I close, the words of his that I have in mind. They were spoken in this city 145 years ago on the fourth of July, 1821. . . . Some of you may be familiar with them but they stand repeating at this moment: "Wherever the standard of freedom and independence has been or shall be unfurled, there," Adams said, will be America's heart, her benedictions, and her prayers. "But she goes not abroad," he went on, "in search of monsters to destroy. She is the well-wisher to the freedom and independence of all. She is the champion and vindicator only of her own. She will recommend the general cause by the countenance of her voice, and by the benignant sympathy of her example. She well knows that by once enlisting under other banners than her own, were they even the banners of foreign independence, she would involve herself beyond the power of extrication, in all the wars of interest and intrigue, of individual avarice, envy and ambition, which assume the colors and usurp the standards of freedom. The fundamental maxims of her policy would insensibly change from liberty to force. . . . She might become the dictatress of the world. She would no longer be the ruler of her own spirit."

Now, gentlemen, I don't know exactly what John Quincy Adams had in mind when he spoke those words, but I think that without knowing it, he spoke very directly and very pertinently to us here today. . . .

SENATOR FULBRIGHT: Thank you, Mr. Kennan. If I may say so, I think you have spoken very pertinently and very wisely to this Committee today also, and your statement raises a great many questions which I know members of the Committee would like to pursue further. . . . One observation which interests me particularly because of your own experience in Yugoslavia, where I know that you served with great distinction and where in a Communist country you were largely responsible for helping this country establish cordial relations which I think are greatly in our own interest. . . . You say, "Given a situation that exists today in the relations among the leading Communist powers . . . there is every likelihood that a Communist regime in South Vietnam would follow a fairly independent political [*sic*] course."

It came to my mind, when you stated that, you may have thought of Yugoslavia, which is a Communist country which is following an independent course of its own, which is not inimical to our own interests. Is that what you have in mind? If we wisely, I think, approach this problem, this could be created there or could have been created and still might be created and would not be to the detriment of our own interests. Is that what you had in mind?

KENNAN: Yes. I meant to say with this statement that we must not always assume that any Communist faction that comes into power anywhere in the world will function simply as the spineless executor of the orders of one of the great Communist powers. It is true that in the years that I spent in Yugoslavia, while I certainly did not see eye to eye with its government, while I sometimes resented and had bitter arguments over statements made by its leaders concerning our foreign policies, nevertheless it was my conclusion that the present policies of that government, especially the policies it follows in its relations with its neighbors, the neutral policy that it followed between East and West in military matters, all this taken in conjunction with the highly strategic position that it occupied in the Balkans, operated to our interest, and that we might have been worse off.

Now, I simply want to point to the possibility that these considerations might apply in other cases, too. I realize that such a statement, Mr. Chairman, is easily open to misinterpretation. I would not like to convey the impression that I think it would be fine if the Communists took South Vietnam. I think it would be regrettable. I think that we should do all that we can with due regard to our own security and to our own interests in world peace to prevent that, but I think that we should also be careful not to overrate or to misinterpret the possible implications of it. It is not so that when men call themselves Communists, some sort of magic transportation takes place within them which makes them wholly different from other human beings or from what they were before. Feelings of nationalism, ordinary feelings, still affect them to a large extent. I think these—this reality plays a part in all of Vietnam. I don't think they want domination by the Chinese. I think the fact that there is an alternative to the Chinese within the Communist world in the form of the Soviet Union, and an alternative which incidentally is in a much better position to give them the economic aid they need, I think all this represents a state of affairs which would be very, very carefully and sensitively taken into account by any South Vietnamese Communists, and I merely wished to say, therefore, that while their domination there would not be desirable, it might not be perhaps quite as tragic or as fatal as many of us assume.

FULBRIGHT: Of course, I don't think many of us are under any illusions that any settlement can be a desirable one in the sense that it is perfection and exactly like we would like it. It is going to be, if any settlement is reached, one that is only tolerable but not satisfactory. Is that not true?

KENNAN: Absolutely true.

FULBRIGHT: One other comment you made—there are many comments that arouse my interest—but you stated . . . that you are not looking at this purely from a moral standpoint, but a practical one, what can be achieved, and you call attention to the great differences in the culture and race and language and so on between this area and other areas which I can think of in which we have become involved. I take it by this you mean that this is simply not a practicable objective, as I understand it in this country. We can't achieve it even with the best of will.

KENNAN: This is correct, and I have a fear that our thinking about this whole problem is still affected by some sort of illusions about invincibility on our part, that there is no problem—a feeling that there is no problem in the world which we, if we wanted to devote enough of our resources to it, could not solve. I disbelieve in this most profoundly. I do not think that we can order the political realities of areas in a great many other parts of the world. So far as I can see we are not being very successful in ordering them on islands very close to our own shores, and I deeply doubt that we can enter into the affairs of people far, far away like this, and by our own efforts primarily determine what sort of political conditions are going to prevail there.

Now, this is separate from my sympathies. I have seen as much as anyone, I dare say, in this room of people living under Communism, and I think I know as well as anyone here does what that means. These people have my sympathy. But as John Quincy Adams says, there are limits to what our duties and our capabilities are, and our first duty is to ourselves, and if we get lost in the attempt to rescue or even to establish, in many instances, the liberties of others and particularly of people who have never known them as we know them in this country, who don't even know what the words mean that we use, we can lose our own substance and I think we can have very little to show for it when it is all over.

FULBRIGHT: You are familiar, I am sure, with a statement made by General Ridgway in his Book [*Soldier*] on this subject . . . that we could [win] a military victory, but he thought such a victory would be completely out of proportion to what could be gained by such an activity. Are you familiar with that statement?

KENNAN: No, I wasn't, but I would agree with it.

FULBRIGHT: Well, we have quoted him before. It occurs in his own book recounting his experiences in 1954. General Gavin also—we discussed this the day before yesterday. General Gavin, as you know, was associated with him and was on his staff when he was Chief of Staff of the Army. . . . And as I understand his statement it was, well, if we wished to we could with a great deal of sacrifice of men and material, blood and money, conquer this country, even China, but that it would be a great mistake if we undertook to do it. Would you agree with that?

KENNAN: Generally, yes, and certainly when it comes to the question of conquering this country. I am not sure about China, because I don't know what conquering it would mean. If it were an effort to occupy the country, I would go even further than General Ridgway and I would say that we probably couldn't even do that. . . .

SENATOR MORSE: . . . In an article last December in the *Washington Post* you stated that since Vietnam became a critical issue, "a pall of discouragement has been cast over those responsible for the conduct of the work of the United Nations." Would you tell us what you mean by that language and if you foresee the United Nations as being able to play an effective role in trying to bring a negotiated settlement of this war?

KENNAN: The reference to the pall of discouragement reflected my feeling that a great many people at the United Nations saw the possibilities for peace rapidly deteriorating as this conflict in Vietnam became more intensive, and had a great sense of helplessness about it, because, after all, this was to have been the principal function of the United Nations organization, to be able to prevent precisely this sort of a deterioration of the international atmosphere.

I personally do not think that the United Nations itself could be useful in writing the terms of any compromise solution to the Vietnam conflict. But it was my hope, and I think it was the hope of many people at the United Nations headquarters in New York, that perhaps this recent initiative in enlisting the interest of the Security Council in this problem might lead either to the revival of the Geneva arrangements or to some other approach to this problem outside of the United Nations, to which both we and the people on the other side could respond in a useful way.

MORSE: Mr. Kennan, is it your view that if the elections had been held in South Vietnam in July, 1956, as provided by the Geneva Accords of 1954, the people of Vietnam would probably have voted in officials that would have established a Communist regime but would have done so under the election procedures set forth in the Accords?

KENNAN: I don't claim to know a great deal about these realities there, and I go largely on the statement in the book of a respected ex-President, who said that in everything he could learn indicated that the election would have gone 80 per cent in favor of the Communist side had it been held at that time. I cannot judge the correctness of this, but from all I could learn I think it likely that elections held at that time would have gone in favor of the Communist side. On the other hand, I am not sure that they would have been entirely free elections.

MORSE: If the people of a country decide to vote themselves a Communist regime or decide that they are willing to support a Communist regime, do you think it is a wise policy for the United States to use its great power to prevent those elections or to intervene to prevent those people from having the kind of government that they want?

KENNAN: No, Senator, . . . I do not think it was a wise policy. I recognize that this can create, depending on the place where it would happen, it could create very difficult problems for our government, but it seems to me that as people who profess to believe in the democratic process, we are in a poor position to object to the consequences of any free expression of opinion on the part of peoples elsewhere in the world. . . .

MORSE: I would like to ask if you think that part of the concern you express in respect to foreign attitudes toward us and misunderstandings toward us, irrespective of what the facts are, is based somewhat upon a fear in many places of the world that we may be headed in a—in the direction of a war with China?

KENNAN: Yes, I think this is true. I think this fear exists in many quarters. . . .

MORSE: . . . Do you know of any justification for an American foreign policy that would cause us to follow a policy of escalation in Southeast Asia that would really increase the danger of the United States unilaterally becoming involved in a war with China?

KENNAN: Senator, I can see why reasons could be offered for such a policy, but in my opinion these reasons are overweighed by other ones, and it would—such a procedure, such a policy, is not warranted by the considerations that present themselves to me. . . .

SENATOR HICKENLOOPER: . . . Mr. Kennan, leaving out the—or without discussing the background of how and why we got into this Vietnamese involvement at the present time, I think everyone will concede that it is a fact that we are involved, and we are very deeply involved. Now, there are problems facing us and others. I am not quite clear what you would recommend that we do about it. How we disengage ourselves without losing a tremendous amount of face or position in various areas of the world.

KENNAN: Senator, I think precisely the question, the consideration that you have just raised, is the central one that we have to think about; and it seems to me, as I have said here, that a precipitate, sudden, and unilateral withdrawal would not be warranted by circumstances now.

HICKENLOOPER: What do you think the result of a sudden precipitate withdrawal of our activities in South Vietnam would be?

KENNAN: I think it would be exploited mercilessly by the Chinese and the North Vietnamese . . . in world public opinion, as a means of humiliating us.

HICKENLOOPER: Do you think it would have a substantial effect on Indonesia and its future political attitudes?

KENNAN: No, sir, I do not. It seems to me that what has happened in Indonesia in recent weeks has been of such finality that we are not going to face much of a Communist danger there for some time. . . .

HICKENLOOPER: Do you think it would have an effect on Cambodia and Laos?

KENNAN: You know, I am not sure that I am really qualified to answer that question. I should not think that it would have a great effect on Cambodia because it seems to me that the government of that country is already so concerned to stay close to the Chinese that I don't think they could get much closer without submitting to inclusion in to the Chinese state. I think that probably the most dangerous effect of this might be on Thailand, but I don't know. I agree that the effect would be unfortunate.

HICKENLOOPER: Do you think there would be an ascertainable effect on the Philippines because of the enhanced Chinese influence and standing in their propaganda, that they had been instrumental in supporting the defeat of the United States or its withdrawal there?

KENNAN: Senator, I ought to emphasize as I answer these questions that in my opinion a great deal depends on how these things are done. If we get out in a gradual way, if there is some sort of political compromise which can help to explain our departure, that is one thing. But if we simply turned tail and fled the scene, obviously we would do great damage around, and I am not advocating anything of that sort. I personally think that even if we were to withdraw at an early date from South Vietnam, there is no reason for the Filipinos to get jittery. The Viet Cong have no amphibious capacity and are not going to pursue us across the Philippine Islands or anything like that. It depends largely on the Filipinos themselves. They have the wherewithal to assure their own security if they want to do it; it is a question of their morale and their determination. They have done it before and they can do it again if they had to.

HICKENLOOPER: Mr. Kennan, I am discussing this with you because of your vast experience with Communist mentality and this—their aggressive tendencies, their programs and their influence upon surrounding areas. Now, manifestly, I think, let's say the Viet Cong haven't any navy with which to attack the Philippines. They can't transport troops over there. That isn't what I mean at all. . . . But here sits China with six, seven hundred million people. It is basically international Chinese in its orientation, I believe. Do you agree with that?

KENNAN: Of course, it is.

HICKENLOOPER: That is as differentiated from purely a nationalistic Communism, which doesn't intend to extend its influence beyond its borders.

KENNAN: Well, the government is certainly Communist-oriented and I don't know how much of the population.

HICKENLOOPER: Well, when I speak of China, I speak of the governing forces of China. . . .

KENNAN: May I put in a caveat there? I believe that the Chinese would certainly like to have influence, dominant influence, all over the mainland of Asia, the Chinese Communists that is, and they would certainly like to have Taiwan. I am not sure that they are anxious to launch invasions against these other countries and to take them under the Chinese sovereignty at this stage of the game anyway.

HICKENLOOPER: Well, they also extended their influence in the disputed area of Tibet, did they not?

KENNAN: Yes.

HICKENLOOPER: They also invaded India—

KENNAN: Yes.

HICKENLOOPER: —with force of arms.

KENNAN: But the areas to which they have extended their power through these actions were ones for which they claimed the argument that the areas had been under Chinese sovereignty before. I don't excuse it by this. I merely say that it puts them somewhat in a different category.

HICKENLOOPER: Do you think that the withdrawal of the United States from South Vietnam—again realizing that you have entered the caveat—that the way it was done and matters of that kind . . . would have some influence?

KENNAN: Yes.

HICKENLOOPER: But do you think the rather immediate withdrawal of the United States forces and our activity in South Vietnam from that country could be used effectively as a propaganda tool and weapon in Africa and in the emerging nations of Africa? . . .

KENNAN: Senator, it would be a six months' sensation, but I dare say we would survive it in the end, and there would be another day. Things happen awfully fast on the international scene, and people's memories are very short. If we run our mind back over the crises of recent years and ask ourselves what has become of them, we can realize, I believe, the truth of that statement. There was a time when we were all hot and bothered over the Lebanon and landing troops there. A year or two ago no one would have —ever have thought that the Cyprus crisis would be as quiet as it is today. These things pass more rapidly than one might think. . . .

SENATOR GORE: Ambassador, for reasons which you have stated more eloquently and with more erudition than I have been able to summon, I have long thought this was an unadvisable adventure for the United States. Behind the closed doors of the Senate Foreign Relations Committee, a long while ago, I asked this question of Secretary Rusk. I cannot give his reply now, but I would like to ask you the same question today: "Now, to view this problem in the context of a decade hence: what is your assessment of its bearing upon the possibility that the Soviet Union may or may not continue on the course of rapprochement with the Western powers which has been under way now since the confrontation of 1961, thus possibly reëntering the European society or conversely becoming more closely aligned with Red China, not only in a push into the Pacific but aligned more closely in a more aggressive international Communist thrust?"

KENNAN: Senator Gore, a year ago this month in a public lecture at Princeton University, which was repeated on one of the two occasions in which I have spoken publicly I believe on this Vietnam problem, I tried to make the point that if we pressed our intervention in Vietnam the Soviet Government would see no choice but to come down strongly against us, and to enter into a sort of a competition with the Chinese to see who could look most critical of our policies, and most dedicated and violent in their defense of the Viet Cong. I said that they would do this even if it had to proceed at the expense of Soviet-American relations.

Now, this is exactly what has happened. The effect of the Vietnamese crisis, conflict, is not to restore the unity between the Soviet Union and Communist China. I think things have gone too far for that. But it is to give to their rivalry a form very undesirable from the standpoint of our interests and the interests of world peace, namely, the form of a contest to see who can look the most anti-American, the most critical of our policies, who can appear to be the most violent defender of what they call the national liberation movements. The reasons why the Soviet leaders have seen themselves compelled to move in this direction are ones for which I can take no responsibility; they don't commend themselves to my sympathies, but I can see why they exist if you try to look at it from their point of view, and this seems to me a most unfortunate development of world affairs generally.

I think that we have more important problems than Vietnam to thrash out eventually with the Soviet Union, problems of disarmament, and problems of the halting of the proliferation of nuclear weaponry, and the still great and vital problem of Germany, which is, to my mind, the most important specific political geographic problem in the world. All of this, as I see it, is in suspense while this Vietnam conflict proceeds, and the effect of the Vietnam conflict on the Soviet Union has been, I fear, to make it more difficult for us to discuss these things in a useful way with the Soviet leaders.

I am not saying that if Vietnam—if the Vietnam conflict did not exist, I am sure that we could have agreements with the Soviet leaders on these points. I think this would take a long time and a great deal of patience, but I think we should have kept the pressure on, and I think we might make progress slowly. At any rate, that was the way things looked a year or so ago. Unfortunately, they do not look that way today, and I attribute this to the operation of the logic of the situation which we have in South Vietnam.

GORE: If the war in Vietnam should be escalated or by some unfortunate incident, God forbid, becomes war between the United States and China, would it be within the purview of possibility that Russia would again, seeing us bogged down, press her point of view in Berlin, and seek to work her machinations in Latin America and elsewhere?

KENNAN: It is certainly within the realm of possibility, and one of the things that worries me most about an extension of our present commitment in Vietnam is that it might leave us very poorly prepared to face crises that might arise in other areas of the world. I think it has already caused a diversion of our attention and our resources to a point that holds dangers for the balance of our world responsibilities elsewhere, and if we are now, as some people fear, to double the amount of the manpower and the resources we are putting into Vietnam, I am afraid that we would not be in a good position to defend our interests in other areas if they were suddenly challenged.

GORE: As unwisely as you think these commitments have been made, I remind you that through three administrations we have inched or been inched into this unfortunate situation. . . . Upon many occasions the Congress has been led to believe that a subsequent step would not follow a step presently being taken. This is behind us. We are now in Vietnam in the situation which you have so eloquently described.

The real issue, it seems to me, is whether this conflict in Vietnam is to be held within bounds which we think we can reasonably master, maintaining control of events. You referred this morning to the damage to America's prestige around the world, the pictures of great damage that is wrought; of course, all of us know that war is hell, but the pictures of a great power, with big bombers, big bombs, big money, wreaking havoc upon a small nation is one which we all regret. Is this element, plus the encroaching threat of China, a benefit to the Chinese Communist apparatus in more effectively regimenting her people and engendering hate of the United States?

KENNAN: Yes, sir, in my opinion it is.

GORE: Then, you conclude, and I conclude with you, that it is in our national interests and in our national security if at all possible to prevent this conflict from further major escalation, and most of all to prevent it from becoming a war between the United States and China.

KENNAN: This is precisely my position, and I think you have stated it in a way that I couldn't possibly improve upon.

GORE: Well, you have improved in many respects on my thoughts. I agree 100 per cent with your presentation here. . . .

SENATOR CARLSON: Mr. Ambassador, first I want to express my personal appreciation for your appearance here. You have been in this field of diplomatic problems affecting our international policies for years and, therefore, I have a very high regard for your views. I would not say I have always agreed with them, but I can assure you I have read many of your books and I have heard many of your lectures. I was interested in the colloquy you had with . . . Mr. Morse this morning, and I may not have understood you properly. Did you say you had some question of referring this and the final negotiations to a conclusion by the United Nations?

KENNAN: What I meant to say, Senator Carlson, was that I did not think that the United Nations constituted itself the forum in which the negotiations could hopefully take place, which would lead or could lead to a peaceful solution of this problem, but that I thought the United Nations might be instrumental in finding other forums and stimulating discussion of this problem in other forums where the discussion would be more hopeful.

CARLSON: Then on that basis, we get, I assume, to the Geneva Conference of 1954. Can you give us any reason or any thoughts why the Soviets have refused to agree to call a reconvening of that conference?

KENNAN: I am puzzled by this myself, and perhaps the difficulties lie with Hanoi. I do feel that if the pressure were kept on in a suitable way that it would become very difficult for the Soviet government to continue to hold to that position.

CARLSON: Just following that thought, then, in a more general sense, why have the Soviets appeared to be reluctant to play any sort of peacekeeping role similar to the one that they played at Tashkent recently?

KENNAN: I believe it is because they are being pushed so hard by the Chinese. It is my observation that any Marxist detests being outflanked to the left by any other Marxist. . . . And they are very sensitive to criticisms that they are aiding the imperialists, doing the work of the imperialists, this sort of silly semantics that goes back and forth between them. The Soviet government is, I think, very apprehensive [that] if it does not take a very strong anti-American line, if it appears to be in any way aiding us in our purposes, it will lose its authority within the world Communist movement and its appeal to other nationalist semi-Communist movements in other developing countries, and this, I think, explains its rather curious conduct in this respect. . . .

CARLSON: Well, following your thoughts along that same line, if we cannot expect any help from the Soviet Union in regard to negotiations on the Geneva Conference of 1954, is it possible that—or is there a likelihood there might be Soviet [military] intervention in this situation we are in? . . .

KENNAN: I see no likelihood of that. . . .

CARLSON: I would like to ask you what you base it on, in view of the fact that I think everyone must agree this must be settled through negotiations. Maybe it will be years but someday we are going to negotiate a settlement, and the Soviet Union refuses to now. Are they just going to sit idly by and let us continue to waste our manpower —and when I say waste it, it is a poor word to use—but have our young men destroyed and have the financial sacrifices in this area, is that their thought?

KENNAN: I think it is. I think they probably reckon we have more to lose than they do from the present situation and they do not want to appear publicly as being in the position of pressuring Hanoi and the Viet Cong to agreements with us which these two factions might themselves not wish to enter into.

CARLSON: . . . What are your thoughts on Chinese intervention?

KENNAN: I think the Chinese, too, obviously would like to stay out of it, and will unless they feel that our military operations are taking forms that become really dangerous to them, either in the straight military sense or in the sense of prestige. I think that if we bomb too freely or if we get operating too close to their borders, it will bring them in. Now, whether it will bring them in in a formal sense, as I have already said, or whether they will do what they did in Korea and send troops in under the flimsy and shabby excuse that these are volunteers, I couldn't say. I would suspect it might be the latter. But it doesn't matter much from the standpoint of the problem this presents for us, whether they come as volunteers or as regular Chinese troops. . . .

SENATOR LAUSCHE: Ambassador Kennan, is has been said frequently that you were the designer and architect of the policy of the United States that we cannot suffer the expansion of Communism, and, therefore, there must be adopted a plan of containment. Were you a participant in the design of that plan?

KENNAN: Senator Lausche, I bear a certain amount of guilt for the currency this word has—"containment"—has acquired in this country. I wrote an article, an anonymous article, in 1947, written actually in '46, in which this word was used, and the article got much more publicity than I thought it would get, and it is true that in this sense I am the authorship, at least of the use of this word with regard to our policy toward the Soviet Union.

LAUSCHE: Right. Now, then, isn't it a fact that when this policy was announced, it was predicated upon the belief that the security of our country required that there be a stoppage of the aggressive advancement of Communism. into different areas of the world than those in which it was then prevalent?

KENNAN: Yes, sir. At that time—

LAUSCHE: Now, then, if that is so, has your view changed?

KENNAN: No, the situation has changed. There was at that time—

LAUSCHE: Well, if there is a change in the situation, has your view changed and that it would now be within, let's say, the general security of our country to permit an expansion of Communism by aggression?

KENNAN: It would certainly not be in our interests to encourage it. But I did not mean to convey in the article I wrote at that time the belief that we could necessarily stop this at every point on the world's surface. There were things I failed to say, I must admit, in that article which should have been said, and one of them was that certain areas of the world are more important than others; that one had to concentrate on the areas that were vital to us. But in addition to this, I must point out that at that time there was only one center of Communist power, and it was to this that I was addressing myself. Today there is more than one, and that makes a great deal of difference.

LAUSCHE: Right. Now, then, there was more than one, and with that I agree. But the nation included in the more is Red China, and Red China does not believe in peaceful coexistence, but urges the expansion of Communism by whatever means are necessary. Do you agree with that?

KENNAN: I agree with that.

LAUSCHE: That is, the split between Red China and Russia has come because Khrushchev believed in peaceful coexistence, thinking that by ideological combat Communism would be triumphant, and the Chinese did not subscribe to that theory, is that correct?

KENNAN: I think this could stand as an explanation of one of the reasons for the Russian-Chinese conflict, but by no means all of them.

LAUSCHE: All right. Now, then, if China is the real aggressor now, doesn't the policy of containment become more demandable than it was when you announced it twenty years ago?

KENNAN: Senator Lausche, the policy of containment certainly has relevance to China, but it is a question of what and where and what lies within our resources. If we had been able—without exorbitant cost in American manpower, American resources, in the attention of our government, in the emphasis of our foreign policy—if we had been able to do better in Vietnam, I would have been delighted and I would have thought that the effort was warranted.

LAUSCHE: That brings us down to this plateau. Do you advocate pulling out of Vietnam?

KENNAN: If by that you mean an immediate and sudden and unilateral withdrawal without any sort of a political arrangement and simply permitting to happen what will in that area, I do not advocate it.

LAUSCHE: Under present conditions, you would not advocate pulling out. Would you advocate allowing the people of South Vietnam by open, free elections, supervised either by the United Nations or by an international body so authorized, to hold elections and determine whether they want a Communist government or a government leaning to the free world?

KENNAN: I think it would be very fine if one could have such a test of opinion, but I doubt that it would be possible in the conditions that prevail to date.

LAUSCHE: Who stands in the way of it? Does the United States or Red China and Hanoi? Who stands in the way of it? Isn't the President and the United States urging that course?

KENNAN: Senator, it seems to me that the whole situation stands in the way of it. You could not have such an election in a civil war situation.

LAUSCHE: All right. All right, if that is your answer. Now I ask you, hasn't the United States government and the people of the United States probed every avenue through which there could be discussion towards reaching a settlement and that there has been constant rebuttal of those efforts by China and by Hanoi?

KENNAN: It is correct that we have gotten nowhere. . . . Perhaps the reasons go deeper than a mere question of blame on either side. Obviously, it seems to me, the other side have much more blame for this than we have.

LAUSCHE: Now, our government has stopped bombing, it stopped fighting. Can you point out to a single act on the part of the North Vietnamese and Hanoi, which collaborated with this policy, of stopping activities, point out one act of the North Vietnamese and Red China where they have tried to help towards bringing the subject to the negotiating table?

KENNAN: They have shown to my knowledge no interest whatsoever in negotiations at this time. I must say that I did not expect that they would, and I believe that I said in the article which was published, written at the end of November before this bombing pause was announced, that I saw no interest on their side in negotiations and did not think that in the immediate future they would be interested.

LAUSCHE: . . . In addition to what the President has done, what would you propose that we do now to bring this to a settlement without damage to our prestige and without danger to our security. What would you propose?

KENNAN: I would propose that we limit our aims and our military commitment in this area, that we decide what we can safely hold in that region with due regard to the security of our forces, that we dig in and wait and see whether possibilities for a solution do not open up. I am fully prepared to agree. . . . I do not see the possibilities for a peaceful solution of this today. But I have seen too many international situations in which possibilities of this sort were not visible at one time, but in which they were visible at another time if one showed a little patience and had a reasonably strong position. . . .

SENATOR WILLIAMS: Mr. Kennan, as I listened to your statement and your answers to the questions, I gather that you think over the past two or three years we have made several mistakes in decisions of our government policy in Vietnam. Is that correct?

KENNAN: I think the totality of our action in this situation as it has developed over the past few years has been unfortunate and in error, but I must say that I have great sympathy for our government. This has not been an easy problem for it to handle, and it has not been easy to find any one place where we could have put the hand to avoid these mistakes. . . .

WILLIAMS: But had you been in a position of authority at the time, what decisions do you think you would have made that were any different from those that were made?

KENNAN: No, I think probably if there was any point where we went wrong, it was in putting fighting men ashore for purposes of combat. Possibly even the instructors for the South Vietnamese forces were warranted by the situation. It is difficult for me as an outsider far away to tell. But I—perhaps we should have thought much more carefully before we put combat units ashore. It has been my belief for many years—and it is a belief based on the fact that I had at one time to make a very careful study of our difficulties in connection with the intervention in Russia in 1918—it has been my belief that one should be very, very careful about ever putting American forces ashore into a situation of this sort unless one can see clearly how and at what point one can get them out again, and unless the arrival at that point appears fairly plausible and material, and here is—if at any point, this is where we made our mistake.

WILLIAMS: Recognizing that we are at this point, we do have a couple of hundred thousand men in there. What would you recommend that we do now?

KENNAN: I would recommend that we not expand either our own commitment of men and resources to this conflict; that we try to limit the conflict rather than to expand it; that we adopt in general a defensive strategy and put ourselves in a position where we cannot be hurried, where we cannot be panicked, where we can afford to wait, and let the logic of this situation then gradually sink in on our opponents. And I think then there is a possibility that with a little greater patience than we have shown thus far, possibilities for an acceptable resolution of the conflict may open up. By an acceptable resolution of it, I do not say that this will be one which will hold any triumphs or indeed any great satisfaction from our standpoint.

I think that there is no happy way . . . out of this conflict. I think the best we can expect is that it be resolved in a manner which does not shake the stability of the area too much, and which permits us to extricate ourselves with a reasonable degree of good grace and retained prestige.

WILLIAMS: When you speak of digging in and holding what we have, you never know what the other side is going to do, and they may add, too. What would you do then? Would you retreat, withdraw, or would you add enough more men to hold so that it wouldn't turn this into just a sword's point of waiting?

KENNAN: This involves military considerations to which

I am not competent to speak, but I must say that I do find it hard to understand that this—that our government does not have it within its power and that our forces that we have out there today do not have it within their power to hold some areas of this country in a secure way. I note that the Viet Cong having approximately, I suppose, the same number—that is, the Viet Cong and their North Vietnamese helpers having about the same number of forces—are said to control completely 25 per cent of the country, and if they can do that with about the same number, it is hard for me to understand why there is nothing that we could hold with our present forces there.

Now, I don't know enough about military matters to say how this should be done. Perhaps you would have to have forward sweeps occasionally with our people. Perhaps it couldn't be just a state of siege, but it does seem to me that it should not be beyond the power of ingenuity to find a way in which the formidable forces which we now have in that country could settle down to a more or less defensive strategy for the coming period, and could create a situation in which nobody else could hope to dislodge us. If they hope to dislodge us at some point in the future they will have to talk to us because they won't get us out.

WILLIAMS: You think there is a possibility that such a holding action could actually develop into more costly both in dollars, material, and lives than would defensive action? . . .

KENNAN: I have heard it argued that it could—again this is a military question—but I cannot imagine that what it might cost in lives and effort could be more than what could possibly be involved if we continue to go on into what appears to be an unlimited escalation of this conflict into an unlimited area. Because this is almost infinite in its possibilities as related to our resources. . . .

SENATOR CHURCH: . . . My questions won't relate to Vietnam as it is in the present state of affairs. I think that what has been done cannot be readily undone. That the options now open to the President are limited, and I am confident that the President is striving to keep this war confined within manageable limits. And he certainly has indicated his sincere desire to bring about a political settlement that will restore peace to Southeast Asia. Rather I would like to question you about some of the underlying premises which led us into Vietnam in the first place, and which could, if they remain unchanged, lead us into other guerrilla wars, indeed, endless succession of guerrilla wars in the future.

I think to get this point clearly made on the record, we have to compare the policies you advocated in Europe with the situation that confronts us in Asia, which has just so recently thrown off European rule. Now, isn't it true that in Europe, following the Second World War, we were faced with a problem of Russian aggression, with the Red Army in occupation and control of much of eastern Europe? . . . And at that time Russian aggression and Communist aggression seemed to be somewhat synonymous, did they not? . . . And isn't it true that the NATO alliance was designed to put a stop to Russian aggression, that is to say, the movement of the Iron Curtain westward across the face of Europe? . . . And isn't it also true that when we intervened militarily in Europe, we intervened in an area where we shared with the Europeans a common culture, and a common civilization, and commonly held attitudes against Communism?

KENNAN: This is absolutely right.

CHURCH: Now, it seems to me we have made no mistake so fundamental in American foreign policy than concluding that a design that was suitable for Europe would also be suitable for those regions of the world that have just thrust off European rule, and that we failed to take into account how very different the underlying situation was in Asia and in Africa, the ex-colonial regions of the world. Would you agree with that?

KENNAN: I couldn't be more strongly in agreement, and at the time when the containment policy with relations to

Europe was being thrashed out in a practical way, and that was the time when the Marshall Plan was devised, we in the policy planning staff of the Department of State who had something to do with the Marshall Plan were pressed repeatedly, and sometimes by people here in Congress, to produce a similiar plan for China and for Asia, and we always resisted this, precisely for the reasons you have given, not because we did not want to see Communism contained in Asia, but because we felt that the devices that were effective in Europe would not necessarily be effective here.

CHURCH: May I suggest here that we just briefly review the basic condition in Asia to contrast it with what it was in Europe? Isn't it true that in Asia and in Africa we have governments that are very unstable, having just been newly established? We have popular aspirations for a better life that often outrun by a considerable distance the capacity of the governments to fulfill. We have, in addition, a situation quite different with respect to popular attitudes toward Communism. That is to say, would it be your judgment that in these areas of the world the people may be less concerned or less fearful or less opposed to Communism as such as they are to imperialism, colonialism, which they have just experienced for two centuries in which with great sacrifice and oftentimes with great struggle they have finally overthrown?

KENNAN: Oh, yes. The power of these various semantic symbols is entirely different in Asia than it is in Europe, and not only that, but the Europeans have things to lose by Communism, by a Communist form of rule, which the Asians are not conscious of having to lose.

CHURCH: They have freedom to lose, do they not, Mr. Ambassador?

KENNAN: Precisely.

CHURCH: Is there freedom as we know freedom in most of the countries of Asia and Africa today?

KENNAN: There is not, and I recall reading only two days ago an article by one of our greatest authorities in this country on Chinese culture, in which he pointed out that the Chinese language has only one word which remotely resembles our word "freedom," and that conveys the sense of license and rather turbulent indiscipline.

FULBRIGHT: Who was that?

KENNAN: John Fairbanks.

CHURCH: Now, in these countries which are mostly totalitarian—although we always like to include them in that phrase we use continuously, "the free world"—isn't it true that change, if it is to come at all, will often have to come through violence, that is to say, through revolution, rather than through the process of free elections?

KENNAN: I am sure that this is inevitable in large parts of the world. . . .

CHURCH: Then, Mr. Ambassador, apart from what happens in Vietnam, and you and I both hope that the best possible solution can be achieved there for our country, but apart from what happens in Vietnam, aren't we going to be facing a situation in this vast region of the undeveloped world which will be fairly beset by revolutions for many years to come?

KENNAN: Yes. By violence of all sorts, I think.

CHURCH: And don't you think, then, we have to begin to devise a new policy?

KENNAN: Yes. . . .

CHURCH: Do you think we have yet begun to develop that new policy?

KENNAN: No, I don't, and I think we find ourselves hampered in that by the slogans and the semantic symbols of the past. I wish we could drop all these things and look at these situations realistically. I think we could perhaps devise an approach to these problems, let's say, rather than a policy, which would be much more effective than the sort of talking we have been doing among ourselves in recent years. . . .

SENATOR CLARK: . . . In my opinion, the major thrust of our American foreign policy today should be the most difficult task of arriving at an over-all détente with the

Soviet Union in the interests of world peace. I wonder if
you would agree with that and whether you would care
to elaborate?

KENNAN: I agree very strongly with that because I think
that the greatest dangers to world peace still lie in the area
of our relations with the Soviet Union; not that I think
that either of us wants a great war, but when you still
have such unresolved problems as the continuing proliferation of nuclear weaponry, and the great outstanding
differences over Germany, differences which are becoming
after all potentially more explosive and dangerous from
year to year as the military strength of the Western
German government increases, so long as you have those
problems, I think that the most important questions we
have to face lie in the field of our relations with the Soviet
Union.

CLARK: I take it, sir, that you would also be of the view
that Russia's present problems and needs, economic and
social, are not so different from our own but that such a
détente would be in the realm of a very skillful diplomacy
exercised over a considerable period of time.

KENNAN: Yes, in the realm of a skillful but a very patient
diplomacy. I don't think these successes are to be had at
any early date. I think some sort of a resolution of the
Vietnam conflict is a prerequisite for them, but I am not
unhopeful about the long-term future of our relations with
Russia. May I just say there that I have never looked for
any utopia in our relations with Russia. We are two great
different nations in different situations in different parts of
the globe. The relations between two such peoples are
always complicated and there always will be elements in
which we do not see eye to eye. Furthermore certain
traditional differences of approach to problems of international policy will always cause some difficulty.

But, when I look back on those days when the so-called
containment policy was formed, it seems to me we have
made a good deal of progress in our relations with Russia
since that time, and that things are better than they were

then, and this is a very important recognition, and if we could make that sort of progress over the past twenty years, I think there are possibilities that we could make it over the next twenty, and we ought to cherish them.

CLARK: You would agree, I take it, that the Soviet leaders and, indeed, the Soviet people, need both peace and reasonably good relations with Western countries almost as much as we need the same thing from them?

KENNAN: They do, and I think they are conscious of that need.

CLARK: Now, my understanding is that you feel the present situation in Communist China is somewhat different on the ground; that they are in the early stages of a revolution, a belligerent stage. I wonder if you would state for the benefit of the Committee on what you think the capabilities and intentions of the Chinese Communists are with respect to the possibility of in due course arriving at a détente or an adjustment with them.

KENNAN: I think that at the moment the Chinese Communist leaders are in an extremely difficult and almost hysterical state of mind. They have had frustrations of one sort and another both internally and externally over the course of recent years. I believe they are really weaker than they like to admit. They are very troubled by what does seem to them to be a sort of encirclement, and an exclusion for which admittedly they are themselves mainly to blame, from the councils of the world. But this puts them into a highly excitable and irritated state of mind, and I think there is very little opportunity of talking with them or dealing effectively with them today.

On the other hand, I do not feel that they have the capability to create much mischief beyond the Asian land mass. I am not really too terribly worried about the island territories of the Pacific. I think they have suffered an enormous reverse in Indonesia, and one of great significance, and one that does rather confine any realistic hopes they may have for the expansion of their authority—confine it pretty much to the Asian land mass, most of which in East Asia they already occupy.

I think it will take a long time before we could deal with them effectively. But meanwhile, I think that we should leave them alone. I don't think that it is necessary for us to, or desirable for us to, try to solve this vast problem by military means. I don't think it is susceptible to solution by military means any more than the problem of Vietnam is. I am quite prepared to recognize that we face a great and serious problem in the cultivation by the Chinese Communists of a nuclear striking capacity. I don't wish to minimize that for a moment. But I would prefer to see us pursue the—or let me correct that—I would prefer to see us tackle that problem and approach it by finding as soon as we can an acceptable ending to the conflict in Vietnam, and then pursuing with the Soviet government, and even with the French, agreements which would permit us to bring the pressure of world opinion to bear a little more effectively on the Chinese.

CLARK: With the ultimate hope that we could get into a meaningful dialogue with them as well as with the Russians?

KENNAN: Yes, with an ultimate hope that we could at least bring this terrible problem of nuclear weaponry under some measure of control. And then, I think, things will change in China as they changed in Russia. They always do. A new generation of Chinese leaders will come. They could scarely be worse in their attitude toward us than the present ones. And as I look over the history of international affairs, it seems to me that the counsels of patience and restraint have been more effective as a general rule than the counsels of violence and unleashing unlimited violence.

Now, there has been great confusion sowed precisely in this respect by Hitler and the nationalists, and no statement of this sort that you make can be without its exceptions. There are no universally valid generalizations here.

There are—there can be threats to the peace that have to be faced in the way that Hitler should have been faced. But, by and large, especially when one is dealing with conflicts which threaten to develop into great world conflicts on a scale that has never been known before in history, surely it is better to exhaust the counsels of patience and restraint before one plunges into the others. . . .

SENATOR PELL: . . . Having followed you all these years in your thinking and spent most of my time in the Eastern European area when I was in the State Department, I was wondering, to return to this area, which is also the area of your specialization, if you believe that the course of events we are following now—which would seem inevitably to lead to a commitment of many more troops than we have in Vietnam, and with the steady escalation, the erasing of Hanoi and Haiphong that we could do in an hour or so, and the placement of the North Vietnamese with the Chinese and the eventual decision we would be forced to face—whether we will fight the Chinese on a man-to-man basis or whether we will go to nuclear weapons; probably thinking back to the public opinion at the time of Korea, going to nuclear weapons. Do you believe the Soviet Union will feel compelled to retaliate or will it stay out of that one?

KENNAN: If we do not resort to nuclear weapons, and merely get into a conflict on land between our forces and the Chinese Communist forces in Southeast Asia, I should not think that the Soviet Union would intervene in any formal sense. But, if nuclear weapons come to be used, I simply cannot predict the effects on world opinion, the effects on our own opinion, the cumulative quality of such a conflict. It could lead us to anything, and I am afraid that I can only say to you that the consequences of such a development are unpredictable. They could be anything. They could be an entrance of the Soviet Union, and I am afraid if it went to the bitter end we probably would

create a situation in which the Soviet Union would be almost forced to come out against us in the strong military
way. If that again would develop into a nuclear exchange
as between the Soviet Union and ourselves, I do not know.
But this represents, all of it, a fringe of apocalyptic danger
on which I should never like to see this country play, if
you see what I mean. This is the edge of a precipice, of
an abyss, and we ought never to get near this edge. . . .

SENATOR CASE: . . . There are just two lines of questioning matters that I would like to explore with you a
little bit, and I hope you will do most of the talking. One
of them is a question of analysis. I take it that one of our
problems here is that we are facing a kind of aggression
which is not so easy to recognize and not so clear perhaps,
what the Communist Chinese particularly call wars of
national liberation, as opposed to the kind of aggression
where armies mobilize along a frontier and then cross and
we have this very direct physical occupation of foreign
territory. Now, I take it you do not disagree that the
former, that is, the kind we face now, is just as much aggression as the latter. It that correct?

KENNAN: Senator Case, I think the use of the word "aggression" with what we are facing today in Vietnam is
confusing. I think that this present conflict has so complicated a background, so long a background, so much of
it does result from things that have happened within
South Vietnam, and not outside of it. Not only that, but
the border between North and South Vietnam is of a
curious quality; it was not meant originally to be the
border between states. All these things seem to me to indicate that when one uses the term "aggression" as our—
some of the people in our own government have been
using it, one confuses the issue. This is, of course, in part,
if you will, the invasion of one country, if one wants to
describe it that way, by forces of another country, although all of these things involve stretching of terms.
But in any case, it is not just that. It is also a civil conflict

within South Vietnam, and one of greater seriousness, I think. I do not think that we can afford to delude ourselves that the Viet Cong are simply an external force or a force that would not exist if there were not external encouragement. They might not be so strong, but all accounts indicate that they were fairly strong years ago before they had this help from the North Vietnamese.

CASE: Well, this, as applied to this particular area and this particular situation, is a question basically of fact.

KENNAN: Yes.

CASE: You would not disagree that there can be as serious aggression by means of bribery, by means of terror, by means of other use of native dissident elements as there is, has been historically, by crossing another country's border with your troops.

KENNAN: I would certainly agree that the effects can be no less serious and final and that this presents a great problem. But I think we ought to be careful to identify it insofar as it is that as a question of internal unrest and insubordination, if you will, rather than a question of external attack.

CASE: Well, I appreciate that distinction. . . . I agree we must attempt to define it. I think, I take it you disagreed rather sharply with Under Secretary of State Ball recently in his Northwestern University speech, in which he said that "North Vietnam and Hanoi systematically created the Viet Cong forces in matters of their equipment, in the guerrilla war and supporting that war on a day-to-day basis, and," Mr. Ball declared, and I am reading from an editorial in one of our radio stations, quoting again, "is purely a fictitious organization created by Hanoi to reinforce a fiction, namely that it is the legitimate spokesman for the people of South Vietnam." You disagree basically with that.

KENNAN: This is not the impression I have. I have the impression this is something that has existed for quite a time there in the South and probably has regardless of the means by which—which are no doubt democratic means—but are a considerable degree of what you call support from the population. By support, too, I would not wish to be misunderstood, this may not be sympathy with its political aims even, but it mainly runs on the part of people that call upon them and bring them to support this sort of force, but many other things enter in there.

CASE: I remember—of course, you know much more about it than I do—but I remember from my rather slight touch with it after the war, in West Germany there was very great concern that Germany was going to be Communist very soon and great timidity on the part of the people there who had no interest in Communism but took care not to make their Western sympathies at all obvious. . . . For this very reason, so this kind of thing can be, can happen, and it is a technique which is embraced within the term, as I understand it, of the Chinese use of the words "war of liberation," actual liberation, I take it, and this is in a sense the kind of thing we have got to find some ways of dealing with. . . .

KENNAN: That is correct. And, Senator, I would like to say I have great sympathy on the way you have described this. On many occasions, talking with Russian Communists, I have tried to impress upon them that this type of thing, stimulating and encouraging and organizing rebellious minorities within another country and seizing power through them, could be just as much a matter of real aggression as anything else.

CASE: And requires whatever handling we can apply to it within reasonable limits.

KENNAN: Yes. But one always has to bear in mind that there is usually in these situations some ingredient of real local injustice out of which these people profit, so that it is never just a clear case of some outsider going in and doing some sort of a magic transformation, as I said this morning, in people and making Communists out of them. There is usually something on which they can work, which is an indigenous situation, and for this reason it is always confused. . . .

SENATOR SPARKMAN: . . . Right now we are confronted with a very difficult problem. I am sure you recognize that fact. We have our men in Vietnam. We are involved there. There is a situation that prevails. Now, I do not see how we can adopt calm attitudes and so forth, now, at this point of the game. So what I had in mind was if we do adhere to the principle of containment, want to practice it, what are the things that we do at this point?

KENNAN: Well, my answer to this would be that we try to establish in South Vietnam some position, militarily, that we can be fairly sure of holding over a long period of time, with due regard to the security of our own forces, and that having established that, we do not try to expand this conflict, give things a chance to simmer down, and let other people who are interested in the resolution of this conflict, see what they can do in trying to find some sort of a compromise solution.

I do not think that we can hope in the present circumstances to negotiate any such solution ourselves. I think it will have to be done by other people, and when the proposals have been made, we will have to decide whether we can accept them or whether we cannot. As of today, I think the chances for any such compromise solution are very poor. But I think time might change that, and my concern is most, at the moment, that we should consolidate our existing presence in South Vietnam in some such way that we can be sure of holding it without great danger to our forces.

I believe, Senator, that we have now done something which is very important, and which perhaps had to be done at some stage here, if we were ever to find our way out of this difficulty, and this is to demonstrate the seriousness of our purpose there. I think no one doubts that any more today, and this is the positive side of an effort of the past year, which has had many negative sides, too. But having demonstrated that seriousness, I think we do not need at this time to go further. I would like to see us try to stabilize as much as we can the situation that exists today, to make it clear to these people that they cannot kick us out of there, and that at some point they are going to have to talk to us, if they want us to get out of there. Once they digest this lesson, I think we may be on the road toward an acceptable resolution of this whole miserable problem. This will not be a resolution which will, I am afraid, contain any triumphs for us or any great satisfactions. This is not the kind of situation that is.

SPARKMAN: Now, in your statement you refer to a satisfactory peaceful resolution of the conflict, and you have referred to it here. Could you state to us what the elements of such a settlement would be?

KENNAN: They are not entirely visible to me today, I must admit that, and I am only hoping that perhaps the future would reveal them because I have seen other cases in the past where solutions which were not visible at one time proved to be possible at another. But it would seem to me that eventually there must be some sort of a political compromise between the various factions involved in South Vietnam. And I am afraid that others, as I say, are going to have to work this out and the South Vietnamese themselves. But there are a number of factions there. It is not the Viet Cong and their opponents. There are Catholics, there are Buddhists, there are Montagnards, and there are a lot of people who have fingers in that pie, and at some point, perhaps, they—who I must say are rarely lacking in political resourcefulness when they want to do something—they may cook up compromises which today look impossible to us.

I do not think that anything of this sort can occur in the present atmosphere of sharp conflict and great nervousness on both sides, and this is why I would like to see things quiet down. I have seen a number of other international situations which looked hopeless at the moment look better after one has simply halted the violence for a few moments. Things always change and pressures and impulses break through then which cannot break through in a highly militant and excited atmosphere.

Now this may sound like a poor suggestion, and no doubt it is in many respects. It certainly contains no great glory for us. But I am measuring it against the two alternatives, one of which would be to launch ourselves in a growing involvement of unlimited dimensions in a part of the world that is very unfavorable to us, and the other would be to get out in a disorderly and abrupt and unilateral fashion presenting our adversaries with a gratuitous prestige victory; and I do not favor either of those alternatives. This is all I can see to do. . . .

SENATOR AIKEN: . . . I notice [in the prepared text] of your formal statement . . . you say, ". . . I fail to understand how it is possible for us in entering into any such commitment to bypass the process of Senatorial advice and consent which were meant to come into play when undertakings of even lesser import than this were entered into." Now, that recalls what someone has said, told me recently, and I have no knowledge of whether it is true or not, that at Munich that Chamberlain failed to—that he bypassed the processes that were provided for in the British Constitution and made decisions by himself. Do you know anything about that? Of course it may not have anything to do with this at all.

KENNAN: I can't judge it from the British standpoint of British constitutional law, which is quite different from ours. . . . But I think perhaps the same principle is involved. What I meant to say here is that I may have missed something, but it seems to me that no doubt without deliberate intent, and probably with the most worthy of intentions, we have nevertheless involved ourselves here in a situation which, according to the consensus of the fathers of our Constitution, would certainly have called for a great national debate and a very solemn decision in the Senate as well as in the Executive branch.

. . . I am not aware that this has taken place, and for this reason I always find myself caught up short when I see the way that this struggle is often referred to today in our public debates, and people talk about our living up to our commitments, and we must fulfill our commitments to these people.

Well, these commitments as we now interpret them, go very far indeed. They go, as I pointed out here, farther than the normal military alliance. To commit yourself in any way, to assure the internal security of another government, means to commit yourself to interference in the most vital process of its own internal political life, and this seems to me a commitment of such seriousness that it should not be lightly or casually slipped into. This is what I meant to say by it.

AIKEN: I would think that to commit ourselves without limitation . . . is certainly a pretty heavy responsibility for anyone to assume, particularly when processes are provided for for Senatorial advice and consent, and I think it well to frequently remind ourselves that these processes are provided for by our own Constitution and our laws, and trust that anyone carrying the responsibility will remember it. . . .

CASE: . . . What I had in mind . . . was your thoughts about the extent to which we have a responsibility in the world for world peace, the extent to which in the absence of world order run by law, with courts and a system of enforcing court orders, this country has to act as Britain did at the time gone by, and other countries perhaps earlier, as to whether we are engaged in this function, whether we are not engaged in this function here, to what extent it contributes to performance of that function, if you think it does or does not. Now, in a sense you have answered all of this in a way before, but not quite so pointedly toward that performance of that function.

Now, the other side of the coin, I suppose, would be to say we have no function, no responsibility in this matter at all. So long as our fairly immediate security is not involved we can wash our hands of the world. Do you move in this direction in your thinking? I wish you would try to put us into some kind of a—put our position as a world power, the greatest, perhaps, certainly on the free world side, in the world today. . . .

KENNAN: What I would say is simply this: that I think we have an enormous responsibility with regard to world peace. We are in many respects the most powerful nation in the world, and in most important respects, and there certainly is no nation which, if its affairs are handled prudently and well and thoughtfully, can contribute more than we can to preserving the peace of the world. I do think, though, what we have to bear in mind here mainly is preserving the peace between the great powers, hostilities among whom might really have appalling effects for the world at large, and set our entire civilization back by goodness knows how much.

I do not have any illusions that we can stop all violence everywhere in the world. I think that the slogan which Litvinov, the Soviet foreign affairs commissar, used to mouth so frequently in the thirties, that peace is indivisible, that this is not correct; it is in fact a horrendous doctrine. Men have always fought; they are always going to. We must hope now that the great powers such as ourselves and Russia are aware of the fact that the weapons in our hands are of such terribleness that we cannot afford to do this any more. And I think we are coming to this realization that we simply—what we have in our hands is so terrible that we cannot afford the luxury of settling affairs with each other the way people have traditionally all through human history. But there are a great many new nations, small nations, nations with inexperienced governments, nations with shallow traditions of national life, dotted all around this world. Believe me, they are going to fight with each other, and it seems to me that our role here as a great power must be to try to isolate, to moderate these conflicts, to settle them as quickly and as easily as we can, not to worry too much about the issues because they will be right and wrong on both sides, but to try to keep these local conflicts from doing great damage to world peace.

Now, the problem we face with relation to Vietnam today is, how do we best serve world peace at this moment? Do we serve it best by increasing the measure of our involvement in Vietnam? By trying to root out the Viet Cong by fire and sword? By increasing the intensity of this conflict in a single area to the neglect; I must say, of our world responsibilities, our responsibilities in other areas? Or do we serve it better by trying as best we can to bring about some sort of a resolution of the fighting in Vietnam and applying ourselves then again imaginatively and courageously and enthusiastically to the solution of the great, really great, and fateful problems that we still have outstanding with the Soviet Union. There is, as I see it, the question, and my own answer would be that it is the last. I agree that—I understand that people can differ about this. . . .

FULBRIGHT: This matter of China, actually something has been said; I want to clarify it just a step further: the nature of the commitment to South Vietnam, and you have already described it considerably, seems to me so out of proportion [to] what is involved there that surely some other consideration beyond Vietnam must be involved. I can't imagine a commitment, such as has been described, could have been just for this rather limited purpose. I think it does involve China and I think previous questions have indicated this; and there was some passing reference made this morning to the aggressive nature of China. Now, as a historian, is it your impression that China, when she was a strong country in the past, has been inclined to military aggressiveness such as was characteristic of Germany in two instances recently and other countries from time to time?

KENNAN: No. It is my impression that the Chinese are

tremendously preoccupied with what used to be called "face," with prestige, with the outward aspects of authority and respect; and sometimes, as in the present situation, their language can be very violent and extreme, but that by and large they are very prudent people when it comes to action, and when it comes to military action.

FULBRIGHT: Perhaps I didn't phrase my question as carefully as I should have. I was really trying to exclude the present, as you said this morning, hysterical state of the present Communist regime. I was trying to make this a historical question. We realize that they are under very different circumstances now from what they were fifty years ago or a hundred years ago or a thousand years ago. They are suffering from what you described very well this morning as a kind of a hysterical state. But traditionally they have not been noted as very aggressive people militarily. Is that true or not in your view?

KENNAN: That is my impression, yes.

FULBRIGHT: Now, even more recently, a statement was made the other day and was this morning referred to—the Indian matter—and I thought I remembered a statement made by General Taylor. That is while he was Chairman of the Joint Chiefs. This was made on February 14, Thursday, February 14, 1963, before the Committee on Appropriations. I think it bears upon the question. . . . This is page nine of that hearing. Mr. Sykes of Florida asked him: "Let me talk about Red China and the Indian operation. Did the Indians actually start this military operation?

"General Taylor. They were edging forward in the disputed area, yes, sir."

And then it goes on. I would be perfectly willing to put it all in the record. I don't wish to burden, take the time.

General Taylor on page ten says: "Mr. Sykes, where is it with relation to the generally accepted international boundary?"

They were talking about the Northeast boundary that this incident referred to.

"General Taylor. That is hard to say because there is no generally accepted international boundary. I am sorry to be vague about this but I can assure you that I spent several hours trying to find out where the McMahon Line is. Actually you find the maps differ on this. The terrain is so terribly rugged there has been no accurate mapping and no accurate boundary lines or markers."

And so on. This is all available. I won't burden the record with it. But it strikes me to say, to use this as an example of an aggression is a rather tenuous one. And with regard to Tibet, has not the status of Tibet been a matter of considerable controversy for a long time?

KENNAN: Yes. Of course it has, and the Chinese did regard it as part of their area of sovereignty. I don't say this excuses what they did there. It puts it in a different category.

FULBRIGHT: But I mean a long time ago, and not with the Communist Chinese.

KENNAN: Yes.

FULBRIGHT: Is it not true that the Nationalist Chinese regarded Tibet as a part of China, not since Mao Tse-tung came in.

KENNAN: Senator Fulbright, there have been very few of the troubles we have been having in the last few years which I don't think we would not have had with any other Chinese regime. A lot of this is national.

FULBRIGHT: I don't wish to overplay this but I think when we look at the specifics, the specific cases and examine the circumstances surrounding them, that their actions as distinguished from their words have not been unusually aggressive or even as aggressive as many of our Western countries', and in view of the history of China during the last century, beginning with the opium wars, running up to the Second World War, would you not say there was considerable reason for their having some dislike to Western nations?

KENNAN: Yes. I think we have to remember that we deal with the Chinese today at the end of a century in

which they had very, very unhappy experiences with
Western powers generally. I don't think that the blame for
this was entirely on the Western powers. There was usually a good deal of connivance on the Chinese side at
these relationships of imperialism. But, by and large, these
were very unhappy experiences. They were humiliating to
the Chinese people, and there has accumulated a fund
here of sensitivity and resentment which we are probably
harvesting today, and we have to bear that in mind.

FULBRIGHT: My time is up, but I would like to clarify
that one point about our having—the Western countries
having been—that their connivance that irritated us or
provoked us, if I remember my history at all. Take, for example, the opium war. Do you see any excuse for waging
a war to force a country to accept opium for the use of
their people?

KENNAN: No, Senator, I don't. All I meant to convey
by that was something which is also relevant to the opium
war, which was that a number of highly placed Chinese
also profited very well from the opium trade and this was
not so simple.

FULBRIGHT: Ah, yes, that is true. They were bribed.
They had a number of their people that were bribed,
there is no doubt about that. . . . But for a country to
take advantage of a country, another country, that was so
weak, and she was very weak in the dying days of the
Manchu Dynasty, and to subvert their local officials and
to wage a war for this reason seems to me about as outrageous as any war I can think of.

KENNAN: Yes.

FULBRIGHT: And you know there was a succession of,
in effect, occupations and invasions on a very weak and
helpless country. Isn't that generally so?

KENNAN: Yes, I think this is true.

FULBRIGHT: Did they attack any other Western country
during that period?

KENNAN: No, I fully agree with you here. I think that
the ferociousness of Chinese policy in the past and some-

what today is often a matter of words rather than of actions. I just would say this: it seems to me that the Chinese, if you look back historically, have not been an easy country to deal with. They have had ideas of being the center of the universe. . . . And all that which have presented problems for other people, and my own feeling is that I think a long period in which we had perhaps as little as possible to do with them, and kept our distance and tried to be reasonably restrained and polite might be helpful in our relations with them. . . .

MORSE: Mr. Ambassador, before I ask you my next question I want to buttress your impression as to what our military policy in South Vietnam is when you speak about it as a policy of victory or to win. I completely share that impression. I only want to point out we started out with thirty thousand and fifty thousand and seventy-five thousand, and then one hundred thousand, a hundred and fifty thousand, now two hundred thousand men, who haven't been sent over there to play checkers; and now we get out of the Pentagon building and out of this military headquarters in South Vietnam talking about four hundred thousand, and we have a chairman of a subcommittee talking about six hundred thousand.

But I want to find out what the President says and what I consider to be the very unfortunate welcoming speech he made at the airport in Honolulu. He said in part: . . . "If we allow the Communists to win in Vietnam, it will become easier and more appetizing for them to take over other countries in other parts of the world." He goes on to say: "We will leave here"—Mr. Ky and Mr. Thieu there with him—"We will leave here determined not only to achieve victory over aggression but to win victory over hunger, disease and despair." He said later in his speech: "In all these endeavors we will give all the support possible to the energetic effort of our Vietnamese allies."

I find nothing there but the conclusion we are out to

win, and then we have in today's press in a statement attributed to the President. The President said, "in South
Vietnam Chief of State Thieu and Ky understand and we
understand that the war we are helping them fight must
be won on two fronts: one front is military and the other
front is the struggle against social justice."

Then we have the communiqué, a most unfortunate
historical document in my judgment because I think in
this document the President exceeded his constitutional
power. I think he flaunted constitutional processes, and I
do not think that he has the constitutional right to make
the commitments that he has made in his communiqué.
But he says in it: "We must defeat the Viet Cong and
those illegally fighting with them on our soils"—it has become "our soil" now—"we are victims of an aggression
directed and supported from Hanoi. That aggression and
so-called war of national liberation is part of the Communist plan for the conquest of all Southeast Asia"—on
which they buttress their plan we are going to stop Communism wherever we unilaterally decide it ought to be
stopped. Then in the communiqué he says, or he agreed
to: "It is a military war, a war for the hearts of our people. We cannot win one without winning the other."

I don't think there is any question about . . . what our
present course is, and I happen to think we ought to
change that present course. We ought to follow the constitutional processes, and we ought to follow the course of
action such as you and General Gavin have told the
American people. And I think that in a democracy if you
are going to have full public disclosure of the public's
business you need just this kind of a forum, and this kind
of a forum, in my judgment, backs up the boys in South
Vietnam because it may lead to the stopping of the killing
of them in increasing numbers that they are going to suffer if we continue to escalate the war which in my judgment will go along with their communiqué.

I am at a loss that my President has yet to repudiate
this statement of Ky in Honolulu. They are not going to

sit down in any negotiations with the Viet Cong, and I want to say, as one member of this Committee, that I do not . . . share a very high opinion of Mr. Ky, being a great lover of Hitler, as he said to the London *Mirror* he was. I don't think we ought to let Ky tell us how many boys are going to die in South Vietnam because of any refusal on their part to negotiate with the Viet Cong that are a real force in South Vietnam or are part of the negotiations, and if that is the position of the South Vietnamese, I have no doubt what our policy should be: get out.

I come to the question of constitutional processes. You mention [in the prepared text] of your statement this morning: "I fail to understand how it was possible for us in entering into any such commitment"—you were speaking about the commitment—"to bypass the processes of Senatorial advice and consent which were meant to come into play when undertakings of even lesser import than this were entered into." You have no doubt, do you, that the President admits we are at war in Vietnam?

KENNAN: It seems to me this has been said many times—

MORSE: —by the President. Do you know of any declaration of war against any country in Asia that we have taken through our constitutional processes?

KENNAN: I do not, Senator Morse.

MORSE: Are you at all disturbed or concerned about the fact that Article I, Section 8, of the Constitution hasn't been complied with by the President and by the Congress? That the President has sent no war message, as did Woodrow Wilson on the night of April 17, 1917, to the Congress in which he said that he lacked constitutional authority, that is his language, to make war in the absence of a declaration of war, and that Franklin Roosevelt, after Pearl Harbor, sent a war message to the Congress asking for a declaration of war? Does it concern you that we have boys dying in South Vietnam, in a war which I have called an "executive war," without a declaration of war?

KENNAN: It has puzzled me, and the whole situation has concerned me.

MORSE: Well, Mr. Ambassador, let me tell you something about Japan. I took a congressional–senatorial delegation to Japan, was there for a good many days. We met with all the Japanese political parties in separate sessions with them, and I want to say in the majority party we got a little lip service. In the other parties we got open opposition to our policy in Vietnam, and most of the Japanese press, the academic world, most of it is against our policies in Southeast Asia; and as to the majority party, there sits behind me Dr. Marcy, head of the professional staff of this Committee, and after our conference with the majority party was over, where they had pretty much one spokesman on the subject, got back to my hotel about four-thirty in the afternoon and Dr. Marcy called me at five in my room, he said, "Senator, we have got two members of the majority party down in my room and they said they must see you."

So I said, "What about?"

He said, "I think you ought to come."

I went down, and these two members of the majority party didn't want me to leave Japan without knowing that they were badly split in their majority party over the war in Vietnam, but that they were in a position of a parliamentary system where they had to go along with the majority leader. But there was great concern even in the majority party, and I want to say their great concern is . . . that we are leading the countries of Asia into a war with China, and they don't want a war with China, and they can handle China, they can live with China, they can get along with China; that is their view, and they are concerned that the U.S. course of action in South Vietnam is going to escalate us into a war with China. And that is why I am putting to you the question in regard to your own reference to constitutional processes. Don't you think it is about time we make up our mind whether or not we are going to legalize this war by going through our constitutional processes?

KENNAN: Yes, Senator, I think we have a fundamental

decision to make and it ought to be a conscious decision and we ought to be aware of the gravity of it when we are making it.

MORSE: I happen to think the American people are entitled to be told whether we are going to take them into war by a declaration of war and get that debate. That will stir up the grass roots of America.

Very quickly, one question more. We hear a lot of comparison with the situation in Vietnam with Munich. Those of us who . . . are against this escalation and this unilateral American war in Vietnam, we are told we are a bunch of Chamberlains. Would you give us your view as to what the analogous relationship, if anything, between this war and the situation at the time of Munich or between Mao and Hitler might be?

KENNAN: I think they are entirely different things, and I think that no episode, perhaps, in modern history has led to—has been more misleading than that of the Munich conference. It has given to many people the idea that never must one attempt to make any sort of a political accommodation in any circumstances. This is, of course, a fatally unfortunate conclusion. Hitler was, thank heaven, a unique phenomenon, I think, and circumstances existed there that did indeed make the fatuous to think that you could arrive at that point at an agreement with him that would preserve the peace of Europe.

But these were specific circumstances and I think the wrong conclusions have—can be drawn and have been drawn time and time again from this. Hitler was a man who had made up his mind that he was going to conquer Europe by force of arms according to a certain timetable. I have never seen the evidence of anything comparable to that state of mind on the part of our Communist opponents, and for this reason, I have had to struggle for years against the attempt of people to apply the Munich precedent to the problem of containing Soviet power.

MORSE: One more question. I want to take you to the United Nations for a moment because you made mention of it. I think it is very doubtful that the Security Council, if it should vote to take jurisdiction over it, would probably get Hanoi and Peking in a conference on it as a Security Council format, but it might very well be able to pass a recommendation or a resolution calling for a reconvening of the Geneva Conference, and Great Britain and Russia might respect that. We must not jump to the conclusion, if that were the proposal, that you couldn't get acceptance of it. We have had some acceptance in Security Council for peacekeeping purposes and there also is the open door then, if they do reject it, of calling for an extraordinary session of the General Assembly, which in turn might even be a better format to try to bring some negotiations with Hanoi and Peking. Do you think there is any basis for my feeling thus?

KENNAN: Yes. I think the first alternative is the more promising one, and if there were a strong demand from the unaligned countries and a wide variety of countries around the world for a reconvening of the Geneva Conference, it would be harder for the Soviet government to stand in the way of it. I think, however, that it would be very desirable, if not absolutely necessary, that there be some sort of a political, internal political accommodation of the various factions within Vietnam before we could get a peace.

MORSE: There has to be?

KENNAN: Yes.

MORSE: Of course, you might be able at this point, if you can see the possibility of getting them to agree to a reconvening of the Geneva Conference, to accept some recommendations from the Security Council for the terms of a cease-fire, because I don't see how you can get anywhere even with the reconvening of the Geneva Conference until you can first bring the killing to a halt. That is what we ought to be urging, and I want to say most respectfully although I disagree with my President I really love him, I think he is dead wrong in the course he is following. I have a suggestion that he might counteract the Honolulu trip with a trip to New York City; and to ask for an extraordinary session, to hear our plea from the President himself, to demonstrate a course of action that we think we ought to follow quite different from what is proposed in this communiqué of suggesting a cease-fire with reasonable terms of a cease-fire, and let them debate that. . . .

HICKENLOOPER: Ambassador Kennan, can you give me your evaluation or your opinion on the political ambitions and orientation of China? Do you think that it follows what we have generally considered to be the international Communist theory of world dominion, extending its dominion of international Communism more and more and more?

KENNAN: Senator Hickenlooper, I think that it is the conviction of the Chinese Communists, as good Stalinist-Marxist-Leninists, that Communism is the future form of government for all the world, and that it is their duty to try to promote the hastening of this state of affairs. But I feel that one has to draw a very significant distinction, when one talks about these things, between what people think would be nice and what they actually expect to achieve within their lifetime and to what they are addressing their efforts.

HICKENLOOPER: Is the Communist timetable limited to the lifetime of any particular people or . . . is it limited only by the progress which they think will make, whether it is one lifetime or two lifetimes?

KENNAN: There is no timetable for this. The Russian Revolution took place nearly fifty years ago, fifty years ago next year, and theoretically ever since that time they have been waiting for the world revolution to occur. They know perfectly well that they are a lot farther from it so far as Europe is concerned. And I think, so far as the world is concerned, than they were then in 1917. They still cling to this as a sort of a respectable doctrine of religion with them. . . .

HICKENLOOPER: . . . How about the Chinese? They

are not as far along in their social and political development as the Russians.

KENNAN: The Chinese are more sanguine. The Chinese
know even less than the Russians do, and that means they
know very little indeed, about Western countries, about
the situation here in the West, and I have no doubt that
the Chinese leaders—cut off as they are, isolated as they
are today, fanatics as they are by training—that they
really believe that there are possibilities for this doctrine
gaining ground and coming to dominate the world.
Whether they expect that this would mean that this
would have disciplinary control of Communist party all
over the world is another thing. I think they hope that
Peking would stand as a great inspiring center in the way
that Moscow did in the early years of the twenties and
the thirties.

I think they do entertain these ideas. These are profoundly hostile to us, and I think they put limitations on
what we could expect to have in the way of friendship
and good relations with them, but I draw a distinction between these sort of long-term aims, which, after all, lie at
the heart of any sort of quasi-religious militant movement,
and sometimes they last for centuries. If you take the
Muslims and people like this, they have entertained aims
which have never been fully achieved. Just as the Chris-
tians have in this world. Well, so it is with these people,
and I would feel that we would do well, if we want to
make headway in coping with world problems, to address
ourselves primarily to what these people are doing, to
what occupies them, their mind, from the standpoint of
tomorrow and the day after, rather than from their long-
term aims. . . .

SENATOR CARLSON: This morning you stated in response
to a question, and this is not an exact quote but as I
took it down, "We cannot order the political realities
or views of other nations by our military power." Would
you want to elaborate a little on that? If we are not going
to do it by military power in this age when we are con-

fronted with nations who seem to respect only military might, what can we do?

KENNAN: I am talking about the internal affairs of other peoples here, and about the—our entering into those internal affairs and deciding what sort of political conditions shall prevail, and this gives me opportunity to say something that I feel very strongly about. When it comes to helping people to resist Communist pressures of all sorts—whether you call them aggression or whatever you call them—it has been my conviction for many years that no assistance of this sort can be effective unless the people themselves have a very high degree of determination and a willingness to help themselves. The moment they begin to place the bulk of the burden on us, I think the whole situation is lost. So strongly do I feel about this that I have often said publicly that the only people worth helping in this world are the people who say, "We propose to survive whether you help us or not, and just because you don't help us doesn't mean we are going to go under. It means that we are going to fight to the last ditch anyway but it may be a little easier if you help us."

Now, the people who take that standpoint, there is something you can latch onto. But I am extremely suspicious every time I hear it said that "If you Americans don't give us more than you have given us or if you slacken your efforts on our behalf, we will become fainthearted, and then what will become of you." And I think there is only one answer to this, and that is, "Whatever becomes of us will not be as bad as what becomes of you yourselves if you become fainthearted."

In other words, I do not believe in the possibility of helping people when it comes to problems that are partly problems of their internal political life, unless they themselves have a very high degree of determination and of internal self-discipline; and if things have deteriorated so far in these countries that they can't mobilize this sort of public morale and determination, I don't think any foreign force can put it into them. I think, then, the entry of a foreign force into the situation confuses it and creates new confusing elements which make it all the more difficult, and I think this is what has happened in Vietnam, and I have seen it happen in other situations in history.

We intervened in Russia in 1918 amid debates and doubts very much like these today, and the effect of our intervention was this: there, too, the problem was Communism, the problem was Communistic forces. We intervened partly to—at least a lot of us thought we were intervening then to keep these forces from taking over. Now they had, the Communists had, opposition in Russia. They had a conservative opposition, they had a more liberal opposition, and the effect of our entry into this situation was to cause these two opposition groups to stop fighting the Communists and begin to fight each other because each of them said to himself, "Ah-ha, the Americans have come in; they are going to save us now from the Communists. Now we can concentrate on sewing up our domestic position and on getting rid of our domestic rivals."

And I think this happens in a number of situations. I think this occurred in China around the time of the Chinese Revolution. In other words, I think it is very, very difficult for outsiders to come into a situation like this and to do only good. I think their presence is apt to confuse the political realities, rather than to be helpful to the resolution of them. . . .

SYMINGTON: [This morning you said], "There seems to be an impression that if we bring sufficient military pressure to bear, there will occur at some point something in the nature of a political capitulation on the other side. I think this is a most dangerous assumption. . . . The North Vietnamese and the Viet Cong have, between them, a great deal of space and manpower to give up if they have to, and the Chinese can give them more if they need it." That is a recognition of the one place that they have equality, if not superiority, namely in numbers of people. Is that correct?

KENNAN: Yes, sir.

SYMINGTON: Nevertheless, even though that is where they exceed us, and we exceed them qualitatively in sea and air power, you would not use that sea and air power in North Vietnam. Is that correct?

KENNAN: We have not spoken of sea power here at all today.

SYMINGTON: Well, all sea power today is air power except for the Polaris, and—

KENNAN: Well, it would depend on the purpose, Senator, for which you are doing this. I do not . . . entertain very optimistic feelings with regard to the purpose of trying to put an end to the Communist pressures in this part of the world by any military means. I have a feeling that you can bomb these oil supplies and means of communication in North Vietnam. I must say that it seems to me that the results of bombing of this sort, not just in this war but in others, have not been quite what we were led to expect or to hope that they would be. But let us say that they were effective. I still do not think that this would solve the problem. I think you are going to be faced with the fact that the Viet Cong will go on controlling bridges at night which we control during the daytime. I do not think we get to the guts of the problem through this. . . .

SYMINGTON: . . . Am I correct in feeling that you would want to withdraw to these enclaves in South Vietnam?

KENNAN: That strikes me as the most hopeful alternative that we face. . . .

SYMINGTON: . . . I notice that you say at one point, "I am not looking at this whole problem from the moral standpoint but from the practical one." And I think practically you would find a good many thousand young Americans in South Vietnam who, regardless of your theories of the relative importance of Europe as against Asia or the relative importance of people in one part of the world as against another, they would feel a moral ob-

ligation not to desert these people, who every day are
risking the lives of themselves and their families to promote the policies of the United States, even though it is
clear to me that you do not think those policies are sound.

Now, I would like to go back to another point . . . ,
where you talk about France giving an impressive exhibi-
tion of statesmanship in withdrawing from North Africa,
and about the British wisely and tolerantly liquidating
great portions of their colonial empire. Do you feel that
the position of the United States today in the world, with
our economy and our obligations, whatever they may be,
to free people is comparable to that of the British today?

KENNAN: Well, it is sufficiently comparable so that I
should doubt, and this is all that I meant to say with that
statement, I should doubt that we would be receiving any
bitter reproaches from the British over giving up an individual position like that even if we were to do it, because they have been all through this, as have the French
and others and, incidentally, as far as that is concerned,
this has usually been digested somehow or another. . . .

The Statement and Testimony of

GENERAL

Maxwell D. Taylor

Thursday, 17 February 1966

GENERAL TAYLOR: Mr. Chairman and gentlemen. I want to thank you, Mr. Chairman, and the members of the Committee for your willingness to hear my views on the situation in South Vietnam. I am afraid that they will not be new to many of you since you have often heard me express them in the days when I was an official of the government. I agree thoroughly with the motivating purposes of these hearings, namely, to analyze the reasons why we are involved in South Vietnam, the importance of this involvement, and the effectiveness with which we are dealing with the resultant problems. If my personal views can assist in clarifying these points, I shall be most happy to present them.

For the purpose of providing a basis for our subsequent discussion, with your permission I would like to make a continuous statement which will undertake to answer three basic questions.

First, what are we doing in South Vietnam?

Secondly, how are we doing it?

And, finally, can we improve upon what we are doing?

A simple statement of what we are doing in South Vietnam is to say that we are engaged in a clash of purpose and interest with the militant wing of the Communist movement, represented by Hanoi, the Viet Cong, and Peking. Opposing these Communist forces, in the front rank, stand the government and people of South Vietnam supported primarily by the United States but assisted in varying degree by some thirty other nations.

The purpose of the Hanoi camp is perfectly clear and has been since 1954. It is to absorb the fifteen million people of South Vietnam into a single Communist state under the leadership of Ho Chi Minh and his associates in Hanoi. In the course of accomplishing this basic purpose, the Communist leaders expect to undermine the position of the United States in Asia and to demonstrate the efficacy of the so-called "War of Liberation" as a cheap, safe, and disavowable technique for the future expansion of militant Communism.

Our purpose is equally clear and easily defined. In his Baltimore speech of April 7, 1965, President Johnson did so in the following terms: "Our objective is the independence of South Vietnam and its freedom from attack. We want nothing for ourselves—only that the people of South Vietnam be allowed to guide their own country in their own way." This has been our basic objective since 1954. It has been pursued by three successive administrations and remains our basic objective today.

Like the Communists, we have secondary objectives derived from the basic one. We intend to show that the "War of Liberation," far from being cheap, safe, and disavowable is costly, dangerous, and doomed to failure. We must destroy the myth of its invincibility in order to protect the independence of many weak nations which are vulnerable targets for subversive aggression—to use the proper term for the "War of Liberation." We cannot leave while force and violence threaten them.

The question has been raised as to whether this clash of interests is really important to us. An easy and incomplete answer would be that it must be important to us since it is considered so important by the other side. Their leadership has made it quite clear that they regard South Vietnam as the testing ground for the "War of Liberation," and that after its anticipated success there, it will be used widely about the world. Kosygin told Mr. Reston in his interview last December: "We believe that national liberation wars are just wars and they will continue as long as there is national oppression by imperialist powers." Before him, Khrushchev in January, 1961, had the following to say: "Now a word about national liberation wars. The armed struggle by the Vietnamese people or the war of the Algerian people serve as the latest example of such wars. These are revolutionary wars. Such wars are not only admissible but inevitable. Can such wars flare up in the future? They can. The Communists fully support such just wars and march in the front rank with peoples waging liberation struggles." General Giap, the commander-in-chief of the North Vietnamese forces, has made the following comment: "South Vietnam is the model of the national liberation movement of our time. If the special warfare that the United States imperialists are testing in South Vietnam is overcome, then it can be defeated anywhere in the world." The Minister of Defense of Communist China, Marshal Lin Piao, in a long statement of policy in September, 1965, described in detail how Mao Tse-tung expects to utilize the "War of Liberation" to expand Communism in Latin America, Africa, and Asia.

These testimonials show that, apart from the goal of imposing Communism on fifteen million South Vietnamese, the success of the "War of Liberation" is in itself an important objective of the Communist leadership. On our side, we can understand the grave consequences of such a success for us. President Eisenhower in 1959 stressed the military importance of defending Southeast Asia in the following terms. He said: "Strategically, South Vietnam's capture by the Communists would bring their power several hundred miles into a hitherto free region.

The remaining countries of Southeast Asia would be menaced by a great flanking movement. The loss of South Vietnam would set in motion a crumbling process which could, as it progresses, have grave consequences for the forces of freedom." Now, this view has often been referred to as the domino theory. I personally do not believe in such a theory if it means belief in a law of nature which requires the collapse of each neighboring state in an inevitable sequence, following a Communist victory in South Vietnam. However, I am deeply impressed with the probable effects worldwide, not necessarily in areas contiguous to South Vietnam, if the "War of Liberation" scores a significant victory there. President Kennedy commented on this danger with moving eloquence: "The great battleground for the defense and expansion of freedom today is the southern half of the globe—Asia, Latin America, Africa, and the Middle East—the lands of the people who harbor the greatest hopes. The enemies of freedom think they can destroy the hopes of the newer nations and they aim to do it before the end of this decade. This is a struggle of will and determination as much as one of force and violence. It is a battle for the conquest of the minds and souls as much as for the conquest of lives and territory. In such a struggle, we cannot fail to take sides." Gentlemen, I think a simple answer to the question, What are we doing in South Vietnam?, is to say that for more than a decade we have been taking sides in a cause in which we have a vital stake.

My second question was: How are we doing in the pursuit of our objectives in South Vietnam? Both sides in the struggle have over the years developed the current strategies which are now in confrontation.

During 1964 and 1965 the Hanoi leadership attempted to exploit the political turbulence which followed the fall of President Diem in November, 1963. Greatly encouraged by the disorder which marked the political scene in Saigon, the Communist leadership made a massive effort to press on to victory. To meet the growing needs in military manpower, they began the infiltration of personnel of the North Vietnamese Army, first as individual replacements, later as formed tactical units. Utilizing this new strength, they intended to make the monsoon offensive of 1965 a major drive for significant military victories.

Concurrently, they increased the sabotage directed at the land communication system in South Vietnam for the purpose of hampering the distribution of commodities and thus adding to the economic stresses in the South. Terrorism was stepped up and directed with added frequency at United States personnel and installations. They apparently hoped to be able to seize and hold politically important localities, such as district and provincial capitals, to demoralize the Vietnamese people and government and to demonstrate to the United States that we were backing a cause which must inevitably fail.

Faced with this growing threat, the Vietnamese government and our American officials were obliged to develop a counter-strategy to blunt and defeat the intensified efforts of our adversaries. It evolved out of the experience of the preceding months and years, and assumed its full form with the critical decisions in 1965 to introduce United States ground forces and to initiate the bombing campaign against military targets in the North. Both of these courses of action had been under consideration at least since November, 1961, when I presented my report to President Kennedy following a visit to Saigon to appraise the growing criticality of the situation there.

We did not take either action at that time but my report contained the following comment with regard to the possible necessity of using air power against the source of the Viet Cong support in North Vietnam: I quote: "While we feel that the program recommended represents those measures which should be taken now, I would not suggest that it is the final word. If the Hanoi decision is to continue the irregular war declared on South Vietnam in 1959 with continued infiltration and covert support of guerrilla bands in the territory of our ally, we will then have to decide whether to accept as legitimate the continued guidance, training, and support of a guerrilla war across an international boundary.

Can we admit the establishment of the common law that the party attacked and his friends are denied the right to strike the source of the aggression after the fact that external aggression is clearly established?" By February, 1965, it became clear that we could no longer tolerate this clandestine support from the immune sanctuary in North Vietnam which served as the external base for the Viet Cong insurgency.

In brief, the strategy which we have been and are pursuing consists of four components. The first includes the many activities directed at increasing the effectiveness of our ground combat against the Viet Cong and North Vietnamese units in South Vietnam. For this purpose we have made the utmost efforts to increase the indigenous forces of South Vietnam, always mindful that this is a Vietnamese war in which we should do only those things which the Vietnamese cannot do for themselves or cannot do in time to avert defeat.

From July, 1964, to July, 1965, the armed forces and police of South Vietnam were increased by some 140,000 trained men, a very creditable effort on the part of this small country where military leadership and administrative experience are inevitably in short supply. As of today the over-all military strength in South Vietnam is approaching seven hundred thousand, the largest military force in being among all of our allies, worldwide.

Encouraging though the results have been in increasing the Vietnamese strength, during the year cited, our intelligence authorities believed that the Viet Cong increased their total strength by some sixty thousand. In other words, we were advancing at a rate only a little better than two to one in our favor. Since history has shown that the government forces successfully opposing a guerrilla insurgency in the past have required a much greater preponderance of strength, ten to one or twelve to one for example, it was quite clear the Vietnamese could not raise forces fast enough to keep pace with the growing threat of the Viet Cong in time. It was this sobering conclusion that led to the decision to introduce American ground forces with their unique mobility and massive fire power to compensate for the deficiency in Vietnamese strength. With such forces available, it was felt that the ratios of required strength cited above would lose much of their validity.

I am thoroughly, Mr. Chairman, aware of the concern of this Committee over the growing requirement for American troops in South Vietnam. Is this an endless requirement in an open-ended war? I do not believe that anyone can give a completely satisfactory reply to this question, but I can suggest the consideration of certain limiting factors which have a bearing on the matter. First, on our side, we are not setting as an objective for our ground forces the occupation of all South Vietnam or the hunting down of the last armed guerrilla. We are in Vietnam to safeguard the people who are the real target of the enemy. Terrain has little meaning except insofar as it supports people. Thus the extent of control and protection of population is the true measure of progress rather than control of territory. By the former indicator we are not doing too badly.

Senator Mansfield estimates in his recent report that the government controls about 60 per cent of the population, the Viet Cong about 22 per cent, leaving 18 per cent contested. When I left Saigon last July, those figures were 53 per cent, 25 per cent, 22 per cent. The point I wish to make is that when one expresses our military objective in terms of securing a high proportion of the population, the troops requirement loses some of its impression of open-endedness. Under this concept the prime target of our United States forces becomes the main-line enemy units which constitute the greatest threat to population, not the entire guerrilla force wherever found.

Another limiting factor is the logistic difficulty of the

Viet Cong in supporting increased numbers of troops in combat. The combination of air attacks on their lines of supply and of increasing ground attacks on their units which must then consume supplies at an increased rate places some kind of ceiling on the forces they can maintain in South Vietnam.

I wish I knew exactly where that ceiling is but our basic data on Viet Cong logistics are too uncertain to permit precision. But the point is that there are factors which tend to keep our troop requirement finite and limit the capability of Hanoi to support large numbers of additional forces in the South.

The second component of our strategy relates to the use of air power against military targets in North Vietnam. It is well to remind ourselves the reasons which impelled us to this decision. There were three which we recognized perfectly at the time of the decision and which remain valid today. The first was to give the people of South Vietnam the assurance for the first time of imposing a direct penalty on the source of the aggression. For eleven years they had suffered the depredations of the Viet Cong without exacting any price from the country which provided the direction and support. The morale of the people and that of the armed forces in Vietnam received an inestimable lift from the decision to use the air forces of both our countries against military targets in the homeland of the enemy—a lift which has certainly contributed to sustaining their will to continue the fight.

The second reason for the decision was to use air power, insofar as it could be effective, to limit and render more difficult the infiltration of the men and supplies from North Vietnam to South Vietnam. It was perfectly clear from the start as it is clear today that air power would not be able to stop infiltration. We were quite sure, however, that it could impose a ceiling on the forces which could be sustained in combat in South Vietnam. I do not believe that anyone who has reflected on the effect of the destruction of bridges, ports, railyards, and similar facilities, and on the effect of the limitation of daylight movement on the roads throughout a large part of North Vietnam can avoid the conclusion that the air campaign has had an important effect in slowing down infiltration and in raising its price. A testimonial to its effectiveness was the feverish activity in North Vietnam during the bombing pause to repair bomb damage and to move transport in daylight.

The third reason for the decision to use our air power was to provide a sobering reminder to the leaders in Hanoi that progressively they must pay a mounting price for the continuation of their support of the Viet Cong insurgency. In spite of their defiant statements of determination to endure these attacks forever, I for one know from experience that no one derives any enjoyment from receiving incoming shells and bombs day after day, and I have no doubt that the warning message is getting through to the leadership of Hanoi. In a very real sense the objective of our air campaign is to change the will of the enemy leadership.

We hope that, in due course, the combination of the Viet Cong failure to win victory on the ground in South Vietnam and the effect of continued air attacks will present to the Hanoi leadership a situation so disadvantageous that they will decide that it is in their interest to halt their aggression, redefine their aims, and join with us in discussing ways and means of improving the lot of all Vietnam.

The third component of our current strategy includes all of those non-military activities which are so important but which receive too little public attention. It is not that our leaders have been unaware of the importance of better government, better living conditions, and the promise of a better future for the people of this country. Unfortunately, lack of security and governmental instability were for a long time factors limiting the effectiveness of the many programs for development and reconstruction. But now, with the growing military effectiveness of our forces on the ground and the slowly developing maturity of the civil leadership in Saigon and in the provinces, I hope that conditions will permit much greater progress than in the past in bringing the benefits of a comparatively normal life to this war-weary people. As you know, the recent Honolulu Conference devoted most of its time to a consideration of these non-military activities. If we are to leave a viable country after the end of the Viet Cong insurgency, it is essential that we make progress even under the conditions of war in stabilizing the government, the society, and the economy.

The fourth component of our strategy is that which relates to our political and diplomatic efforts to initiate the discussion of a peaceful settlement of this conflict. The so-called "peace offensive" is so well known as to require no discussion at this time, as is also the discouraging lack of response from the other side. I am obliged to feel that the Hanoi leadership is not yet convinced that it must mend its ways. Perhaps they still hope for some kind of military victory in the South. Certainly, they are not convinced that in some way the United States cannot be detached from the support of South Vietnam. They hope against hope that through international or domestic pressures our government can be forced off course.

They have not forgotten that the Viet Minh won more in Paris than in Dienbienphu and believe that the Viet Cong may be as fortunate in Washington. They doubt the will of the American public to continue the conflict indefinitely. In a contest of patience, they expect to win even though North Vietnam like the South has been constantly at war for over twenty years. Until it becomes perfectly clear to them that we are going to stay on course regardless of anything they can do, I am afraid we are not likely to see them at a conference table. Or if they come unconvinced of the inevitability of the failure of their present course, we can expect them to stall, delay, and maneuver just as they did at Panmunjom in Korea for over two years.

In summary then, our four-point strategy consists of a complex but coherent package of measures designed to improve the effectiveness of our forces on the ground in South Vietnam, to exploit our air superiority by attacking military targets in North Vietnam, to stabilize the politcal, socal, and economic systems in South Vietnam, and to seek an honorable negotiated settlement of the conflict. It is limited as to objective, as to geographical scope, as to weapons and forces employed, and as to targets attacked. All parts of it are interrelated; all parts are indispensable; we must be successful on all fronts. The key, I believe, is inexorable pressure at all points, directed at the will, the ability and the means of the Communist aggressors.

It is a fair question to ask, whether this is the best strategy to attain our basic objectives. I am the first to concede that we can and must do better in all four categories of our efforts; and, unhappily, progress toward peaceful negotiations is a bilateral affair which can progress only with some cooperation from Hanoi. As you know, thus far that cooperation has been withheld. Having conceded the need and possibility for improvement within the components of our current strategy, I must add in honesty that I know of no new strategic proposal which would serve as a better alternative to the one which I have described—that is, provided we do not sacrifice our basic objective. There are, of course, the two old alternatives which we have always rejected and I hope will continue to reject: to withdraw and give up our basic objective or to widen the war by massive air attacks on the North Vietnamese or even on Chinese targets. These two courses of action appear so to contravene our national and international interests that I shall not take the time of the Committee to discuss them here.

The only new proposal of which I am aware is the so-called "holding strategy," which in its least extreme form calls for a cessation of United States reinforcements and a limitation of military operations to those necessary for the security of our forces and for the maintenance of our military presence. On several occasions I have expressed myself in opposition to such a course of action. To button up our troops in defensive positions and thus to sacrifice their unique attributes of mobility and fire power would constitute the abandonment of our allies on the battlefield and would assign a most inglorious mission to our troops who, for the present, have high morale and complete confidence in their ability to cope with the Viet Cong in the field. The effect of such behavior on our Vietnamese allies could be disastrous. At a minimum it would destroy all confidence in Vietnam in ultimate success and would encourage the timid and the wavering to turn to the Viet Cong for protection and to the Liberation Front for political accommodation. Another serious result of such passivity would be the impossibility of obtaining honorable terms at any peace table. The Communists are tough enough to deal with when one has the upper hand. They would never give us acceptable terms if the military situation reflected weakness on our part and a readiness to withdraw. Our only alternative would be to accept dishonorable terms or to continue to sit out the war indefinitely on a supine defensive. I can hardly see the American public or this Congress long supporting such a course of action. Thus I am obliged to conclude that the so-called "holding strategy" is really not an alternative way of reaching our objective of an independent South Vietnam free from attack. We could never reach it on such a course. Rather than being a true alternative, it amounts to the modification and erosion of our basic objective and hence appears to me to be unacceptable.

In conclusion, I feel that our present strategy is the best that has been suggested and that it is important that we adhere to it, always striving to improve our performance within the confines of its general concept. Certainly it is not without risks, but little of value in this world is accomplished without risk. It seems to me that the risks entailed are warranted by the importance of our stake in Southeast Asia. Congress recognized this importance in the wording of the Joint Resolution of August, 1964: "The United States regards as vital to its national interest and to world peace the maintenance of international peace and security in Southeast Asia." I subscribe to these words and believe that we should live by them and by the words of President Johnson when he said in regard to our commitment in South Vietnam: "We will not be defeated. We will not grow tired. We will not withdraw either openly or under the cloak of a meaningless agreement." . . .

SENATOR SPARKMAN: General Taylor, I followed your statement with a great deal of interest. It seems to me it should clear up some misunderstandings that a great many people have, I believe.

First, let me ask you an elemental question. Who are the Viet Cong?

TAYLOR: The Viet Cong are, in terms of military categories, they are the so-called main-line units who are really the hard corps, the tough professional fighters, and then they have both provincial and local units who are more paramilitary in character than strictly military. Then they have a large cadre of political cadremen, some forty thousand.

Now, insofar as race is concerned, the majority—exactly what percentage I don't know—are South Vietnam, but a large majority are South Vietnamese. The important South Vietnamese who, particularly those in the main-line units, have been taken north and trained in the North, and sent south. So that their leadership, regardless of ethnic origin, came out of North Vietnam. Now, since the end of '64 in addition to the Viet Cong themselves, we have the so-called PAVN units, the units of the Army of North Vietnam who were brought there as I mentioned, first as individuals, then later in formed units, even in division size. So you have them as a very important reinforcement and they are all from North Vietnam.

SPARKMAN: We hear a good bit from time to time about this being simply civil war within a country, and that we are in effect intervening in the internal affairs of that country. What would you say about that?

TAYLOR: I would say that is simply not the case; that we have indeed a foreign aggression supported from Hanoi, the Viet Cong simply being the military arm of North Vietnam, being utilized initially clandestinely to overthrow—to impose a Communist rule upon the people of South Vietnam. The leadership, the direction, the important supplies, all come from North Vietnam.

SPARKMAN: In other words, they are directed by another power, and under the Communist ideology. Is that right?

TAYLOR: That is perfectly clear, I think, now, Senator. . . .

SPARKMAN: We were not a party to the Geneva Conference, were we?

TAYLOR: We did not sign the . . . Agreement. Neither did South Vietnam.

SPARKMAN: Did we make an agreement with the South Vietnamese government that we would help them if they needed help?

TAYLOR: Shortly thereafter. There was an exchange of letters in which President Eisenhower agreed to assist the government in response to the request of President Diem.

SPARKMAN: Was it under that promise that we went into South Vietnam originally at the request of the government of South Vietnam?

TAYLOR: I think that was the basic action which initiated our aid. Again, I have not researched all the documents, but that, as I recall, is the principal document which [is] the starting point for the programs which we have carried forward.

SPARKMAN: . . . When did we first give military assistance to South Vietnam?

TAYLOR: Almost at once. After this agreement in '54 we established a small mission which gradually grew. For a while the French remained in a training capacity in South Vietnam. Eventually they withdrew that formal participation and we took over the entire training task of the armed forces. At the same time there was economic aid going on. . . .

SPARKMAN: That increased later to advisors, even to the men in the field.

TAYLOR: It grew rather substantially, as the result of the visit of my mission in '61. President Kennedy and his government decided to increase the numbers of advisors, not to change the quality of our support, but to increase the quantity of it, and very shortly thereafter the total number went as high as seventeen thousand.

SPARKMAN: And then it was some time later that we put in sizable units?

TAYLOR: Yes. That was not until 1965, because of the inability to create additional adequate South Vietnamese forces to compensate for the added infiltration from the North, that we decided to put in our own combat forces in a combat role.

SPARKMAN: They were increasing their military manpower but not fast enough to match the infiltration from the North, is that correct?

TAYLOR: That is correct, sir. I think the increase has been very good. The limiting factor is not so much manpower but leadership. It is almost impossible to create a trained officer corps, and noncommissioned officer corps, quickly. So that the dearth of leadership has been the restraining factor on the increase of their forces. But even so, as I mentioned in my prepared text, they have almost six hundred thousand men now in the army, the paramilitary forces, or the police.

SPARKMAN: Now, General Taylor, I notice in your statement that you do not subscribe to the so-called domino theory, but you do admit, do you not, that Communist success in South Vietnam would have a tremendous effect on other nations around there?

TAYLOR: I certainly do. I don't like the domino phrase,

because it suggests an automaticity—the neighbor goes
down next. . . .

SPARKMAN: In your opinion, can we win in South Vietnam?

TAYLOR: Senator, I always ask, when asked that question first, I want to say what I mean by winning. I think
the word "win" tends to mean Appomattox, Yorktown,
the signing of a peace on the deck of the battleship *Mis-
souri.* That doesn't mean that to me at all in this kind of
situation. To win means to obtain our basic objectives,
the ones which I underlined in my prepared statement—
namely, the ability to offer freedom and self-determination to South Vietnam. I think we could do that, yes, sir.

SPARKMAN: . . . You mentioned some of the advocacy
of withdrawing to enclaves, create the holding action.
Could we win, as you see it, with that kind of action?

TAYLOR: Definitely not. I think that it inevitably—if
indeed our objective is to get to a conference table, to
come to a conference table from that posture means we
could never get the kind of agreement which would attain the basic objective we have been discussing.

SPARKMAN: You recognize that military winning alone
is not sufficient.

TAYLOR: We must be successful on the ground against
the Viet Cong to the point of convincing the leadership in
Hanoi that the Viet Cong insurgency cannot possibly win.
So in that sense the military is very important. It is also
very important in creating that security behind which we
can do these nation-building acts which are also very important. I would like to stress the point, our strategy is
a package and we have to do well in the military field,
the political field, the economic field, and the psychological field.

SPARKMAN: Are we beginning to move, do you think,
in this field of pacification? . . .

TAYLOR: We have always been able to move in the
areas where the security was good enough. But I have
often said it is very hard to plant the corn outside the

stockade when the Indians are still around. We have to get the Indians farther away in many of the provinces to make good progress. But I do think that our increased military effectiveness and, of equal importance, the growing capability of the South Vietnamese government to administer, to do all these actions, civic actions necessary to support the military program, that the increased capability in both of those fields is encouraging as we look to the future. . . .

SPARKMAN: Do you believe there has been some growth in the stability of the government?

TAYLOR: Almost anything would be an improvement over what I saw while I was Ambassador. I had to work with five prime ministers in the course of my thirteen months. Since this present government is now, I believe, in its eighth month, clearly it has done better in terms of stability than any government since that of President Diem. I think we have missed one reason, one explanation, namely, the fact that this is the first government which is solidly backed by the armed forces; and as long as they are behind this government in the present sense, it is not going to be overturned by some noisy minority as some governments were overturned in the previous years. So I do feel there is some encouragement, indicators of growing stability in the political scene.

SPARKMAN: By the way, you hear the complaint made often that the government of South Vietnam and the action in fighting the Viet Cong is not supported, does not have popular support in South Vietnam. What is your answer to that?

TAYLOR: In a certain sense of the word I would agree. In the sense that because of the war conditions, present leadership, the individuals are not generally known throughout the country. Saigon historically has always been an unpopular place to the peasants in the field: that is where the tax collector lives. So I don't think the commitment really is to this government, or particularly to the leaders, although Prime Minister Ky now is showing a considerable political sense. He gets out among his people. He obviously has their interests at heart. But the real commitment of the people is against the Viet Cong, against Communism. They know that kind of life is not progress but retrogression. So they are deeply anti-Communist, although with no deep personal devotion, I would say, to the present government. They simply don't know the government. . . .

SENATOR HICKENLOOPER: . . . With regard to the situation we find ourselves in now, and I have asked this question before but I would like to put it to you: In my view it seems we have three broad courses of action. They may have some ramifications, but one would be to withdraw. The other would be to follow the idea of a strongpoint security in a defense-limited area, and just sit there and hold that strongpoint and hope that they wouldn't lob mortar shells in on us, that they wouldn't get close enough. The third is to either increase or continue the active destruction of military targets which go to the North Vietnamese and the Viet Cong's ability to carry on the war. Would you say those are three general courses that are open to us?

TAYLOR: Well, I mentioned a fourth and then immediately threw it out; namely, the unlimited use of our air [power] in all targets in North Vietnam or even in China.

HICKENLOOPER: I would use the fourth as a potential part of the third, perhaps.

TAYLOR: I think it is so different, Senator, that I think you ought to make it a separate category.

HICKENLOOPER: Well, it may be. It has been my philosophy if you get into a hassle of this kind, you want to win. Do you think if we, speculating now, if we just withdrew, withdrew our forces and our support there and then said, let's come to a conference table, do you think the North Vietnamese would come to the conference table?

TAYLOR: It is hard to say. They would have won, anyway. I wouldn't think they would win anything more at a conference table. I wouldn't be sure. We would be sunk, of course.

HICKENLOOPER: In the history of struggles between nations or peoples, do you know of any great number of instances where a nation that believes it is at least holding its own in the struggle or perhaps winning is willing to come to a conference table and make a lot of concessions that are against their interests as they see it?

TAYLOR: Well, all conferences or all settlements of course simply record the assumed balance of power at the moment, so obviously no one should go to a conference table from a weak position unless he is ready to come out with a weak solution. . . .

HICKENLOOPER: Now we have had, we had about a thirty-seven-day lull in the bombing of military targets. . . . Do you think much was accomplished there except to enable the North Vietnamese and the Viet Cong to rehabilitate themselves in the field and get in new supplies and repair their damage, so that they could return to the fray with greater vigor?

TAYLOR: Well, Senator, I think a great deal was accomplished. I was for the pause. I was asked my opinion and I said I think it is well worth the try. Whether it was worth thirty-seven days or not I think is a matter of judgment, but certainly a substantial pause was clearly ample to sound out the opinion of the other side, clearly ample, when you have all the consultations which were made, I am sure was a good thing.

It is quite right, as you suggest, there was some military price paid in terms of allowing the other side to recoup, to repair damage, to build up stocks. I think all of those things, however, can be remedied if indeed our subsequent conduct from here on out shows the leadership in Hanoi that we are inevitably unalterably committed to our course of action; we are going to stay on until they mend their ways.

HICKENLOOPER: I think you said a little earlier . . . that, after all, this is nothing new in South Vietnam. They have been at it for twenty years over there, been fighting. Well, having become acclimated to twenty years of fighting over there, is it going to mean so much to them to continue for another ten or twelve years? Aren't they rather used to it now, unless they get hurt rather badly? . . .

TAYLOR: I have been exposed to war situations; one never gets used to war. The first shell coming in is rather exciting and rather interesting, but the thousandth shell is very dull and unattractive. . . . Another point: while they have been at war for twenty years—either at war with the Japanese or French, and feeding the war in South Vietnam—North Vietnam has never been touched in the last fifteen years. And there is something new: the bombing attacks forces the homeland to pay a direct price, which was not true in the past. . . .

SENATOR MORSE: General, prior to Dienbienphu, were the French people growing restless and [was] increasing opposition developing in French public opinion to the war in Indochina?

TAYLOR: There was a great deal of opposition developing, Senator. As you can recall the governments were changing rapidly and it became a political issue.

MORSE: It was my recollection, and I wonder if you share it, that Mendès-France really stood for office on the pledge to the French people that he would bring the war in Indochina to an end? . . .

TAYLOR: I think that is true, sir. I had not reviewed that situation.

MORSE: He was elected and interpreted it as a mandate and went to Geneva, following Dienbienphu, and joined in negotiating in those Accords carrying out what he considered to be the mandate that the French people gave him. I think that is a fair observation on my part.

TAYLOR: I do not recall whether he had a clear majority or not. But certainly, as you say, he took office with the intent of doing this, and furthermore made the negotiation most difficult by fixing a date by which he was going to withdraw his forces. That virtually sold out any chance of getting a reasonable settlement from the point of view of the non-Communist Vietnamese.

MORSE: Now, when the people of a country demonstrate an opposition to a foreign policy of that country, and make clear, as I think they did to Mendès-France, that they wanted the Indochina war stopped, do you interpret that as a weakness on the home front?

TAYLOR: The question, as I understand it, was that if indeed Mendès-France had a clear majority of the will of the French people, whether I should call that a weakness on the home front. . . . If one attaches importance to success in Southeast Asia, it certainly is a legitimate act on the part of any people to change the policy of their government.

MORSE: You know we are engaged in historic debate in this country, where there are honest differences of opinion. I happen to hold to the point of view that it isn't going to be too long before the American people as a people will repudiate our war in Southeast Asia.

TAYLOR: That, of course, is good news to Hanoi, Senator.

MORSE: I know that that is the smear that you militarists give to those of us who have honest differences of opinion with you, but I don't intend to get down in the gutter with you and engage in that kind of debate, General. I am simply saying that in my judgment the President of the United States is already losing the people of this country by the millions in connection with this war in Southeast Asia. All I am asking is, if the people decide that this war should be stopped in Southeast Asia, are you going to take the position that is weakness on the home front in a democracy?

TAYLOR: I would feel that our people were badly misguided and did not understand the consequences of such a disaster.

MORSE: Well, we agree on one thing, that they can be badly misguided, and you and the President in my judgment have been misguiding them for a long time in this war. . . .

General, I take you to the final declaration of the Geneva Conference on July 21, 1954. Before I do that, I want to point out that General Eisenhower on August 17 is reported, and I think accurately, in the press, and I read what it says: "Although asserting strongly at a news conference that the Communists must be stopped in Vietnam, Mr. Eisenhower denied that he had ever given a unilateral military commitment to the government of South Vietnam. His administration saw no need for such a commitment in 1954, he said, and he was offering aid, not military programs."

Later it says, When asked about the view today, Mr. Eisenhower said, and in my second round, I probably won't have time to get into the Eisenhower letter, but I want to mention it in the first round, Eisenhower said, we would help that country. We were not talking about military programs. But foreign aid, so our original program was not a military program under Eisenhower but a foreign aid program.

TAYLOR: Senator, first in 1954 we had no vision of what was going to take place. We did not realize we were about to face a clandestine aggression directed out of Hanoi; obviously there was no commitment made to cover that contingency. We didn't foresee it. Secondly, I would say in 1954 the program initiated was not just aid but also had the rather limited military factor in it which Senator Hickenlooper mentioned.

MORSE: I will take you to paragraph four of the Declaration of Geneva which reads, "The conference takes note of the clauses in the agreement on the cessation of hostilities in Vietnam prohibiting the introduction into Vietnam of foreign troops and military personnel as well as all kinds of arms and ammunitions."

TAYLOR: I would say that, one, there was never a cessation of hostilities to begin with. The North Vietnamese left behind five to six thousand men in South Vietnam, and large caches of ammunition. They proceeded almost at once to infiltrate armed men from North Vietnam, so I would say that the whole provision was never effective.

MORSE: But the signatories to the Treaty thought so. They signed it.

TAYLOR: They didn't know what was going to take place, sir. The ink was not dry on that piece of paper before North Vietnam was violating it.

MORSE: You haven't heard France or the other signatories to the charter take America's position that a course of action in violation of these sections was justified? . . .

TAYLOR: Well, their objection is not being gored, Senator; ours is.

MORSE: But their treaty is being torn up by us.

TAYLOR: It was not our treaty, nor did the Vietnamese people, and let me remind our listeners that the South Vietnamese leaders present at the time denounced the treaty in advance, and indicated, I think with considerable perspicacity, that the other side would never adhere to the provisions which were actually signed.

MORSE: I will ask later some questions about what this government is and how it came into being and where Diem came from but I want to hold longer to these articles of the declaration. The paragraph, paragraph five, says, "The conference takes note of the clauses in the agreement on the cessation of hostilities in Vietnam to the effect that no military base under the control of a foreign state may be established in the regrouping zones of the two parties, a latter having the obligation to see that the zones allotted to them shall not constitute part of any military alliance and shall not be utilized for the resumption of hostilities or the services of an aggressive policy." Do you think the bases we have established in South Vietnam and the military forces we have put in there are consonant with that section of the declaration?

TAYLOR: I would say that by the time we put in any

forces and establish anything that might be called a base, the entire Geneva Accord had been nullified by the action of North Vietnam.

MORSE: Taking paragraph six, and I respectfully dissent, and we will discuss it later, Section 6 says, "The conference recognizes that the essential purposes of the agreement relating to Vietnam is to settle military questions with a view to ending hostilities, and that the military demarcation line is provisional, and should not in any way be interpreted as constituting a political or territorial boundary. The conference stresses its conviction that the discussion of the provisions set out in the present declaration and the agreement on the cessation of hostilities creates the necessary basis for the achievement in the near future of a political settlement in Vietnam." Do you think our support of Diem—that we had much to do in setting up in the first place—was a violation of this paragraph of the declaration?

TAYLOR: No, sir, I do not. I think we all feel that a day may still come and would hope for the day when unification could still be possible under terms freely reached by the Vietnamese people. It was clearly impossible after the action of Hanoi in establishing a police state in North Vietnam that partition for a long period of time was inevitable and unhappily it is today. . . .

MORSE: The demarcation line of the 17th Parallel was a demarcation of zones, military zones; south of it the French forces were to repair thereto. It was contemplated there should be nothing but two zones and it was the United States and Diem that proceeded to set up this first government in South Vietnam in clear violation of the treaty. Now we have got Ky saying he is for reunification, but it is going to be under Ky's terms later. It is all right if it is going that way, but it is wrong if it is coming from the North–South.

TAYLOR: Senator, it is your position that elections, free elections internationally supervised could have been held in 1956?

MORSE: I don't think there is any doubt about it. I think if India, Canada, and Poland would have supervised those elections—they were set up and we should have tried it and then if it turned out into chaos we would have had a case; but the fact is history will record that my contribution and yours stopped those elections and it is a black mark on our history.

TAYLOR: The fact is that tens of thousands of North Vietnamese citizens were murdered and the International Control Commission could do absolutely nothing to control the situation at the time. . . .

SENATOR AIKEN: . . . General Gavin told us that he thought the problem was how to make a truce consistent with the military effort. Now, is this the way you appraise the problem or do you think of it in terms of what kind of settlements may be possible if the Viet Cong are defeated? . . .

TAYLOR: I wouldn't say defeat, because again I am afraid we are thinking about Appomattox or something of that sort, but I would say until it is quite clear that their course of action is a losing one and they can profit by changing the course of action.

AIKEN: In other words, we have to really put them in a mood to negotiate before we attempt—before we do negotiate with them?

TAYLOR: This is true. I think this is applied in all military confrontations in history.

AIKEN: Is that consistent with President Johnson's position that he will negotiate with anybody, anywhere, anytime, and go anywhere to conduct negotiations? It seems to me that your position is somewhat at cross purposes with that of the President. . . .

TAYLOR: No, sir, I don't detect that. . . .

AIKEN: In view of the fact that in 1962 seventeen thousand American troops were considered adequate to deal with the situation over there, would you venture a guess as to how many troops, exclusive of supply lines, air force, navy, would be necessary to deal with the situation within the next year?

TAYLOR: I wish I could give you an accurate estimate. I just can't. Certainly the present strength, 205,000 I believe, which includes your supply type, is not sufficient, and some increase is going to be required. How far it will go I just don't know.

AIKEN: I am sure it is not sufficient even to hold their own there, and also assuming there is no escalation of the enemy forces.

TAYLOR: Well, I think it is most important that we move aggressively on the ground against these Viet Cong units in order to impose this attrition on them which increases their supply problems, and adds to the difficulties of the Hanoi leadership. Having embarked on their course, I hope we strike them hip and thigh and be as effective as possible in order to shorten this.

AIKEN: You evidently take exception to the position which some have taken that we should hold the bases which we now have, and stay there for as many years as is necessary. Of course we stayed in the Philippines fifty years. I don't know whether we have got out or not yet, but we stayed there for fifty years. We have been quite fortunate in holding those bases, haven't we, in the last few months?

TAYLOR: No, sir, we have absolutely no chance of being overrun. Our lads are in charge of this war situation, Senator. We are not being licked. There is too much of a situation we have to run away and hide some place. We are looking for these people and destroying them at the greatest rate that has ever taken place in the history of the struggle.

AIKEN: Aren't all our bases surrounded by the Viet Cong?

TAYLOR: Not in the way "surrounded" suggests. They have mortar; six men can have a mortar attack and get away with it. But forty thousand Marines being in danger of the Viet Cong—I am sure all forty thousand Marines would rise in anger at the suggestion.

AIKEN: I think you are right. But on the other hand, it isn't safe for American soldiers at least to venture out in bases.

TAYLOR: Senator, there are bases in Washington that are not safe to walk around at night. . . .

SENATOR CARLSON: . . . I think [you said earlier] you were not using your air force outside of Vietnam, is that correct?

TAYLOR: I was commenting on the fact that in 1961, although we were perfectly aware that North Vietnam was the source of the support of the insurgency, we did not recommend the air strikes outside of the country, hoping to be able to cope with the situation within the confines of South Vietnam.

CARLSON: Well, the reason I bring it up is that I have here a dispatch from Saigon dated February 15, and I shall now read it. It is written by Jack Foisie, *Los Angeles Times* reporter. It read this way: The U.S. Air Force has stepped up its attack on the Ho Chi Minh Trail in Laos by using spray planes to destroy foliage with chemicals. My only reason for bringing it up—I wonder if it is an extension or escalation of the war outside of what we are calling our Vietnam area.

TAYLOR: I am not aware of this operational activity, Senator. We have been flying armed reconnaissance for a long time with the agreement of the Laotian government. Whether reference is to that kind of activity I am not sure.

CARLSON: If this statement is correct, would this be an expansion or escalation of the war even to another country?

TAYLOR: Escalation, I believe, represents a rather dramatic change in tactics or strategy. I would say it is simply an extension of the kind of thing we are doing in the North, namely, the infiltration of men and supplies. . . .

CARLSON: . . . General Gavin . . . told us, in his opinion if we become further involved to the extent of vastly increasing our troop strength, that the Chinese would surely open up in Korea Do you have any comment on that?

TAYLOR: I—it is purely a matter of opinion; neither one of us can prove our case. I would not agree with that. There are so many reasons why the Red Chinese would want to avoid a military confrontation with us, and, of course, on our side, we are certainly not seeking one. Since both parties would be against a military confrontation, I would be surprised if it arose. There is always some risk, as I conceded in my statement, but when you look at the problems of China, there are enormous population [and] food problems, their extreme vulnerability to air attack, to the fact that they can't afford to have their own strength diminished in relation to the Soviet Union with whom they are engaged in a bitter competition. And all these factors, when they are looked at, it seems to me that the likelihood of deliberate military involvement in confrontation of the United States on the part of Peking is unlikely. . . .

SENATOR MUNDT: Mr. Ambassador, [you made] a statement which might need a little clarification or, perhaps, some expansion, because it sort of changes the context of the opposition we confront in Vietnam, if I understand that opposition correctly. You said that a simple statement of what we are doing in South Vietnam is to say we are engaged in a clash of purpose and interest with the militant wing of the Communist movement represented by Hanoi, the Viet Cong, and Peking. I do not think you completed the roll call. I think you have got to add Moscow to that to present a realistic picture, if I understand it.

TAYLOR: Moscow is, of course, an important factor in

the situation. . . . I think the relationship of Moscow to the problem, however, is quite different from that which links those three elements together, the three mentioned in my statement.

MUNDT: Would you care to define the difference? . . .

TAYLOR: I would say that it is the Peking Chinese wing of the Communist block which would gain primarily by success in this part of the world. Actually their success to some extent might even embarrass the Soviet Union because they have—they are known to be the conservative force tending to discourage any escalation, to use that overworked word, in this part of the world. The Soviet Union has no national objective to gain here, and they have a great deal to lose if, in the course of events, it brought them into confrontation with the United States. So their interests are quite different, and I suspect that their role is quite different from that, say, of Peking.

MUNDT: If that indeed is the true condition of affairs, and I am one who believes the evidence supporting [that] that hypothesis is a little bit on the skimpy side; but if, in fact, we accept that hypothesis, why don't they implement it by discontinuing shipping in the supplies of a military nature into the harbor of Haiphong? . . .

TAYLOR: I think they are in a dilemma, as I see it, Senator. But while they have the factors which I mentioned, which incline them in one direction, on the other hand, they have to contend with Peking as the flag banner of world Communism. They cannot stand by entirely inactive and not assist in South Vietnam, even though they do not enjoy doing it. . . .

MUNDT: Having in mind the increase of troops, which you set out so clearly in your presentation, where we seem to be gaining in terms of over-all numbers on our side, I wonder if you have in mind the ratio of losses which, it seems to me, also must be moving favorably on our side. I am not now thinking about American losses. I am thinking of South Vietnamese losses versus the North Vietnamese losses. . . .

TAYLOR: Very hard to say, except, of course, we would like to see a continuation of the heavy losses inflicted on the North Viet Cong. I saw the figures quite recently of those killed, the Viet Cong killed, in action since January first, and I quote the figures, although always with a warning that there can be a considerable factor of error in the figures. It is 5,748 since January 1 to mid-February. That is a monthly rate of thirty-eight hundred. Now, let us say we do not know how many wounded there were, but if the average is about what it is on our side, at least three wounded to one killed would be a fair assumption. If that is the case, in a month they lost over eleven thousand wounded. Now, furthermore they are defecting at the highest rate ever encountered. For the last two or three weeks the average has been around eighty a day. . . . So that I am assuming then, in this month that I am checking on, perhaps fifteen hundred defectors might be added. Hence, the total loss that would have to be replaced by the Viet Cong would be over sixteen thousand. I do not guarantee the accuracy of this, but it is a very suggestive figure, and I would answer your question then, if we could increase, maintain or increase, this rate of loss for the next year, I would say that the Viet Cong are indeed in very serious difficulties in manpower.

MUNDT: Would you give us that in ratios, Mr. Ambassador; in terms of South Vietnamese losses; would it be two to one, or three to one?

TAYLOR: It is around four to one, probably . . . I have not checked the record recently. . . .

MUNDT: . . . What are we doing in this area of pacification? We hear a lot about that. Are we making any progress? Every once in a while we hear we have got it buttoned down pretty well, but then you hear about some mayor in a community we have held for several years who gets assassinated.

TAYLOR: Of course, pacification, by that I assume you

mean all the effort, in the military, political, and social field.

MUNDT: Economic, social.

TAYLOR: It is not something, I am sure you will say, that we suddenly recognized the need for progress in this field. We have always recognized it, but we have been inhibited by two factors. One, is the lack of security. One cannot build in this country without some level of protection. Second is the inexperience of the government in Saigon. Since both of those situations are improving, I think we are going to move forward better. The present situation is that the pacification goes well in about eight or nine provinces, does virtually nothing in about the same number, and in between the remaining provinces of the forty-four, uneven fluctuating progress.

MUNDT: Some of us believe, General, we are limited by a third factor that you did not mention. You and I have discussed that before in the Foreign Relations Committee, and that is to develop in this country a recognized, competent, and thorough training facility for the kind of political, economic warfare we are having to fight and want to fight in lieu of a military fight. We have all the training institutions we need militarily. But I think we are also lacking in a cadre of sufficiently trained people in that area to carry out this job. And that is the reason we have been trying for at least as long as we have been fighting in Vietnam to create something we call a "freedom academy" in this country, to provide for our non-military operatives the same kind of training that the Army, the Marines do, and that the others get. And I wish you would use your considerable influence and your capacity as a general counselor at the White House to encourage the State Department to take its foot off the brake so we can enact legislation, which already once has passed the Senate, to create here the training facilities required to carry out this important aspect of the war.

TAYLOR: I quite agree with you, Senator, that the

training of the civilian expertise required is most important. I am very proud of the twelve hundred, roughly twelve hundred American civilians who are scattered all through this country, working in very exposed conditions, often situations just as dangerous as those occupied by our military people. They are doing a first-class job. But what I am concerned about, as I am sure you are, is the rotation question. They cannot stay out there indefinitely, and how to replace these people by men equally motivated, equally skilled, will be difficult. . . .

SENATOR SYMINGTON: Now, I would like to ask, why did you state in your recent New York speech that General Gavin's enclave strategy would more likely lead to overt Chinese Communist involvement in Southeast Asia than our current strategy? That interested me. . . .

TAYLOR: First, I do not think I referred to it as General Gavin's. I never have mentioned General Gavin in my comments on the enclave strategy because he is not the only one who has supported it. I am frankly not sure to what extent he does today. The comment there simply indicates that the sureness of our eventual elimination from Southeast Asia under the enclave strategy would encourage the other side to take greater advantage, to exploit the weakened situation on our front, and to expand through Southeast Asia and elsewhere.

SYMINGTON: Would the enclave concept allow us to deploy fewer forces into South Vietnam?

TAYLOR: I suppose it would if we arbitrarily said, we will send no more than those at the present time. I think, in the long run, we might then have to be shoved off, one by one, these coastal enclaves if the enemy massed against us and if we had major defections from the South Vietnamese, which would be quite possible.

SYMINGTON: What would be the results for the South Vietnamese and ourselves, political and military, if we adopted the enclave theory?

TAYLOR: I think, in the first place, the South Vietnamese

government would fall. I do not see how it could subsist after the American ally had abandoned their forces on the battlefield. I would think that the timid and the wavering would seek an accommodation of the enemy and, I think, this would probably, there would probably be, defections among the armed forces, feeling that all was lost in the long run, and they had better adjust to the Viet Cong and the enemy. So, in combination, I think it would be disastrous.

SYMINGTON: What have been the effects of the B-52 air strikes in South Vietnam?

TAYLOR: I think they have been very effective in keeping the Viet Cong moving. In the good old days, as they would refer to them, I am sure, it was possible for a Viet Cong battalion to get into a fight, have a good brisk one for two or three days, then break off and go back into base areas where that battalion was relatively secure; in fact, it was completely secure. It could train, rest, recruit, and prepare for the next operation. The B-52 strikes now have been used on a scale supported by, I think, reasonably good intelligence, with the result that no battalion is ever secure. We find from the prisoners—they complain about the fatigue, of constantly moving for fear of a B-52 strike, and from that point of view, I am sure, they are very effective. I would doubt if we would find many of the bombs hitting exactly where we would like them to go simply because of the fact this is area bombing, and, as I say, based on generalized intelligence; but the over-all effect has been very helpful.

SYMINGTON: In your statement you mentioned a couple of alternatives that you hope we continue to project. One of those included massive air attacks on the North Vietnamese or even on Chinese targets. By massive air attacks, you are talking about bombing Hanoi, are you not, that kind of thing?

TAYLOR: Yes, sir. Removing all restraints and removing the restraints on urban bombing because of the command centers and industrial targets of various kinds.

SYMINGTON: There is nothing in that statement that infers you would be against attacking military targets of any type in North Vietnam?

TAYLOR: No, sir. I would favor it and I would favor a gradually increasing scale of attack.

SYMINGTON: What is the true risk that we are running vis-à-vis Red China? Do you think there will be a direct confrontation?

TAYLOR: No, sir. I said, on numerous occasions, one cannot write off the possibilities, but I would think when one analyzes the pros and cons from the point of view of the other side, the likelihood is quite low.

SYMINGTON: And is the air campaign against military targets in North Vietnam integrated in a complementary [way] to the allied military operations in South Vietnam?

TAYLOR: It is an essential part of the strategy which I described in my opening statement. We must not only convince Hanoi they cannot win in the South, but we must also remind them they will pay an increasing price in the North. The two go on concurrently, and we must be effective in both areas.

SYMINGTON: To what extent have allied forces seized the initiative from the VC, the North Vietnamese forces, in South Vietnam since the midsummer of 1965?

TAYLOR: We have done increasingly well, more or less in proportion to the numbers of American forces engaged. Not only do our American units add their weight to the battle, but also their presence has had a stimulating effect on the Vietnamese units, so that the net result has been clearly an advantage. . . .

SENATOR CASE: . . . You refer [in your statement] to the historic suggestion that or theory that you need ten or twelve times as many anti-guerrilla forces as the guerrilla forces to be successful against guerrillas, as an historical generally accepted thing, with some indication of your support. And then you go on to say that with the addition of fire power, et cetera, et cetera, this can be cut down. How much can it be cut down, General?

TAYLOR: I just do not know, sir. When the decision to bring in American forces was taken, the direct head-count ratio between friendly strength and hostile strength was about three and a half to one. On a battalion basis the ratio was even more unfavorable, around two to one, perhaps less than that. All I can say, at that time it was not good enough. Yet I do not think we had anything like the ratios that were necessary to, say, have in Malaya, because we have available this great mobility which allows the battalion to fight in Province A, and tomorrow Province B, two hundred miles away. Obviously mobility affects the effectiveness of these forces. So somewhere between three to one and ten to one. Only experience will tell. It will have to be cut and tried, in my judgment, to reach the point when our advantage has been reached great enough to serve our purpose. . . .

SENATOR PELL: I would like to develop your point . . . that you said you felt there was a finite limit to the amount of people that the North Vietnamese could put in, if we continue to bomb in North Vietnam. Would you be more explicit as to what in your view is that finite limit?

TAYLOR: I have been asked frequently to try to put a number on that, and I just cannot, because of the fact that the data bearing on the consumption of supplies by the Viet Cong, for example, are very few. I am quite sure, however, in a qualitative sense, that a combination of continued intensive attacks on the lines of communications of the North, utilizing our air power, accompanied by increased attacks against the ground forces, so that they must consume supplies, they must take greater casualties, will lower the ceiling which probably exists today. In other words to some degree we control where the ceiling is.

PELL: In other words, if we keep going as we—you feel that they have reached their finite limit now?

TAYLOR: Well, it is very interesting. A study of the combat rate of the Viet Cong battalions reveals that a Viet Cong battalion is rarely in action over one or two days a month, which almost raises a question whether they pay off, so to speak, whether or not it would be better to have fewer battalions, and make them fight five times a month or ten times a month. I am sure the Communist leadership have a sensible answer to that conundrum, but I don't see it. In a certain sense you could say that even now the ceiling is preventing their utilizing fully the forces they have available.

PELL: Isn't there a human limit, too, to the number of days in a month or a week that a man is willing to be in battle?

TAYLOR: Very much so. But they are not even approaching the breaking point in terms of direct combat. I do suspect, however, as I said this morning, that the B-52 and the use of our other aircraft against their bases does take away the rest periods which has allowed them to be a very durable force in the field in the past.

PELL: General, in connection with the bombing, particularly in the North, one of the purposes, as I understand it, is to make their will flag, and make them more willing to come to the negotiation table. Where—and this is a point that other witnesses would not agree with you —where in history do we find other examples of where general bombing, or bombing has brought people to the —made people more willing to come to the negotiating table?

TAYLOR: Since the days where we have had aircraft in quantity, so that it is a formidable weapon, we have never had a situation like this. You recall in World War Two it was unconditional surrender, it was fight to the end or be destroyed, and many people preferred to be destroyed rather than to accept unconditional surrender. Here we are not doing that at all. Just the contrary. We are constantly pointing out the better life that awaits the North if they will end their aggression against the South. We are deliberately keeping a golden bridge open behind them, so they are never in the trapped position that the Germans or the Japanese found themselves in.

PELL: But then would you bear with me in my view that bombing per se has not at least in the past—I am not just thinking of World War Two—but in the past tended to bring countries to the negotiating table?

TAYLOR: Well, I think it certainly did in the sense the destruction of bombing, both in Europe and in Asia, weakened the ability of our opponents to continue the war. I don't think anyone would suggest that in itself the bombing brought the enemy to the peace table, but it certainly was an important part of it.

PELL: You don't feel that in some cases the bombing can be, as I think the British found in Malaya, that it can be counterproductive.

TAYLOR: I don't know the circumstances there. But if properly used, certainly it is a great advantage to us to present to the leadership in Hanoi this very dismal picture of continued destruction of all they have been constructing in the last ten years, and always giving them an alternative; but you don't really have to accept this indefinitely—you can stop it yourself.

PELL: I appreciate your view, and I hope you are right. I just have this feeling in me that it can be in many cases—is counterproductive. I think for those of us who have been campaigning in the past, we think back a year ago, and we campaigned against escalation and defolia-tion, and the bombing of North Vietnam, it puts us in a rather odd position, because we want to support our President, and we believe in the objectives. And witnesses like you may be able to persuade us that the premises of 1964 were incorrect.

One point in connection with the counterproductivity of bombing—I am trying to find out what the casualties are in South Vietnam from the war, because I agree with you, many people were horribly murdered and assassinated by the Viet Cong, and many murdered and assassinated in North Vietnam. But for the person who is killed, for his immediate relatives, it doesn't matter if it is napalm, bombing, or some other way. You are just dead. Why is it so hard to get an estimate of the casualties of the South Vietnamese from the war?

TAYLOR: Because of the very nature of the war. Our weapons are used in the jungles and the forests, generally in areas where the population is very sparse. There is no way to count—to visit the battlefield and count the casualties. But I would say it is significant. I know of no protest on the part of any of the leaders of South Vietnam, any newspaper in South Vietnam, over the use of our bombing. The great concern, which I respect here in the United States, as to whether or not we are needlessly destroying civilians, is not felt in South Vietnam. And any suggestions that we limit the use of our weapons I am sure would be very strongly resisted by the people and the leaders in South Vietnam. . . .

SENATOR FULBRIGHT: I know that you cannot be positive in these matters. But it is anything but certain just how this is proceeding—whether it is optimistic or not. One thing I wanted to explore, I think is not important, is this question of limited objectives that was discussed earlier this morning. I am confused about this. It strikes me the way you described it, although not using that language—but if it means that you are going to use whatever is necessary to eventually make them give up, this is just another way of saying "unconditional surrender"—

TAYLOR: No, sir, I don't agree.

FULBRIGHT: —which to me means an unlimited objective. But I know you don't use that language. But the language you do use, it seems to me, logically results in that conclusion as opposed to a disposition to negotiate. Now, recently the Administration has said, I think, from time to time, that it would allow the Viet Cong to be represented in negotiations. But Premier Ky, after Hono-lulu, said that he would never negotiate with NLF, or, as he characterized them, as the National Enslavement Front. These seemed to be different views. And the President's speech yesterday would seem to—it seems to be more in agreement with Mr. Ky's view that we are not going to negotiate, we are not going to negotiate until they give up, which to me means unconditional surrender. Could you just clarify this a little bit?

TAYLOR: First, I would hope you will address these necessities on negotiations to a gentleman who can really speak with authority, the Secretary of State. I would only comment on this, that I think that the exact status of the Liberation Front in any negotiations is going to be a very important point. And I would think it would be a great mistake for us to make too clearly our position until we find out what are the other factors to be arranged in order to conduct meaningful negotiations.

But I would certainly say most positively that the position—I have never heard any official of our government suggest that we will not negotiate until the other fellow surrenders. I do not consider it a surrender to have a criminal surrender his future or his life if he is required to give up his felony. And all we are trying to get is to have North Veitnam cease the aggression against the South, and in exchange, therefore, I can suggest a number of advantages which they might be offered.

FULBRIGHT: Well, in the last World War all we were seeking was for Germany to give up its aggression and be good boys and quit.

TAYLOR: No, sir, we went much further than that. Furthermore, it is quite clear that we were going to try and presumably execute their leadership.

FULBRIGHT: Well, in any case, I am very confused about it. The idea of negotiating a compromise, which is something less than just what we want, seems to me to be consistent with a limited war; whereas if they must give up and come upon our own terms, this is what I would call unlimited commitment to use whatever we need to use to bring about this result. . . .

TAYLOR: "Unlimited" means you could add nothing to the requirement. I am sure you could think of other things we might ask North Vietnam to do in addition to stopping their aggression. We could ask them to stop being Communist. We could ask them to stop being allied to Peking, to abjure their ideology.

FULBRIGHT: You might ask them that at the conference table. You would not expect them to agree to that in advance.

TAYLOR: I am just making a point that when we say, "Stop your aggression," that is far from being unlimited.

FULBRIGHT: That seems to imply, though, that we use unlimited means, even if it means going into China or anywhere else, whatever that takes.

TAYLOR: We are certainly using limited means in terms of the vast resources which we have in reserve.

FULBRIGHT: We are up to now. That is not what I meant. I meant the objective, the ultimate, how this comes out is what I am talking about.

TAYLOR: The ultimate objective is to get the leadership of Hanoi to stop doing what they are doing to the South. And I am quite sure they are not going to wait [for] ultimate annihilation before changing their ways. . . .

FULBRIGHT: I think, General, in all honesty, behind the concern of many of us is not just Vietnam, as much concerned as we are—I don't mean it is insignificant—but is the possibility or even probability of this escalating into a war with China. And we always hesitate to talk about these things. But I am sure that is one of my concerns. I would regret to see us continue this war to the point where we engaged in an all-out war with China. And many people that are wiser than I am believe this is a possibility.

TAYLOR: As we discussed this morning, obviously one cannot rule it out. But I wonder whether our government, or whether the Congress, would suggest complete supineness on the part of our foreign policy in the Far East because of that relatively small possibility

FULBRIGHT: I don't think anyone suggests complete supineness. But there have been several stories in which the Chinese have stated that they are being encircled. And they are exhibiting considerable nervousness about the possibility of a war with us. I believe you said that you did not feel nervous about a war with China; but there is a real question that the Chinese may feel very nervous about a war.

TAYLOR: They should feel nervous about it. If they ever got in a war with us, it would be disaster for them. And we know we are not seeking such a confrontation.

FULBRIGHT: You have confirmed their fears, I think. And this is really, I think, behind us. And my greatest trouble is the feeling of inadequate knowledge and understanding of China and of this whole area to make very sound judgments. I don't profess to have the kind of knowledge to make that kind of judgment. It is more by instinct and feeling. That leads me to believe it would be a great disaster for this country, not only for China, but I mean for this country. I hope, like General Gavin and Kennan said, they are trying to be practical about it, and I think that it would be a great disaster if we became involved in an all-out war on the Asian continent against the Chinese. . . .

SPARKMAN: . . . General Gavin said that if we should get into war with China, it ought to be a place of our own choosing, and that southern China was not the place where it ought to be. If we were going to have a war with China, it ought to be in the Manchuria area. Do you agree with that reasoning?

TAYLOR: Well, first, I don't believe there is any good place to have a war with China. But if indeed we had one, certainly we would not be confined to South Vietnam. I assume this would be general war against China. And if our strategists preferred Manchuria, they could take Manchuria.

SPARKMAN: Of course a war with China would probably—well, I think probably we ought not to speculate on that. I started to say it probably would involve nuclear weapons, would it not?

TAYLOR: It is possible, but not necessarily so. . . .

MORSE: . . . would like to ask you a question in regard to Hanoi. . . . Do you think that there are a considerable number of Russians in Hanoi? . . .

TAYLOR: I doubt there is any great number. Undoubtedly there are some technicians there in connection with the surface-to-air missile.

MORSE: Do you think if we should mine or blockade or bomb the harbor outside of Hanoi, we would increase the danger of Russia coming into the war?

TAYLOR: No, sir.

MORSE: I want to tell you about a report I gave to the President the early part of last August, when a group of us met for about three hours and twenty minutes one night in a rough-and-tumble exchange with the Russian Ambassador here in Washington—and we have an obligation to our President to report such information. And during the course of that discussion, we asked him, if things went from bad to worse, and our government bombed Hanoi, what would be the position of his government. He didn't hesitate to say they would go to war against us, because, as he said, you cannot bomb Hanoi without bombing Russians.

TAYLOR: I would expect him to say that, sir.

MORSE: It was dismissed by the Administration as Russian propaganda. Then we asked him about the harbor; the same answer. Then we asked him about the bombing of the nuclear installations in China, and he pointed out there that they not only would go to war, because they keep their security agreements, but he said,

"It will not be fought in Asia alone." And that was perfectly clear where it would be fought. But I judge from your statements that you are not very much concerned about either Russia or China coming into this war.

TAYLOR: Under the present circumstances, that is correct.

MORSE: And you don't think the circumstances would change—cause you to change your opinion?

TAYLOR: I am not going to go into the future on that, because you will be quoting me here in 1977.

MORSE: I expect to be here in 1977 to quote you.

TAYLOR: I hope my judgment will be better by that time.

MORSE: I hope so, too. But one more question: Do you think if we should get into a war with China, we could beat her by bombing, either nuclear or conventional? . . .

TAYLOR: I wouldn't know what "beat her" means.

MORSE: Force her to surrender.

TAYLOR: I don't know whether we would want her to surrender or not. We could make her pay a tremendous price for aggression.

MORSE: She doesn't have anything to fight back except manpower. Wouldn't we have to meet her on the ground?

TAYLOR: No, sir.

MORSE: Just meet her in the air?

TAYLOR: To a large extent. That is one way of doing it.

MORSE: You take the position—this is very interesting —you take the position that if we get into a war with Red China, we are not going to have to send hundreds of thousands of men on to the mainland of China?

TAYLOR: Not necessarily so. . . .

SENATOR GORE: General Taylor, I undertook this morning, as you will recall, to draw from you a definition of the limits to which you referred. . . . You say that it is limited as to forces employed. Would you be more specific and tell us just why the limits as to the forces employed?

TAYLOR: Well, we obviously have not put in anything

like the forces we have available for commitment in that part of the world if we wanted to. We have put in only the forces which are consistent with our limited objectives, which is the persuasion of the leadership of Hanoi to stop their aggression.

GORE: I was not addressing my question as to what we had done. What are the limits on forces with respect to policy in the future?

TAYLOR: The ultimate limit, I would say, probably the basic limit is the willingness of Hanoi to continue the aggression in spite of the mounting costs. Just at what point they will decide this is not a remunerative course of action I just do not know. But they are the ones really to decide what that limit will be.

GORE: Is it fair for me to conclude from that, that there are no limits on the forces to be employed until Hanoi capitulates?

TAYLOR: I would say that the forces that can be usefully employed, employed for the purpose of bringing conviction to Hanoi in the form of continued increasing loss to the Viet Cong guerrillas, so that they cannot replace their losses—there was a downward trend in their over-all strength—and a clear picture created in the mind of Hanoi they cannot win a military victory in the South. . . .

GORE: Do I correctly understand that the limit on forces employed to which you refer in your prepared statement will be determined by the willingness of Hanoi to capitulate?

TAYLOR: No, I would put it more is determined by the requirement to create a military situation in South Vietnam which makes it clear to Hanoi that they cannot win a military victory in the South.

GORE: Could you give us any specifics at all as to the size of forces which our policy now contemplates in this comment?

TAYLOR: I wish I could but I just don't know. I think

only the experience from month to month will indicate what is required, but it is certainly a finite number of troops in order to continue to—the present rate of loss which the Viet Cong are suffering. I mentioned this morning, if we could continue the rate which has been going on in 1966, theoretically they would virtually run out of trained troops by the end of '66—I would not like the headline to say I predict the end of the war by '66 because the Viet Cong run out of men but it is a significant fact that the rate of loss is now very high—and if our forces can continue to impose this attrition on the Viet Cong, they are going to be in a very serious way for replacement at Hanoi.

GORE: I will ask you again to deduce from your statement that there are no limits on forces employed insofar as our policy is concerned except to use whatever is necessary to bring about the capitulation of the Hanoi government.

TAYLOR: I am sorry, that is not my statement. Our ultimate objective is bringing Hanoi to change its course of action. That will be, in my judgment—I am speaking only for myself—in my judgment when first it is clear that there can be no military victory for the Viet Cong in the South. That does not mean that they are all eliminated, that does not mean they are all captured or rounded up, it means a highly unfavorable military situation in South Vietnam. Secondly, there has to be clear evidence that our air strength in North Vietnam is going to apply continued pressure, and they are going to suffer continuing loss and pain from the air in the North. Third they are—the picture must include also the existence of a reasonably viable, reasonable stable, reasonably efficient government in Saigon. And fourth there must be the picture of a determined United States back home that is not going to be forced off course. When all four conditions are met, I am convinced we will then have brought Hanoi to the point that they are willing to talk in a sincere way at a conference table. So, you see, the military situation on the ground is only one fourth of the entire problem.

GORE: Then there are no limits insofar as policy is concerned except to the sufficient force to achieve the objectives which you have stated in general terms?

TAYLOR: I have stated—we are talking just about ground force requirements in the South; I gather that is what we are concerned about—I am saying we must have enough strength, Vietnamese and American, actively engaged to inflict such continuing loss on the Vietnamese forces that obviously they can't win. I would say that is a fairly restricted objective.

GORE: Well, General, I hope you will not mind my suggesting that I find it a little incongruous that this Committee is advised that the Joint Chiefs of Staff have presented a plan to the Armed Services Committee involving a possible use of six hundred thousand troops and you as the military, President's advisor, seem not to have heard about it.

TAYLOR: I am not the President's military advisor. I am a part-time special consultant, and they have a very qualified Joint Chiefs of Staff—Chairman of the Joint Chiefs—who gives military advice to the government.

GORE: Are you really telling this Committee that you haven't heard such plans discussed?

TAYLOR: I am quite sure there are plans, as I said this morning, for two hundred thousand, for four hundred thousand, six hundred thousand, maybe a million for all I know; it is one thing to have a plan and a conviction that such a requirement exists. And I am not confident of that conviction. . . .

GORE: I wouldn't expect you to tell me the exact number, but can you give me—is it two hundred thousand, six hundred thousand, or a million? Can you give us some order of magnitude?

TAYLOR: I would just say with the force we have we are imposing losses on the enemy which run about, what did I say, some seventeen thousand per month at the present time. Now, that is a very sizable number and I would doubt that this force could continue at that rate. I think it is too narrow an experience base to try to project it. But it does suggest that no extremely large increase is necessary to impose these casualties.

GORE: Well, Senator Fulbright suggested to you, as others have, that a very deep concern on the part of certain members of this Committee and a great many Americans, is this war in Vietnam be escalated until a war with China becomes almost inevitable, a fact. With respect to this particular point, some reference was made to General Bradley's views; I do not know what his views are with respect to the present situation. But I would like to read you a few sentences. . . . I recognize that it is dangerous to draw analogies. A number of people have tried to draw the analogy between the situation in Western Europe after the end of World War Two and the situation in Vietnam. They are not very analogous. We did not try to exterminate the Communists in Italy, France; the largest political party in Italy is still the Communist Party. But in South Vietnam it seems to be the policy to exterminate the Viet Cong. Is that not the case?

TAYLOR: Not as a military objective. There are 125,000, 140,000 of them, I don't think anybody suggests literally exterminating them but we would like to have them so beaten that they would be glad to come in and accept an amnesty.

GORE: So would I. But to get back, with the limitations of analogy which I acknowledge, I would like to read you what . . . General Bradley said, to a joint meeting of the Armed Services Committee and the Senate Foreign Relations Committee in 1951, involving . . . much the same problem of whether or not this war in Korea would escalate into a war with China: "The strategic alternative enlargements of the war in Korea to include Red China would probably delight the Kremlin more than anything else we could do. It would necessarily tie down additional forces, especially our sea power, and our air power, while the Soviet Union would not be obliged to put a single plane into the conflict. Under present circumstances we have recommended against enlarging the war. The course of action often described as a limited war with Red China would increase the risk that we are taking by engaging too much of our power in an area that is not the critical strategic prize." Do you think that would be reasonably relevant to the danger of an enlarged escalated war in Vietnam?

TAYLOR: I would say there would be a very great difference. Let us—first, I agree with General Bradley when he made that statement or would have; I was not present at the time. I would point out he was considering whether or not we would deliberately take on China at that time, when the Soviet Union was a great menace, we were not at all sure what they were going to do in Europe even with a minor engagement in—

GORE: Couldn't she suddenly become a great menace in Berlin if we became bogged down?

TAYLOR: I would say the situation is now—the atmosphere is quite different. Let me continue with my reminder of the situation in '51. . . . We had a very aggressive Soviet Union quite capable of militarily exploiting any commitment we made in the Far East. We had no nuclear weapon stockpile of any great significance at the time. We were utterly unprepared for the land war that we were engaged in in Korea, having great difficulty putting an army together literally on the battlefield. Today what is the difference? Well, first, we are not considering taking on Red China. We are not seeking a confrontation and certainly I would hope they are not either. We are, however, far better, greater military power. We have been preparing for this kind of challenge of the guerrilla war ever since '61. We have a vast stockpile of nuclear weapons to be the ultimate deterrent of any great expansion. So, the problem is quite different although I come out with—the same way as you, Senator—this is not the time, probably there is not the time to take on deliberately Red China in a military confrontation. . . .

SENATOR CHURCH: Well, I would think that China would hesitate very long before entering the war, considering what this would mean to her and to us as well, and the kind of power that we have to bring to bear, should such an eventuality occur. But I am nonetheless concerned about this. One of the reasons, I suppose, is because of the experience we had in Korea. In his book *The United States in the Korean War,* Larson reviews an exchange between President Truman and General MacArthur, the passage of which I would like to read to you. "In your opinion," President Truman asked General MacArthur, "is there any chance that the Chinese might enter the war on the side of North Korea?" MacArthur shook his head. "I would say there is very little chance of that happening. They have several hundred thousand men north of the Yalu, but they haven't any air force. If they tried to cross the river, our Air Force would slaughter them. At the most, perhaps sixty thousand troops would make it. Our infantry could easily contain them. I expect the actual fighting in North Korea to end by Thanksgiving. We should have our men home or at least in Japan by Christmas."

We have had in the course of the last few years some optimistic predictions about how soon we would have our men home from Vietnam. Is there anything in the strategic or tactical situation that would confront the Chinese in Vietnam that would make it less likely for them to enter the war in that region of Asia than in Korea?

TAYLOR: Yes, I would think so very clearly. When our armies moved to the Yalu, there was no certainty in the Chinese mind that they were not about to invade China. We, so far as I know—I do not think the record indicates there was any dialogue, any conversation going on at all as to what our intention was. So in retrospect, and it is always easy to be wise in retrospect, one can see reason for very grave concern on the part of the Chinese as we came rushing forward.

CHURCH: If we were to duplicate or tend to duplicate in North Vietnam what we did in North Korea, that is to say extend the perimeter of the war northward toward the frontiers, then do you think that she might respond as she did in fact respond in Korea?

TAYLOR: Undoubtedly the danger would increase dramatically as our ground forces approached the frontier of China. Again, however, I would say that there are two or three factors in such a situation which did not exist in Korea. The first would be, I assume, we would be talking very vigorously as we are talking now, and did, during the pause, talk to everybody. I do not thank any country ever opened its books as completely to the world as we did in the thirty-seven days, what our intentions were, what we hoped to come out of the situation as we are explaining the world right at this table now; and, finally, the fact that now we are the great military power we are, with a nuclear arsenal of great proportions, is another factor which did not exist before.

CHURCH: At the time of Korea was it not true that we were the only nuclear power?

TAYLOR: Our arsenal was extremely limited, and we were very much worried about what Russia would do in Europe. Finally, the Chinese are extremely vulnerable in other ways, internal because of the tremendous population-food problem. They are also vulnerable in the fact they have worked so mightily to get a limited nuclear capability which is highly vulnerable to elimination. So all of these factors, I would think, would add up—furthermore, they have a great rivalry with the Soviet Union. They cannot afford to be weakened in their strengths in a confrontation with us and thereby fall well behind the Soviet Union when they hope to be the number-one Communist power. So in combination these are all pretty potent reasons, it seems to me, to suggest that

China will not come in, and then we add quickly we have no plan to put our ground forces near . . . the Chinese frontier.

CHURCH: Yes, I think that in view of the fact that an apparent miscalculation was made as to Chinese intentions last time, we ought not to be too confident that we can properly calculate Chinese reaction this time. Would you not agree with that?

TAYLOR: Gentlemen, a general was wrong before, and a general can be wrong again.

CHURCH: Politicians are often wrong, too. General, you referred earlier, I think, to Bao Dai, and I think correctly so, as a French puppet. . . . Is it not true that the pre-Ky regime in Saigon is rather completely dependent upon the massive aid we are giving them both in—

TAYLOR: I am afraid that suggestion is the equivalent of saying he is an American puppet, and I would say he is not. We did not elect General Ky. We did not put him in.

CHURCH: General, if I may frame the question; I was not going to suggest our purpose in Vietnam is anything like the French purpose. . . . What I am try to ascertain is how the Vietnamese themselves may regard the regime of Ky, particularly the peasant folk in the countryside, where the war is being fought, and how they may regard the American presence there. Do you think that the peasantry in the countryside of Vietnam tend to draw very definite distinctions between Americans and Frenchmen?

TAYLOR: Oh, I think there is no question about it, that in the vast majority of cases our presence is welcomed. I would not suggest a village that is about to be the battleground between the two forces enjoys having either of us around. But insofar as recognizing this indispensable character of our presence, I do not think there is any question.

CHURCH: Do you think the Ky regime enjoys widespread support from the people in the countryside?

TAYLOR: No, sir.

CHURCH: You think he does not.

TAYLOR: Let me qualify it because that sounds, perhaps, misleading. I made the statement this morning, the government in Saigon is rarely known to the peasantry; there have been so many Saigon governments since the fall of Diem, I am quite sure that many of the peasants have never heard of the present leaders in Saigon. On the other hand, they are so completely committed to anti-Communism, and they know that government forces, whether they know the leaders or not, represent safety and security. In that sense they are committed to the government.

CHURCH: Are there leaders in South Vietnam today that are committed to the cause of anti-Communism that are known to the people sufficiently so that their prominence in the government would constitute a link between the government and the people?

TAYLOR: Well, it is relatively few, simply by the circumstances of history, that the French never allowed anybody to emerge as a national name. It is quite true Ho Chi Minh is the best-known Vietnamese in the world probably, and also there is considerable regard for him in South Vietnam as the nationalist leader against the French and against the Japanese but not as the head of the state at Hanoi. They distinguish very clearly between the two personalities. . . .

PELL: A question of tactics that I do not understand fully is, why can we not arouse the same terror in the Vietnamese, South Vietnamese, that apparently Ho Chi Minh does in the North Vietnamese? Why does it take, if the ratio is ten to one, to pin down guerrillas; why are there not guerrillas on the north of the line doing exactly what they are doing in the South, only Vietnamese?

TAYLOR: No one thought about this in time. The reason the guerrilla war has been so reasonably successful in the South is that a strong base including caches of arms and ammunition were left in the South, readily available for the guerrillas, the manpower which was later infiltrated from the North. No one had that in mind at the time of partition of North Vietnam; so by the time anyone could think of that, you had a closed police state with all the guards and fences against infiltration by anybody. So if one wanted to pursue that course of action, it was not feasible.

PELL: We also do not seem to be able to stimulate the same terror. What is the reason for that? You were in Vietnam. You saw them and worked with them. How do you account for it?

TAYLOR: I do not know that I would agree necessarily that the Communist terror is higher. It is very hard to measure that because they are under such control that it is impossible for them to show a lack of enthusiasm. In a democracy such as they have in South Vietnam where there is no police state, anybody could go out on the street and carry a banner and demonstrate against the government and against the war. So, one receives impressions of dissidence, if that is the word, in the South which could not possibly appear in the North.

PELL: Do you think that the course of those of us, of men like me, who believe we have a logical commitment to be there—we are there, that is a fact—but feel that we should act as a brake to this indefinite escalation, that this is a harmful or that this view, when expressed publicly, is of harm to the enemy? . . .

TAYLOR: Well, I would not know in exactly what form one would make that statement. I think that if we decided to adopt an enclave policy, as I understand the enclave policy, that would be the best news in the world to Hanoi, and a great discouragement to South Vietnam.

PELL: I must say, I for one was very impressed by General Gavin. I would love to see a debate between the two of you. I think it would be very instructive for us and the American people because you sound very convincing here and he sounded very convincing a few days

back. Finally, I was wondering if you felt that Vietnam
. . . , because of the closeness of the world today every
part to the other, is really a mater of our vital national
interest.

TAYLOR: I believe it is. I know the Congress agreed
with that in 1964. I would phrase it more in terms that
the lives and liberty of fifteen million people is bound to
be a great stake to any country that has committed itself
to the preservation of that particular segment of the
world's population. I think the collateral importance
which we have discussed in the course of the day, the
resistance to a war of liberation, to preventing the worldwide effect of encouraging the Sino-North Vietnamese
aggressors by allowing them a success, all of these together, add up to a vital interest about which I have no
doubt. . . .

FULBRIGHT: General, you stated several times that we
are killing very large numbers, increasing numbers of
Viet Cong. Is it not a fact that there are more Viet Cong
in South Vietnam today than there were a year ago? . . .

TAYLOR: Yes, sir.

FULBRIGHT: I believe the official figure from the Pentagon indicates that beginning in January of '65 there were
a hundred and three thousand Viet Cong; they estimated
forty thousand infiltrators; they also estimated thirty-four
thousand were killed during that year, and eleven thousand captured, which would, I believe, leave about
ninety-eight thousand. Their present estimates are that
there are two hundred forty-three thousand, which would
indicate that they had recruited a hundred thirty-five
thousand during the course of '65, which . . . seems to
me to be somewhat inconsistent with the theory that we
are killing ever increasing numbers, and thereby making
progress. Is that true?

TAYLOR: [We] did not inflict the casualties at the rate
which I discussed for this year in the number you mentioned. It is quite true they have increased, and that

was one of the reasons we decided we had to use our American ground forces to compensate for the deficiency in the Vietnamese.

FULBRIGHT: General, you mentioned a moment ago, I think, in one of the answers, that [this war involves] the nerves, the courage, the patriotism of this country. I don't really believe that is questioned by anyone on this Committee. What we are questioning is the wisdom of the policy, particularly if it leads to substantial escalation of the war. I hope you understand.

TAYLOR: Yes, sir, I do. I hope I did not give the impression of impugning the patriotism or courage of anyone.

FULBRIGHT: Yes, no one on this Committee, I think, is trying to suggest that we ought to turn tail and scuttle and run, as one of our leading columnists characterizes it, because of a lack of courage; it is purely a matter of judgment that we are concerned with. General, there was one other question that was inspired by your reply to a question by [Senator Symington]. General, can you imagine, in your wildest dreams, of a Secretary of Air agreeing to napalm a great city, perhaps a city like Tokyo, with millions of little children, sweet little children, innocent pure babies who love their mothers, and mothers who love their children, just like you love your son, thousands of little children, who never did us any harm, being slowly burned to death? Can you imagine any Secretary of Air or President ordering the burning of these little children right before the eyes of their mothers?

TAYLOR: I am not sure of the situation; I can't visualize the situation you are asking me about.

FULBRIGHT: Isn't it a fact we did just that in Tokyo?

TAYLOR: The fire raid?

FULBRIGHT: Didn't we?

TAYLOR: I am not familiar with the details—

FULBRIGHT: You are not familiar?

TAYLOR: —but we certainly dropped fire bombs on Tokyo.

FULBRIGHT: You hadn't heard about the bombs?

TAYLOR: I had heard about it.

FULBRIGHT: What difference, really, morally or any other way, do you see between burning innocent little children and disemboweling innocent citizens? Isn't it only in the means you use?

TAYLOR: I would say there is no doubt as to the objective in the latter case. In the former case, I would imagine the answer would be that it was an unhappy concomitant of the attack of the targets that happened in the bombing.

FULBRIGHT: Isn't it an objective in war—we mentioned it before—about your seeking the surrender, of the breaking of the will of the opposition? This is the nature of war?

TAYLOR: This is not a factor in the present situation in South Vietnam at all, Senator.

FULBRIGHT: Well, the only implication of this question was that we are the only good people, and I certainly don't think we are bad people, but I don't see any great distinction between using the weapons that we happen to have and others don't, to kill innocent people, to burn them slowly, whether they be babies or brothers or fathers or uncles, and disemboweling with a knife because a knife is all you have got. I mean, I don't see we should claim any great superiority because we happen to have nuclear bombs and fire bombs and the others don't.

TAYLOR: But we are not deliberately attacking civilian populations in South Vietnam. On the contrary, we are making every effort to avoid their loss.

FULBRIGHT: We drop napalm bombs on villages just deliberately.

TAYLOR: In the illustration that was deliberate.

FULBRIGHT: It is not by accident we are doing this. I am not questioning the nature of war; and people use what they have at their command.

TAYLOR: I would just say that the observation does not apply to what we are trying to do in South Vietnam because this is not an unlimited war. This is, as I have often said, a limited war, with a limited objective, one of the objectives being to try to protect the civilian population which we are trying to rescue and not destroy.

FULBRIGHT: I find your answer to Senator Gore is unsatisfactory. You say it is unlimited, but the implication, the only logical conclusion of your objective, would seem to be to surrender.

TAYLOR: No, sir. I am not asking for anyone to surrender.

FULBRIGHT: I don't see how else you can explain it. I don't understand this play on words—maybe I am much too stupid to understand what it means when you say, well, we are going to do what it takes to make them come to the conference table, which to me means they are going to go, as they used to say in the Ozarks, "Holler enough" or "calf rope, I give up."

TAYLOR: This is simply to make them see pursuing their present course of action is so disadvantageous, it is to their interests to come to the table.

FULBRIGHT: Yes, I think that to me means surrender.

TAYLOR: No, sir, it is not surrender.

FULBRIGHT: Let me make the contrary point: I would think a limited war would be where our real efforts are to seek a conference and propose a compromise in which we don't necessarily get our way and they don't surrender. We don't surrender, but we seek a settlement of it.

TAYLOR: How do you compromise the freedom of fifteen million South Vietnamese, Senator? I don't understand that. . . . They are either free or not free.

FULBRIGHT: You can apply that reasoning—how do we compromise the freedom of two hundred fifty million Russians. Why don't we go over there and free them?

TAYLOR: That is not the issue for the moment.

FULBRIGHT: Or the Yugoslavs. You have been talking about Communism. The Yugoslavs are Communists, as you call them. I know it is not the issue and I don't think your answer is responsive. I think that this is a war, a most unfortunate war; I am very unhappy about it. But we are trying to develop just what is our objective. My objective, as I have stated it often, is we try to find a way to a conference table without pursuing this in an un-limited way, which may involve us in a war with China if we persist to the point of forcing North Vietnam to give in. I also think that Viet Cong in South Vietnam being the major opponent on the field is a party that has to be dealt with. I don't agree with their tactics any better, any more than you do. I think they have been very savage. I think most people have been. We said, the Germans were sav-age in World War One, at least we were told so; we were given pictures of cutting off the hands of the children and doing all sorts of things to women and so on. It has been so in every war that I know of, in the last war, the gas chambers. Now the Germans are our bosom friends, our staunch allies, but they killed more people in gas cham-bers, most inhuman and immoral. It seems to me, under ordinary conditions with the weapons at the time all wars have very similar characteristics, no matter we just use whatever means they have at the time to kill people, either by burning or by disemboweling—it is equally, they are equally dead, and I can't see much moral distinc-tion about it. If you wish to examine a particular indi-vidual who has the nerve or whatever it is, a lack of sensitivity to do it in person, why I suppose it is an indi-vidual matter, there is a distinction.

TAYLOR: I think the matter of intent is important, Senator. I think the law recognizes that.

FULBRIGHT: There is a difference. But as a national policy, as a country, and as a government that engages in this and uses its own weapons, I don't see any very great distinction. I don't know that this point makes any difference. The only reason I raised it, I didn't raise it, Senator Lausche raised it first, this morning, and I think it is the kind of inflammatory line which discourages the utilization of what little reason we have left, that is the only reason I comment on it in the first place, and I don't wish to make any point of it. I don't wish to say we are a bit worse than any other country. We use weapons at our disposal. We burned a lot of innocent people in this war. I am not blaming you or anyone else for it. It is the nature of war. This is why I would like to find some way to stop it.

I am not complaining about it. I think both sides have done dastardly things. But I can't see where the emphasis in this policy—as either you have described it or others have—the emphasis is on trying to find a way to stop the war, a cease-fire, the same kind of cease-fire they found in '54, which did bring that particular phase of the war, at least to a temporary end, if we hadn't intervened, the same way they stopped it in Algeria, that is all I am seeking for.

TAYLOR: I am sure, Senator, we would like to have this settlement on the '54 line, if all the Viet Cong would go home and go north and let South Vietnamese lead their own lives.

FULBRIGHT: You are asking them to say, "Well, we are sorry we made a mistake and we beg your pardon. Now whatever you want we will do."

TAYLOR: I think they could have compensations. There are compensations that we could offer.

FULBRIGHT: So could we, and I am not advocating we just stop it out of hand. Maybe it is a matter of degree, but, in all honesty, I get the impression that our policy is directed toward forcing them by force to surrender, and then we will parlay with them, rather than seeking some basis upon which we could obtain a compromise to stop the slaughter. In the long run, I think, the outcome in this area will be probably the same whichever way you follow because I do not think you are or any of our government are capable of creating out of whole cloth the kind of fine democratic regime in this area which some people seem to imagine they can. I think this is an impossibility. They are going to have to create it for themselves, and the sooner we allow them to get about it, I think, the better.

TAYLOR: I quite agree with you, Senator, providing the

fifteen million South Vietnamese choose the kind of government, the kind of life, they want to lead.

FULBRIGHT: The proposal I have made, and the 1954 proposal was to allow them to make their own decision, that is what it provided. It has been interfered with. I would not want to recount all who interfered. We certainly played our part in our support of Diem, and it seems to me that is the most we could ask. We should not presume to dictate it. I think they should be allowed to make their own decision, and that is what I have been recommending, and other members of this Committee have.

TAYLOR: That is what our position is, that is what we are trying to do.

FULBRIGHT: To create a condition that would allow them to do it. Now, a method was stated in 1954, in the 1954 [Geneva] Agreement. Maybe there is a better method. But this excludes, in my mind, it is inconsistent with, the pursuance of an unlimited war to the point where they surrender and come on their knees and say, "Now we have stopped." Well, I have had my say. Do you wish to comment on that? You do not have to.

TAYLOR: I am sorry, Senator, I do not agree with much of what you have said. Certainly our objective is as you have interpreted it. . . .

The Statement and Testimony (concluded) of

SECRETARY OF STATE

Dean Rusk

Friday, February 18, 1966

SENATOR FULBRIGHT: . . . [Since February 4 there have been] three developments which I hope you will address yourself to in your opening remarks. . . . First, we would like very much to know how far our commitments to General Ky have gone in Honolulu; how firm we are to back him in his determination never to negotiate with the National Liberation Fronts; how many troops we have promised and how much money. Two, . . . what commitments [has] the Administration authorized the Vice-President to make in his extended trip to some ten nations, especially whether in return for the $100 million loan to India the Indians will be required to send troops to Vietnam, and the same with regard to the other countries in which he is apparently authorized to . . . extend loans? Three, what [did] General de Gaulle really say in his letter to our government about the war in Vietnam, as reported again in the *Washington Post* this morning? Or to be more specific, I would like to know if General de Gaulle actually said this Vietnamese war is leading nowhere and that it is absurd. . . .

It seems to me we in the public are entitled to know if

that is true, somebody leaked it or gave it to the press, and while I understand from the press it is a private letter, nevertheless it appears in public, that this is what he said, and . . . insofar as you can, I hope that you will enlighten the Committee. . . .

SECRETARY RUSK: Mr. Chairman, the immediate occasion for these hearings is a request by the President for a supplemental appropriation to the AID Administration of $415 million, of which $275 million are intended for South Vietnam. Mr. David Bell, the Administrator of AID, and I have both already testified on this particular request. These hearings, as the Chairman has pointed out, have also entered into the largest and most far-reaching aspects of our interests and involvements in Southeast Asia. So, for my part, I welcome this opportunity to appear again before the Committee to discuss with you these larger issues.

Since World War Two, which projected the United States into the role of major world power, we Americans have had to face a series of difficult tasks and trials. On the whole we have faced them very well. Today we are facing another ordeal in Southeast Asia which again is costing us both lives and treasure. South Vietnam is a long way from the United States, and the issues posed may seem remote from our daily experience and our immediate interests. It is essential, therefore, that we clearly understand—and so far as possible agree—on our mission and purpose in that faraway land.

Why are we in Vietnam? Certainly we are not there merely because we have power and like to use it. We do not regard ourselves as the policeman of the universe. We do not go around the world looking for quarrels in which we can intervene. Quite the contrary. We have recognized that, just as we are not gendarmes of the universe, neither are we the magistrate of the universe. If other governments, other institutions, or other regional organizations can find solutions to the quarrels which disturb this present scene, we are anxious to have this occur. But we are in

Vietnam because the issues posed there are deeply inter-
twined with our own security and because the outcome of
the struggle can profoundly affect the nature of the world
in which we and our children will live. The situation we
face in Southeast Asia is obviously complex but, in my
view, the underlying issues are relatively simple and are
utterly fundamental. I am confident that Americans, who
have a deep and mature understanding of world responsibility, are fully capable of cutting through the underbrush
of complexity and finding the simple issues which involve
our largest interests and deepest purposes. I regard it,
therefore, as a privilege to be able to discuss these problems with the Committee this morning—to consult with
you—and at the same time to try to clarify for the American people the issues we must squarely face.

I do not approach this task on the assumption that anyone, anywhere, has all the answers or that all wisdom be-
longs to the Executive branch of the government, or even
to the government itself.

The questions at issue affect the well-being of all Americans and I am confident that all Americans will make up
their own minds in the tradition of a free and independent
people. Yet those of us who have special responsibilities
for the conduct of our foreign policy have had to think
hard and deeply about these problems for a very long
time. The President, his Cabinet colleagues, and the Congress, who share the weightiest responsibilities under our
constitutional system, have come to certain conclusions
that form the basis for the policies we are now pursuing.
Perhaps it is worth pointing out that those who are of-
ficially responsible for the conduct of our public affairs
must make decisions—and must make decisions among existing alternatives. None of us in the Executive or the
Legislative branch has fulfilled our responsibilities merely
by formulating an opinion; we are required to decide what
this nation shall do and shall not do and are required to
accept the consequences of our determination.

What are our world security interests involved in the

struggle in Vietnam? They cannot be seen clearly in terms of Southeast Asia only or merely in terms of the events of the past few months. We must view the problem in perspective. We must recognize that what we are seeking to achieve in South Vietnam is part of a process that has continued for a long time—a process of preventing the expansion and extension of Communist domination by the use of force against the weaker nations on the perimeter of Communist power. This is the problem as it looks to us. Nor do the Communists themselves see the problem in isolation. They see the struggle in South Vietnam as part of a larger design for the steady extension of Communist power through force and threat.

I have observed in the course of your hearings that some objection has been raised to the use of the term "Communist aggression." It seems to me that we should not confuse ourselves or our people by turning our eyes away from what that phrase means. The underlying crisis of this postwar period turns about a major struggle over the very nature of the political structure of the world. Before the guns were silent in World War Two, many governments sat down and thought long and hard about the structure of international life, the kind of world which we ought to try to build, and wrote those ideas into the United Nations Charter. That Charter establishes an international society of independent states, large and small, entitled to their own national existence, entitled to be free from aggression, cooperating freely across national frontiers in their common interests, and resolving their disputes by peaceful means. But the Communist world has returned to its demand for what it calls a "world revolution," a world of coercion in direct contradiction to the Charter of the United Nations.

There may be differences within the Communist world about methods and techniques and leadership within the Communist world itself, but they share a common attachment to their "world revolution" and to its support through what they call "wars of liberation." So, what we face in Vietnam is what we have faced on many occasions before—the need to check the extension of Communist power in order to maintain a reasonable stability in a precarious world. That stability was achieved in the years after the war by the valor of free nations in defending the integrity of postwar territorial arrangements. And we have achieved a certain stability for the last decade and a half. It must not be overthrown now.

Like so many of our problems today, the struggle in South Vietnam stems from the disruption of two world wars. The Second World War completed a process begun by the first. It ripped apart a structure of power that had existed for a hundred years. It set in train new forces and energies that have remade the map of the world. Not only did it weaken the nations actively engaged in the fighting, but it had far-reaching secondary effects. It undermined the foundations of the colonial structures through which a handful of powers controlled one third of the world's population. And the winds of change and progress that have blown fiercely during the last twenty years have toppled those structures almost completely. Meanwhile, the Communist nations have exploited the turmoil of the time of transition in an effort to extend Communist control into other areas of the world.

The United States first faced the menace of Communist ambition in Europe when one after another of the nations on the boundaries of the Soviet Union fell under the dominion of Moscow through the presence of the Red Army. To check this tidal wave the U.S. provided the Marshall Plan to strengthen the nations of Western Europe, and then moved to organize with those nations a collective security system through NATO. As a result, the advance of Soviet Communist power was stopped and the Soviet Union gradually adjusted its policies to this situation. But within a year after the establishment of NATO, the Communists took over China. This posed a new and serious threat, particularly to those weak new nations of the Far East that had been formed out of colonial empires.

The problems in Asia were, of course, different from those in Europe. But the result was much the same—instability, uncertainty, and vulnerability to both the bully and the aggressor.

Western Europe, with its established governmental and traditional social institutions recovered quickly. But certain of the new nations of Asia—particularly those that had not known self-government for a century or more—continued to face a far more formidable problem which they still face. The first test in Asia came in Korea when the United Nations Forces—predominantly American—stopped the drive of Communist North Korea supported by material aid from the Soviet Union. It stopped the Chinese Army that followed. It brought to a halt the Communist effort to push out the line that had been drawn and to establish Communist control over the Korean peninsula. We fought the Korean War—which like the struggle in Vietnam occurred in a remote area thousands of miles away—to sustain a principle vital to the freedom and security of America, the principle that the Communist world should not be permitted to expand by overrunning one after another of the arrangements built during and since the war to mark the outer limits of Communist expansion by force.

Before the Korean War had ended, the United States, under President Truman, moved to settle and consolidate the situation in the Pacific through a peace treaty with Japan, and through bilateral security treaties with Japan and the Philippines, and through the ANZUS Treaty with Australia and New Zealand. Hardly had the Korean War been finished when France, which had been fighting a protracted struggle in Indochina, decided to relinquish its political presence in Southeast Asia. After a brief negotiation it came to terms with the Communist forces that had captured the Nationalist movement. The result was the division of Indochina into four parts: a Kingdom of Cambodia, a Kingdom of Laos, and Vietnam divided at the 17th Parallel between the Communist forces in the North and a non-Communist Vietnamese government in the South.

Recognizing that the Communists had not abandoned their ambitions, the U.S. government under President Eisenhower took steps to secure the situation by further alliances. Bilateral treaties were concluded with the Republic of Korea and the Republic of China on Formosa. In the Middle East the so-called "northern tier" of countries lying to the south of the Soviet Union entered into the Baghdad Pact which established what is now known as CENTO, the Central Treaty Organization. The United States did not become a formal member of this alliance, which is composed of Great Britain, Turkey, Iran, and Pakistan. But we are closely associated with CENTO and have bilateral military assistance agreements with its regional members, concluded by the Eisenhower Administration.

In order to give support to the nations of Southeast Asia, the United States took the lead in the creation of an alliance embodied in a treaty and reinforced by a collective security system known as SEATO, the Southeast Asia Treaty Organization. In this alliance the United States joined with Great Britain, France, Australia, New Zealand, Thailand, Pakistan, and the Philippines to guarantee the security not only of the member nations but also to come to the aid of certain protocol states and territories if they so requested. South Vietnam was included in this protocol. The United States had not been a party to the Agreements made in Geneva in 1954, which France had concluded with the Communist Vietnamese forces known as the Viet Minh. But the Under Secretary of State, Walter Bedell Smith, stated under instructions that the U.S. would not disturb the Agreements and "would view any renewal of the aggression in violation of the . . . Agreements with grave concern and as seriously threatening international peace and security." Under Secretary Smith's statement was only a unilateral declaration, but in joining SEATO, the United States took a solemn treaty engagement of far-reaching effect. Article IV, paragraph one, provides that "each party recognizes that aggression by means of armed attack . . . would endanger its own peace and safety, and agrees that it will in that event act to meet the common danger in accordance with its constitutional processes." It is this fundamental SEATO obligation that has from the outset guided our actions in South Vietnam.

The language of this treaty is worth careful attention. The obligation it imposes is not only joint but several; that is, not only collective, but individual. The finding that an armed attack has occurred does not have to be made by a collective determination before the obligation of each member becomes operative. Nor does the Treaty require a collective decision on actions to be taken to meet the common danger. If the United States determines that an armed attack has occurred against any nation to whom the protection of the Treaty applies, then it is obligated "to act to meet the common danger" without regard to the views or actions of any other Treaty member.

The far-reaching implications of this commitment were well understood by this Committee when it recommended, with only the late Senator Langer dissenting, that the Senate consent to the ratification of the Treaty. The Committee's report states, in its conclusion, that "The Committee is not impervious to the risks which this treaty entails. It fully appreciates that acceptance of these additional obligations commits the U.S. to a course of action over a vast expanse of the Pacific. Yet these risks are consistent with our own highest interests. There are greater hazards, "the Committee's conclusions stated, "in not advising a potential enemy of what he can expect of us, and in failing to disabuse him of assumptions which might lead to a miscalculation of our intentions."

Following this Committee's recommendation, the Senate gave its advice and consent to the Treaty by a vote of eighty-two to one, the late Senator Langer voting against; all members of this distinguished Committee who were then Senators voted for. . . .

Our multilateral engagement under the SEATO treaty had been reinforced and amplified by a series of bilateral commitments and assurances directly to the government of South Vietnam. On October 1, 1954, President Eisenhower wrote to President Diem offering, and I quote, "to assist the government of Vietnam in developing and maintaining a strong, viable state, capable of resisting attempted subversion or aggression through military means." In 1957 President Eisenhower and President Diem issued a joint statement which called attention to "the large buildup of Vietnamese Communist military forces in North Vietnam," and stated, and I quote: "Noting that the Republic of Vietnam is covered by Article IV of the Southeast Asia Collective Defense Treaty, President Eisenhower and President Ngo Dinh Diem agreed that aggression or subversion threatening the political independence of the Republic of Vietnam would be considered as endangering peace and stability."

On August 2, 1961, President Kennedy declared that "the United States is determined that the Republic of Vietnam shall not be lost to the Communists for lack of any support which the United States can render." On December 14, 1961, President Kennedy wrote to President Diem, recalling the United States declaration made at the end of the Geneva Conference in 1954. The President once again stated that the United States was "prepared to help the Republic of Vietnam to protect its people and to preserve its independence." This commitment has been raffirmed many times since.

These then are the commitments we have taken to protect South Vietnam as a part of protecting our own "peace and security." We have sent American forces to fight in the jungles of that beleaguered country because South Vietnam has, under the language of the SEATO Treaty, been the victim of "aggression by means of armed attack." There can be no serious question as to the existence and nature of this aggression. The war is clearly an "armed attack," cynically and systematically mounted by the Hanoi regime against the people of South Vietnam. The North Vietnamese regime has sought deliberately to confuse the issue by seeking to make its aggression appear as an indigenous revolt. But we should not be deceived by this subterfuge. It is a familiar Communist practice. Impeded in their efforts to extend their power by the use of classical forms of force, such as the invasion of Korea, the Communists have, over many years, developed an elaborate doctrine for so-called "wars of national liberation" to cloak their aggressions in ambiguity.

A "war of national liberation," in the Communist lexicon, depends on the tactics of terror and sabotage, of stealth and subversion. It has a particular utility for them since it gives an advantage to a disciplined and ruthless minority, particularly in countries where the physical terrain makes clandestine infiltration from the outside relatively easy. At the same time the Communists have a more subtle reason for favoring this type of aggression. It creates in any situation a sense of ambiguity that they can exploit to their own advantage. Yet, in spite of Communist efforts to confuse the issue, the nature of the conflict in South Vietnam is very clear.

Let me review briefly the facts. With the benefit of hindsight no one can doubt that in agreeing to the 1954 Accords, the regime in Hanoi fully expected that within a relatively short period the South Vietnamese would fall under their control. The South seemed overburdened with troubles; its formidable economic problems were complicated by the need to absorb almost one million North Vietnamese, who, having seen the true face of Communism, fled South after the 1954 Accords. The North moreover had concealed resources in the South. At the time of the Accords in 1954, many Communists fighting with the Viet Minh had been directed by the Lao Dong Party in Hanoi to stay in the South, to hide their arms, and to devote their efforts to undermining the South Vietnamese government. These efforts of subversion were in the initial years quite unsuccessful. Much to the dismay of the Hanoi regime, South Vietnam made substantial progress in spite of the extraordinary problems it faced, while North Vietnam lagged far behind. As a consequence the Communist leaders in North Vietnam were forced to conclude that more active measures were necessary if the subversion of South Vietnam were to succeed.

During the five years following the Geneva Conference the Hanoi regime developed a secret political-military organization in South Vietnam based on the cadres who had been ordered to stay in the South. Many of the activities of this organization were directed toward the assassination of selected South Vietnamese civilians. More than a thousand civilians were murdered or kidnaped from 1957 to 1959. In 1960 alone terrorists assassinated fourteen hundred local government officials and kidnaped some seven hundred others, while armed guerrillas killed twenty-two hundred military and security personnel.

In September, 1960, the Lao Dong Party—the Communist Party in North Vietnam—held its Third Party Congress in Hanoi. That congress called for the creation of a front organization to undertake the subversion of South Vietnam. Three months thereafter, the National Liberation Front was established to provide a political façade for the conduct of an active guerrilla war. Beginning in 1960 the Hanoi regime began to infiltrate into South Vietnam the disciplined adherents whom the Party had ordered north at the time of the settlement. In the intervening period since 1954, these men had been trained in the arts of sabotage and subversion; now they were ordered to conscript young men from the villages by force or persuasion, and to form cadres around which guerrilla units could be built. All of this was documented by the Legal Committee of the International Commission for Supervision and Control. That body, established to supervise the performance of the Vietnam cease-fire, is composed of Indian, Polish, and Canadian members. The Legal Committee, with Poland objecting, reported in 1962: "There is evidence to show that arms, munitions, and other supplies have been sent from the zone in the North to the zone in the South with the objective of supporting, organizing, and carrying out hostile activities, including armed attacks, against the armed forces and administration of the zone in the South.

"There is evidence that the PAVN (i.e., the North Vietnamese Army) has allowed the zone in the North to be used for inciting, encouraging and supporting hostile activities in the zone in the South, aimed at the overthrow of the administration in the South." That is the end of the quotation.

In the three-year period from 1959 to 1961 the North Vietnam regime infiltrated ten thousand men into the South. In 1962 thirteen thousand additional personnel were infiltrated; and by the end of 1964 North Vietnam may well have moved over forty thousand armed and unarmed guerrillas into South Vietnam. But beginning over a year ago the Communists apparently exhausted their reservoir of Southerners who had gone north. Since then the greater number of men infiltrated into the South have been native-born North Vietnamese. Most recently Hanoi has begun to infiltrate elements of the North Vietnamese Regular Army in increasingly larger numbers. Today there is evidence that nine regiments of regular North Vietnamese forces are fighting in organized units in the South.

I have reviewed these facts, Mr. Chairman, which are familiar enough to most of you, because it seems to me they demonstrate beyond question that the war in Vietnam is as much an act of outside aggression as though the Hanoi regime had sent an army across the 17th Parallel rather than infiltrating armed forces by stealth. This point is important, since it goes to the heart of our own involvement. Much of the confusion about the struggle in South Vietnam has arisen over a failure to understand this aspect of the conflict. For if the war in South Vietnam were, as the Communists try to make it appear, merely an indigenous revolt, then the United States would not have its own combat troops in South Vietnam. But the evidence is overwhelming that it is in fact, something quite different: a systematic aggression by Hanoi against the people of South Vietnam. It is one further effort by a Communist regime in one half of a divided country to take over the people of the other half at the point of a gun and against their will.

Up to this point I have tried to describe the nature of our commitments in South Vietnam and why we have made them. I have sought to put those commitments within the framework of our larger effort to prevent the Communists from upsetting the arrangements which have been the basis for our security. These policies have some-times been attacked as static and sterile. It has been ar-gued that they do not take account of the vast changes which have occurred in the world and indeed are still in train. These contentions seem to miss the point. The line of policy we are following involves far more than a defense of the status quo. It seeks rather to ensure that degree of security which is necessary if change and progress are to take place through consent and not through coercion. Certainly, as has been frequently pointed out, the world of the mid-twentieth century is not standing still: move-ment is occurring on both sides of the Iron Curtain. Com-munism today is no longer monolithic; it no longer wears one face but many; and the deep schism between the two great power centers of the Communist world—Moscow and Peiping—is clearly one of the major political facts of our time.

There has been substantial change and movement within the Soviet Union as well, and perhaps even more among the countries of Eastern Europe. These changes have not been inhibited because of our efforts to maintain our postwar arrangements by organizing the Western Alliance. They have taken place because of internal devel-opments as well as because the Communist regime of Mos-cow has recognized that the Western Alliance cannot permit it to extend its dominion by force. Over time the same processes, hopefully, will work in the Far East. Peiping, and the Communist states living under its shadow, must learn that they cannot redraw the boundaries of the world by force.

What we are pursuing, therefore, is not a static concept. For unlike the Communists, we really do believe in social revolution and not merely in power cloaked as revolution. We believe in constructive change and encourage it. That was the meaning of President Johnson's initiatives at the Honolulu Conference—to encourage the efforts of the South Vietnamese government to transform the country in a way that will correct ancient injustices and bring about a better life for all the people.

In meeting our commitments in South Vietnam, we are using substantial military forces. At the same time we are making it quite clear to North Vietnam and to the world that our forces are being employed for a limited and well-defined objective. What we seek in South Vietnam is to bring about a restoration of the conditions contemplated by the Accords of 1954. We seek, in other words, to restore the integrity of the settlement made between the French government and the Communist forces under Ho Chi Minh—a settlement which was joined in by the United Kingdom, Communist China, the Soviet Union, Laos, and Cambodia. This settlement forms a part of the structure of arrangements that are the key to stability in the present-day world.

Unfortunately, the limited nature of our purpose is foreign to the philosophy of the Communist world. It may be hard, therefore, for them to realize that the United States seeks no territorial aggrandizement in South Vietnam or anywhere in Southeast Asia. We do not wish to maintain our troops in that area any longer than is necessary to secure the freedom of the South Vietnamese people. We want no permanent military bases, no trade advantages. We are not asking that the government of South Vietnam ally itself with us or be in any way beholden to us. We wish only that the people of South Vietnam should have the right and opportunity to determine their future in freedom without coercion or threat from the outside.

For months now we have done everything possible to make clear to the regime in Hanoi that a political solution is the proper course. If that regime were prepared to call off the aggression in the South, peace would come in almost a matter of hours. When that occurred, the people of North Vietnam could safely go about their business. For we do not seek to destroy the Hanoi regime or to force the people of North Vietnam to accept any other form of government. And, under conditions of peace, we would be quite prepared for the North Vietnamese people to share with the other peoples of Southeast Asia in the economic and technical help that we and other nations are extending on a regional basis to that area.

This is the simple message that we have tried to convey to Hanoi through many channels. We have sought in every way to impress upon the Communist world the ease with which peace could be attained if only Hanoi were willing. We have used every resource of diplomacy. I know of no occasion in history where so much effort has been devoted —not only on the part of the United States but of many other nations—in an effort to bring about a political solution to a costly and dangerous war. . . . But to this point the sounds from the other side have been harsh and negative. The regime in Hanoi has been unwilling to accept any of the possibilities open to it for discussion. All we have heard is the constant insistence that they will not negotiate unless we accept in advance their Four Points. Yet the effect of those Four Points, as propounded by Hanoi, would be to give away the very purposes for which we are fighting and to deliver the people of South Vietnam against their will to the domination of a Communist regime. To understand the situation realistically, we should not underestimate the harshness of the Communist side or overestimate the ease of a political solution.

From time to time we have heard it suggested that we should seek a Geneva Conference or enlist the good offices of the Conference co-chairmen or take the problem to the

United Nations or invite the mediation efforts of neutral nations. Well, we have done all of these things, and in most cases we have done them repeatedly, with no result. We have heard it suggested also, by governments and individuals on both sides of the Iron Curtain, that no peace was possible so long as American planes were flying bombing missions over North Vietnam, but that negotiations might be possible if the bombing were discontinued. We did that also, not once but twice. The last pause as this committee will recall, lasted more than thirty-seven days. And again with no response. Certainly, we shall do everything consistent with our national objectives to seek a solution through diplomacy. There is no doubt as to the elements for an honorable peace as we see it. We have made them clear again and again. Most recently we have summarized them in the form of fourteen points:

1. The Geneva Agreements of 1954 and 1962 are an adequate basis for peace in Southeast Asia;

2. We would welcome a conference on Southeast Asia or on any part thereof;

3. We would welcome "negotiations without preconditions," as the seventeen nations put it;

4. We would welcome unconditional discussions, as President Johnson put it;

5. A cessation of hostilities could be the first order of business at a conference or could be the subject of preliminary discussions;

6. Hanoi's Four Points could be discussed along with other points which others might wish to propose;

7. We want no U.S. bases in Southeast Asia;

8. We do not desire to retain U.S. troops in South Vietnam after peace is assured;

9. We support free elections in South Vietnam to give the South Vietnamese a government of their own choice;

10. The question of reunification of Vietnam should be determined by the Vietnamese through their own free decision;

11. The countries of Southeast Asia can be nonaligned or neutral if that be their option;

12. We would much prefer to use our resources for the economic reconstruction of Southeast Asia than in war. If there is peace, North Vietnam could participate in a regional effort to which we would be prepared to contribute at least $1 billion;

13. The President has said, "The Viet Cong would not have difficulty being represented and having their views represented if for a moment Hanoi decided she wanted to cease aggression. I don't think," he said, "that would be an insurmountable problem";

14. We have said publicly and privately, and since this particular point was put through there were thirty-seven days of action, that we could stop the bombing of North Vietnam as a step toward peace although there has not been the slightest hint or suggestion from the other side as to what they would do if the bombing stopped.

These fourteen points are on the public record. Our government has made quite clear what kind of peace we are prepared to accept—a peace that will guarantee the security of South Vietnam, a peace that will stop armed aggression in violation of international agreements and international law. This is the position that we have made known to the other side, both directly and through intermediaries. How does this compare with the position of the Hanoi regime? Both Hanoi and Peiping have repeatedly rejected our proposal for unconditional discussions. They have insisted instead that before any discussions can take place our side must agree in advance to the Four Points of Hanoi's program. The words that they have used have differed from formulation to formulation. Sometimes they have said their points are the "sole basis" for negotiations, sometimes "the most correct basis." But the effect is the same. What they are insisting upon is that we accept in advance their substantive position and then discuss only the ways in which it shall be given effect. The technique of demanding such substantive agreement in advance is a familiar Communist negotiating tactic. It does not mean that the basic points are open for discussion or that they can be loosely interpreted. It means just what it says.

We have subjected these Four Points to the most careful scrutiny. What do they reveal? The first point calls for "recognition of the fundamental rational rights of the Vietnamese people: sovereignty, independence, unity, and territorial integrity." This point also calls for the withdrawal of U.S. forces, dismantling of our military bases, and abolition of our military alliance with the government of South Vietnam, "in strict conformity with the Geneva Agreements." The United States has made clear that we, too, are prepared to support a restoration of the provisions of the Geneva Agreements and that we are prepared to withdraw our troops and dismantle military bases once there is compliance with the Accords by all parties. We have said also that we would not expect or require a military alliance with a free South Vietnam.

The second point relates to the military clauses of the Geneva Agreements, and these, too, we could agree to under the conditions I have indicated.

The fourth point provides that the issue of peaceful reunification should be settled by the Vietnamese people without foreign intervention. This also we could accept if it be clearly understood that conditions must first be created both in the North and South that will make it possible for truly free elections to be held.

It is in the third point that the core of the Communist position is disclosed. That point provides that "The Internal affairs of South Vietnam must be settled by the South Vietnamese people themselves in accordance with the program of the National Liberation Front." To understand the significance of this point, it is necessary not only to examine what is meant by the "Program of the National Liberation Front" but to explore somewhat further the character of the Front itself and the purposes it serves in the tactics of the North Vietnamese regime.

Let us turn first to the Front itself. Both Hanoi and Peiping have made clear again and again, and they have been joined in this by other Communist powers, that negotiations will be possible only when the United States recognizes the National Liberation Front as the "sole genuine representative of the entire South Vietnamese people."

What are the implications of this proposal and why are the Communists urging it so insistently? The evidence is overwhelming that the National Liberation Front is exactly what its name implies—a Communist front organization intended to give support to the deliberate fiction that the war in Vietnam is an indigenous revolt. The Front is, as the facts make clear, an invention of the Communist Party of North Vietnam, to serve as a political cloak for its activities in the South.

As I have noted earlier, the Front was created by the North Vietnamese Communist Party, the Lao Dong Party, in 1960, soon after North Vietnam's military leader, General Giap, announced: "The North is the revolutionary base for the whole country."

The individuals proclaimed as leaders of the Front are not personalities widely known to the Vietnamese people, either in the North or in the South. To suggest that they represent the aspirations of the Vietnamese people is absurd. The significant fact is that at no time has any single individual of political significance in South Vietnam adhered to the Front or to its policies. While some Vietnamese leaders and groups may differ among themselves on how the country is to be led, none of them differs on the fact that the Front does not speak for them.

In 1961 Hanoi sought to strengthen the fiction of the Front's indigenous origins by creating a seemingly independent Communist Party as the principal element of the Front. It therefore established the People's Revolutionary Party. A secret Lao Dong circular dated December 7,

1961, advised Party members that "The People's Revolutionary Party has only the appearance of an independent existence. Actually our Party is nothing but the Lao Dong Party of Vietnam unified from North to South under the Central Executive Committee of the Party, the chief of which is President Ho. . . ." During these explanations, take care to keep this strictly secret, they said, "especially in South Vietnam, so that the enemy does not perceive our purpose."

The People's Revolutionary Party has not concealed its role at the front. It has frankly stated that it is the dominant element. On February 15, 1961, the Viet Cong Committee for the South went even farther, stating that in time the Communist Party would "act overtly to lead the revolution in South Vietnam." In other words, the Communists have told their followers that at the proper moment they would emerge from cover and cast off the disguise of the National Liberation Front. And so the Communists have a clear purpose in insisting that we recognize the National Liberation Front as the sole representative of the South Vietnamese people. For them this is not a procedural question but a major question of substance. They insist on our recognition of the Front as the sole spokesman for the people of South Vietnam, since our acceptance of the Front in that capacity would in effect mean our acceptance of the Communist position as to the indigenous nature of the conflict and thus our acceptance of a settlement on Hanoi's terms, which would mean delivering South Vietnam into the control of the Communist North.

In spite of these clear realities, we have not asserted nor do we assert an unreasoning attitude with regard to the Front. The President said in his State of the Union Message, you will recall, that we will meet at any conference table, we will discuss any proposals—four Points or fourteen or forty—and we will consider the views of any group"; and that, of course, includes the Front along with other groups. To the extent then that the Front has any validity as a representative of a group, the views of that group can be heard and the issue of the Liberation Front should, as the President has said, not prove "an insurmountable problem." It remains a problem only because Hanoi insists on using it to establish its own substantive position—that the Front represents the hopes and aspirations of the South Vietnamese people, and hence should control them.

The significance of this issue is clearly seen when one examines the so-called "Program of the National Liberation Front," as it was announced from Hanoi on January 29, 1961, and revised and amplified in a second publication on February 11 that same year. The first point of this program discloses the full Communist intention. It calls for the overthrow of the South Vietnamese government in Saigon and the establishment of a coalition government from which the government in Saigon would be totally excluded.

In other words the Hanoi regime is demanding the following preconditions to which the United States must agree before the Communists will even condescend to negotiate: First, that the South Vietnamese government be overthrown; second, that the Liberation Front, the creature and agent of Hanoi, be accepted as the sole bargaining representative for the South Vietnamese people; third, that South Vietnam be put under the control of a coalition government formed by the Communists and from which the South Vietnamese government would be excluded.

May I conclude, therefore, Mr. Chairman, with certain simple points which are at the heart of the problem and at the heart of United States policy in South Vietnam.

One, the elementary fact is that there is an aggression in the form of an armed attack by North Vietnam against South Vietnam. Two, the United States has commitments to assist South Vietnam to repel this aggression. Three, our commitments to South Vietnam were not taken in isolation but are part of a systematic effort in the postwar period to assure a stable space. Four, the issue in Southeast Asia becomes worldwide because we must make clear that the United States keeps its word wherever it is pledged. Five, no nation is more interested in peace in Southeast Asia or elsewhere than is the United States. If the armed attack against South Vietnam is brought to an end, peace can come very quickly. Every channel or forum for contact, discussion, or negotiation will remain active in order that no possibility for peace may be overlooked. . . .

FULBRIGHT: One question I thought you might comment upon is the situation that resulted at the Honolulu meeting with regard to the announced attitude, I believe I have quotes, they were in the paper, of General Ky with regard to his attitude toward negotiating with the NLF. . . . How do you reconcile that with the statements you have made of our willingness to negotiate with them if they would be willing?

RUSK: Mr. Chairman, that particular statement was made as a result of several attempts by a newsman to force him to a categorical answer to that question. Now, at Honolulu, Prime Minister Ky was freshly aware of the fact that Ho Chi Minh, in a letter to the heads of Communist governments, declared that the recognition of the Front as the sole representative of the people of South Vietnam was a prerequisite to any political solution.

Prime Minister Ky is leading a nation at war. All of his people are in the front line. The villagers, as well as the soldiers, the local officials as well as high officials in Saigon, are subject to terror and intimidation or assassination. He has the problem of war leadership among a people to whom he cannot promise the prospect of peace next week or next month, and so he felt, and I think we can understand it, that he could not indicate to his own people that he felt that there was a prospect for an early peace through negotiation on the basis of the experience that he and we had during this period of a pause.

Now, what we have said on this has been . . . discussed thoroughly with him and his government. The President's offer of unconditional discussions back in April was discussed in advance with the South Vietnamese government. I do not believe . . . that this is a difference of substance if Hanoi shows it is capable of stopping its aggression and shows some interest in peace.

FULBRIGHT: Do I understand that General Ky's attitude that he would under no circumstances negotiate with the National Liberation Front is not accepted by our government?

RUSK: Well, we have said what our view on that would be. But I think we ought to note that although this is what Prime Minister Ky said when he was pressed on this exact same question six times—and he was trying to point out that the Liberation Front was misnamed, that it was not a liberation front but what he called an "enslavement front"—when he was pressed on it, he gave that categorical answer. Now, the circumstances would be drastically changed if Hanoi indicated an interest in peace, and I have no doubt that those circumstances would be reviewed by everybody concerned if they developed in that direction, and we see where we go on that point.

FULBRIGHT: How can you expect any development in any direction when we pursue, appear to have taken, such an adamant attitude? I don't see how any development can come about.

RUSK: Well, Mr. Chairman, an adamant attitude has to do with one particular and specific and limited point. We are not asking anything from Hanoi except to stop shooting their neighbors in Laos and South Vietnam. We are not asking them to give up an acre of territory. We are not asking them to surrender a single individual, nor to change the form of government. All we are asking them to do is to stop sending armed men and arms, contrary to specific agreements and contrary to international law, into South Vietnam for the purpose of shooting somebody. Now, I have seen in certain columns the remark that to ask them to stop shooting is to ask them to surrender unconditionally. We are not asking them to surrender a thing except their appetite to take over South Vietnam by force. Now, on that, on that I would suggest somebody had better be adamant. . . .

FULBRIGHT: We certainly haven't made much progress. If there is a sticking point about whether or not they should be admitted to the conference, everything we have had in testimony is that the Viet Cong constitute the major fighting force in South Vietnam. . . . I wouldn't minimize the difficulty of getting over this obstacle. And that is why I wished to bring it up to see if we can clarify whether or not we have changed our position with regard to being willing to sit at a conference table with the representatives of the Viet Cong. . . .

RUSK: What the President said last July indicated that this problem of the Viet Cong and its views should not present an insuperable obstacle. . . . For us to negotiate the details of that point, even here in this room, or with the press or with other governments who have no capability of stopping the shooting, is somewhat beside the point. If Hanoi would come to the conference table, that is the kind of thing that could be discussed among other things.

Now, we see a double standard pretty widespread in the world which affects this problem of the effort made to bring this matter to a political solution. The United States has exhausted almost every procedure, every idea; we have traveled all over the world, we have tried to get the assistance of the seventeen neutral nations, the Secretary-General of the UN, the British Commonwealth, the President of India, the President of Ghana. We have made unilateral declarations about discussions, we have had private contacts with Hanoi. In other words, what we have been saying is, Why don't you come to the table and let's see if there is a basis for peace. . . . They say, No, not unless you recognize the Liberation Front as the sole spokesman for the South Vietnamese people. We can't do that, that is what the shooting is all about.

FULBRIGHT: I never had understood they said sole spokesman. Are you quite certain they have said that, if we have a negotiation it will only be with representatives of the National Liberation Front? Is that your position?

RUSK: In the Ho Chi Minh letter to the leaders of Communist governments, they call on the recognition for the Viet Cong as the sole representative of the South Vietnamese people.

FULBRIGHT: And they would talk with no one else at the conference table?

RUSK: These things have been explored in many ways through private channels, and I can assure you we have had nothing else from the other side except that idea.

FULBRIGHT: . . . I wondered if you could tell us about the de Gaulle letter. It was in the [*Washington Post*] this morning. . . .

RUSK: I think that dispatch was from Paris. That tends to suggest it was not us for a change that did a leaking, if there was any leaking. It used some adjectives in that dispatch that I did not recognize in recognizing the communication. It would not be, I think, for me to disclose the specific contents of the communication; but the attitude of France in this situation is pretty well known. They think there ought to be a settlement on the basis of the Geneva Accords; so do we. They think that these problems ought to be solved by political means; we certainly would prefer that. They do not believe that the time is ripe . . . for such political discussions, or at least they do not see any particular steps which they themselves can take at this particular moment to bring this matter to the conference table. But I did not find anything in the letter that justified this word "sever," I believe, that was used—

FULBRIGHT: Well, the paper uses the word, if my memory serves me right. We can get it. It says the war is leading nowhere and it says the war is absurd. . . . The French are really the culprit in this; they were the colonial power that were [the cause of] our original involvement; we came, it was in response to their request that we support them in maintaining their colonial domination of this area. That is the origin of it. You testified before that you were in the Department at the time this took place. . . . So you know all about that. And the French, if anyone, should be qualified to make some judgment about the character of these people who had intimate relationship to them, as their colonial masters, for about what—eighty years, wasn't it? Seventy-five or eighty years.

RUSK: Yes, sir.

FULBRIGHT: Here is what it reads: " 'Government circles in Washington,' Fontaine wrote, 'can compare the friendly public text of [de Gaulle's] answer to Ho Chi Minh with that of his reply to Mr. Johnson. Fontaine said de Gaulle apparently reproached Mr. Johnson 'not only for having ordered the resumption of the raids against the North, but also for persisting in an intervention from which there is nothing to be hoped, the Vietnamese alone being qualified to find a solution for their problem.' " . . .

RUSK: Mr. Chairman, that story is highly inaccurate and it is not . . . my privilege to prove my statement by putting President de Gaulle's letter in the public record here. . . . That story does not bear any resemblance to the letter that I have seen.

FULBRIGHT: In the last paragraph it says, "To an American visitor, de Gaulle confided, in substance, a short time ago: 'My analysis is different from that of your leaders. This war is absurd. It is leading to nothing. But I know the responsibilities of anyone at the head of a great state. I can imagine and I understand President Johnson's problems of conscience." . . . I wanted to know if it was inaccurate and . . . untrue.

RUSK: It is inaccurate and untrue, Mr. Chairman.

FULBRIGHT: I said that the *Post* is sometimes accurate

and I was not about to accept it and I wanted to know whether it was true. What about . . . Vice-President Humphrey, who is traveling to a number of countries? The paper also this morning says that he has made and authorized a loan, I believe, of $100 million, I am not sure, a grant or a loan, to India. What are the—this seems to me rather out of channels. It is not the usual responsibility of the President of the Senate and the Vice-President of the United States to go about making such commitments. Would you explain that?

RUSK: Well, Mr. Chairman, the two loans to India and Pakistan which were announced on the occasion of the Vice-President's visit were development loan fund allotments made and the fund provided for this fiscal year. As you know, certain activities in the economic assistance field began to mark time at the time of the India-Pakistan fighting. Since then there has been the Tashkent agreement between those two countries, and the steps taken by the two to carry out in important ways that Tashkent agreement.

We have been in touch with both India and Pakistan, and the negotiations on these particular loans will continue in the usual channels; that is, they are loans aimed primarily at facilitating the import of certain spare parts and other goods to get the industrial sector of the economies going full speed again. The Vice-President felt he would not undertake the negotiation and would not do that. The release of these funds were announced while he was there.

FULBRIGHT: Are there any conditions that are not public with regard to these loans?

RUSK: No, sir. The loans are of the type with which your Committee is fully familiar under the development loan program.

FULBRIGHT: In your last appearance before this Committee, Mr. Secretary, you said that one of the components in the commitment to Vietnam was approval by Congress each year of the AID program. You repeated this in a speech in Las Vegas on Wednesday. We have, of course, before us the supplemental request for authorization. Do you consider that we are making similar commitments to all fifty-three countries to which we provide military aid?

RUSK: No, sir. I do not. The commitments . . . as far as Vietnam is concerned center on the SEATO Treaty, which I discussed in my opening statement.

FULBRIGHT: You did state that with regard, though, to the AID program.

RUSK: No, but the commitment was there, and President Eisenhower began in 1954 and '55, to provide assistance to South Vietnam, to assist it in building a viable state secure from internal subversion or outside aggression. Now, that bilateral aid was in reinforcements of the purposes of the SEATO Treaty, and the general attitude of the country and of the government has been consistent throughout this period. The most recent formal affirmation of that same policy was, of course, the resolution of the Congress of August, 1964. And I would think that the economic and military assistance which we have given to South Vietnam over the years has been consistent with the purposes stated both in the preamble of that resolution and in the resolution itself.

FULBRIGHT: Then in case I do not approve of the policies being followed in Vietnam, then I am forced to vote against this authorization, if I accept that as a proper interpretation. . . . I don't wish to do that.

RUSK: Mr. Chairman, you and others would want to consider very seriously the declaration of policy which the Congress itself, by a vote of 504 to 2 made in August, 1964. Section II of that resolution says, "That the United States regards as vital to its national interests and to world peace the maintenance of international peace and security in Southeast Asia." And that indicated that "the United States is prepared, as the President determines, to take all necessary steps, including the use of armed force to assist any member or protocol state of the Southeast Asia Collective Defense Treaty requesting assistance in defense of its freedom."

Now, that declaration of policy passed in 1964 is entirely consistent with the Southeast Asia Treaty on the same subject which was passed over an overwhelming vote in the Senate, was ratified in 1955; the policy lines are very simple and they have been repeatedly reaffirmed by Presidents and by the Congress, so I would hope that you would take into full account the continuity of policy, and the problem of turning aside from that policy under present conditions.

FULBRIGHT: Mr. Secretary, I wish these things appeared as simple to me as they do to you. I am sure it is due to my own obtuseness but we will pursue this later. . . .

SENATOR HICKENLOOPER: [Is it your view] that the Viet Cong in South Vietnam are sustained and bolstered and encouraged and prodded, if you please, by not only logistical help from the North but by military directional help, and, in fact, by strong units of the North Vietnamese Army, so that the Viet Cong in South Vietnam really are completely dependent upon North Vietnam for continuing this struggle?

RUSK: That is correct, sir.

HICKENLOOPER: Therefore, if we get down to the point of a conference, and if we and the South Vietnamese did have a conference with the Viet Cong, . . . would any agreement with the guerrilla fighters, whether Viet Cong or whatever unit their reference might be, would any agreement with them down there be worth anything at all and, in fact, would it be completely unreliable unless Hanoi were one of the sustaining parties to that agreement on a reliable basis? In other words, the Viet Cong might agree to something, but if Hanoi did not agree, there might be a temporary lull, but Hanoi probably would return to the fray with increased vigor in a very short time. Is there anything to that theory?

RUSK: Senator, this is a very important point because

we have said privately to a good many governments that as far as the United States is concerned, the key issue of peace is with Hanoi. I said this morning that had that infiltration of men and arms not occurred, that we would not have had combat forces in South Vietnam. So, as far as the United States is concerned, Hanoi is the problem. Now, unless Hanoi stops doing what it is doing by way of launching an armed attack against the South, then we have not solved our problem. If they do stop, then I think these other problems will fall into place very quickly.

HICKENLOOPER: But it should go beyond a mere stopping temporarily, should it not?

RUSK: That is correct, sir.

HICKENLOOPER: The settlement would have to be based upon a realization by Hanoi that its adventures are unprofitable, and, in fact, disastrous to them if they continue them.

RUSK: That is correct, sir. And, Senator, I would hope —I do not want to emphasize this point because I undoubtedly will be charged with raising a new precondition of some sort for discussion by some quarters—I would hope that the assurances which would come out of any such agreement would be far stronger than those that we had in Laos, for example, where we had categorical agreements that were not worth anything because they were never complied with by the other side, and the machinery that was supposed to provide the assurance was not permitted to operate. . . .

SENATOR MORSE: You speak about the need for political settlement in Southeast Asia. I agree with you. Unless we have a political settlement in Southeast Asia, I would hope along the format of our institutions of international law, there is also going to have to be a political settlement in the United States, and I think that is the issue that you are helping draw this morning In my opinion now, the American people are going to have to decide this issue, and we will take the case to them . . . .

You rely heavily upon the SEATO Treaty this morning, as did Under Secretary Ball in his Northwestern University speech some time ago. I only want to say that I completely disagree with the conclusions you have reached in regard to the SEATO Treaty. I do not think that we can possibly justify our course of action on the very terms of the SEATO Treaty, and I shall answer your position point by point in a major speech that I shall give early next week in the Senate. Some of the top international lawyers of this country will be involved in that speech, because they take quite the opposite point of view, as international lawyers on your side take the position that you take, and I think we are going to have to draw that issue, too.

You said, Mr. Secretary, in answer to Senator Sparkman's questions about the course of action that we have followed in the United Nations, is it not true that when we took an issue back in 1964, I believe it was, to the United Nations, that we circumscribed that presentation on the basis of the alleged violations of our rights in the Tonkin Bay incident?

RUSK: That was the immediate issue on which the matter was taken to the Security Council, but we were prepared for a full discussion of the entire problem.

MORSE: We may have been prepared for it, but did we file an official resolution at any time before the United Nations prior to the resolution that we filed recently that is now pending before the Security Council that raised the issue to the threat of the peace of the world in Southeast Asia for a taking over by Security Council jurisdiction?

RUSK: We have invited them on repeated occasions to consider what they could do on that, Senator. As you know, we have had considerable discussion of this matter over the years, and the presence of a Soviet veto in the Security Council, the role of the Soviet Union as a co-chairman of the Geneva Conference, and the hopes that expectations of members of the Security Council that

258 The VIETNAM HEARINGS

somehow procedures could be worked out for convening a conference on this matter, has tended to limit the frontal confrontation of this issue by the Security Council.

MORSE: As you know, Mr. Secretary, you and I have had from time to time friendly discussions of this matter. We have disagreed as to what our procedure and course of action should be, and you have told us for quite some time about the veto point you have now made. But it has been the position of the senior Senator that we have had an obligation under the Charter to file a formal resolution before the Security Council, calling for a Security Council takeover of this threat to the peace in Southeast Asia. And I know of no resolution that we have filed that has met that obligation save the last resolution that we filed. These conversations of which you speak are, after all, conversations, and do not—are not based upon carrying out what I think is our clear pledge under the Charter.

I am hoping that we can get consideration in the Security Council, but if we can't, as I have said to you many times, and in hearings before this Committee, then we ought to proceed under the form of procedure of the rest of the Charter for an extraordinary session of the Geneva assembly, because I think our only hope is to try to get it —get this controversy under the canopy of the United Nations for action, and then [indicate that] we are willing to engage in a reconvening of the Geneva Conference. That represents another point of view in regard to this matter. . . . I do not think, until our last steps, we have ever fulfilled what I think has been our clear obligation— to test this matter in the United Nations. I don't think it is too late. There are those who are pessimists that think that we can't succeed now because we have waited too long. I don't think you ever can wait too long if you want to demonstrate to the world we want a peaceful solution; and I want to say that I hope we press for the debate in the Security Council, and if we can't get it, that we press for action in the Geneva assembly.

But, Mr. Secretary, this great emphasis of recent days,

although it has been mentioned before, this great emphasis of recent debate on SEATO interests me, because for a long time we were talking about the commitments of past Presidents, and President Johnson only a few months ago was laying great emphasis on the President Eisenhower letter to Diem. Subsequently, President Eisenhower—paraphrasing, I have the paper here, that purports to report him, and I think accurately—pointed out that his agreement or commitment with Diem was for economic aid and not military aid. Is that your understanding?

RUSK: Well, the commitments that were made bilaterally in terms of the assistance at that time were indeed in terms of economic and military aid. . . . The ordinary military assistance type of program, with training and arms and things of that sort. But the commitment of the Treaty existed at that time. So the problem was, what steps are necessary to give effect to the Treaty if the Treaty itself is brought into play by the action of the other side. And back in 1955, '56, along in there, I think that it would not have been the view that North Vietnam was at that point engaging in an armed attack against South Vietnam. Now, that armed attack is in process at the present time. So I think that the measures to be taken with respect to a policy will vary as the circumstances vary. And specifically will vary with the steps taken by the other side to upset such arrangements as the '54 Agreements or to challenge the SEATO Treaty.

MORSE: Would you disagree, then, unless he is inaccurately reported, that President Eisenhower was mistaken if he voiced the point of view that this alleged commitment to Diem did not involve commitment of military forces?

RUSK: I think his bilateral commitments to President Diem were of the sort that he described. But I am pointing out that in the background and in the contingency of such things as an armed attack, the Treaty which he recommended to the Senate and which the Senate approved by a vote of eighty-two to one did contain a commitment with respect to an armed attack. . . .

SENATOR AIKEN: . . . According to the Department of Defense statistics, there have been a total of 63,300 infiltrators from North Vietnam since 1960, and during that period, again according to the Department of Defense, we have killed 112,000 Viet Cong. The year-end strength of the Viet Cong was 225,000 excluding the North Vietnamese troops. It makes a total of 337,000 Viet Cong including those killed in action. Now, if you subtract from that the total of 63,300 infiltrators from the North, that still leaves 273,700 Viet Cong recruited and trained in the South, according to the Department of Defense statements. Does this indicate that there are civil war aspects to this struggle, and that the appeal of the Viet Cong to his fellow countrymen in South Vietnam is quite strong?

RUSK: There are elements of civil war in this situation, but the heart of the problem of peace is the external aggression. On the matter of the extent of Viet Cong influence among the South Vietnamese, we could debate that or listen to other people debate it at some length. The North claims that the Viet Cong are the sole spokesmen and ought to be treated as such. We can't find any significant political leader or significant groups in South Vietnam, outside of the ranks that you have just described, who want the Viet Cong's answer. But in any event, Senator, we are prepared to see that matter tested at the polls in a free election. We are prepared to let the people of South Vietnam make that judgment.

Now, the Liberation Front is not and Hanoi is not. They say we have got to have another government: "We have got ourselves to be in charge here before there are any elections." They are asking an international conference presumably to impose the Liberation Front upon the people of South Vietnam in some sort of combination. So, whatever the speculation might be, and all our evidence is that the Vietnamese people as a whole simply do not want the Liberation Front, we are prepared to have that matter tested at the polls, and the other side is not.

AIKEN: But do you think there were elements of rebellion, internal rebellion, present before the Communists moved in; or did the Communists move in first and organize the elements of rebellion?

RUSK: Well, at the time of the split between North and South Vietnam, it was agreed that there would be a regroupment of the two sides, and the Communist elements were supposed to go north and, as you know, one million Northerners came south to get away from what was to come in the North. Several thousand of those who were supposed to be regrouped to the north stayed behind. Now, I can't say, Senator, those were the only—that would be the only group that resisted at one time or another the government of the day. Certain of the sects were in rebellion for the time and they worked out a certain modus vivendi, and there are times when a Montagnard group will be disturbed. But the great problem of international peace is the infiltration. The great problem of internal peace is this resulting fight, and the great obstacle to a constitutional choice on the part of the South Vietnamese is the violence that is going on there for which the North must take the heaviest responsibility. . . .

SENATOR GORE: . . . Now I do not wish to engage in an argument with you or an extended colloquy with you about whether the SEATO Treaty binds the United States to do what we are doing in Vietnam, and what may be contemplated. I think that I can present an argument equally as strong as the one you have presented that it does not. But suffice it to say if this Treaty did in fact bind us, as you now describe it, I wonder why President Eisenhower, who signed it, did not interpret it as binding us to send combat forces to Vietnam. And if indeed it is as binding as you today interpret it, why was it that President Kennedy, under whom you served as Secretary of State, gave assurance to the American people that combat forces would not be sent to Vietnam, and indeed if that Treaty is also binding, and if this resolution, your interpretation of which I also disagree [with], is so binding and so specific, why was it that two days after this resolution was approved, President Johnson himself, in a speech to the American people, . . . said, after he had referred to those who said we should withdraw . . . : "Some others are eager to enlarge the conflict. They call upon us to supply American boys to do the job that Asian boys should do. They ask us"—this may have been Senator Goldwater—"to take reckless action which might risk the lives of millions and engulf Asia and certainly threaten the peace of the entire world."

I simply don't understand how three Presidents could take this limited view of our commitment under SEATO in this resolution, or under SEATO, and then one President with respect to the resolution, and now you interpret it as being a binding commitment to do what we are doing in Vietnam. I will not ask questions but I will certainly yield in fairness for you to respond to that. . . . I want to come to what I think is more important: We are there, our forces are there; they must be supported. And the question is, What do we do from now? But since so much has been made of the history of our commitment and the nature of our commitment— . . .

RUSK: . . . The difficulty is that we are not playing this hand of solitaire, and we need to keep our eyes on what the other side is doing during all this period. President Eisenhower did not have to face the question as to whether he should make a finding that there was in being an armed attack by North Vietnam against South Vietnam under the SEATO Treaty. When President Kennedy became President, we have about eight hundred U.S. military there under a U.S. aid mission, and that was within the level provided in the Geneva Agreements themselves of 1954.

But it was President Kennedy who went to Vienna in June, 1961, to talk to Mr. Khrushchev about Southeast

Asia, who found that Mr. Khrushchev agreed in principle that we ought to get out of Laos and leave that alone, but he also found that Mr. Khrushchev and he could not agree on Vietnam. And so when he came back, and you remember this was during a period also when there was a pretty sizable Berlin crisis underway, President Kennedy sent men out to South Vietnam to take a very special look at that situation, because he knew that the other side, as far as anything he could learn from Mr. Khrushchev was concerned, he knew that the other side was going after it.

So by the end of 1961 we had three thousand men there. By the end of 1962 President Kennedy had authorized up to eleven thousand men in South Vietnam. Now, they were advisors but they were also advising combat people in the field, and were themselves engaged in combat during that period as advisors and were getting killed. Our first military casualty, I am informed, in South Vietnam occurred in December, 1961. But the policy has been the same policy. The actions required to meet the steps taken by the other side have had to be different.

Now you mentioned the statement . . . of President Johnson on August 12, 1964. At no stage have we ourselves wanted to escalate this war, as the expression goes. At no stage have we wanted a larger war. But it was in November, December, January, over the turn of the year 1964-65 that North Vietnam moved the 325th Division of the regular North Vietnamese Army from North Vietnam to South Vietnam to up the ante here. . . . That was before the bombing started. . . . That wasn't in response to an escalation by the United States. That seemed to be as the result of a decision on their part that, well, "the United States, maybe they don't want a big war, maybe we can have a big one without undue risk." But in any event the steps that have to be taken in this situation have to be taken against the background of, and in the fact of, action by the other side to carry out a result which we are committed to prevent—namely, the armed seizure of South Vietnam by North Vietnam.

GORE: Thank you, Mr. Secretary. I shall not dwell upon that. I merely wanted to indicate that I did not accept the thesis . . . that we are legally bound to do what we are doing in Vietnam, or what I understand is contemplated, what I am apprehensive is contemplated. Let us come to what I think is a more important and a more current problem. I notice with some concern that in no place in your prepared text did you refer to that [which] has aroused such deep concern in this Committee and the country, to wit, the possibility that this war may be escalated into a conflict or war with China. Will you first indicate why you made no reference to this, and then will you please, sir, address your remarks to the subject. . . .

RUSK: Senator, perhaps I might comment on it at least briefly, . . . because, as you know, we have spent considerable time in the Committee on this problem. The question of how far a crisis can go is of course the final question at the end of the day in handling any crisis. And now [in] all of these postwar crises a possibility of a larger war has always been present, whether it is the Greek guerrillas or the Berlin blockade or the Korean war or the Cuban missile crisis, now here in Southeast Asia. This is also a problem for the other side, and it would work both ways with the other side.

Now we have had to deal with a number of crises in this postwar period with firmness. We have taken 160,000 casualties, 165,000 casualities, now in different parts of the world since 1945, to try to stabilize the peace, literally to try to stabilize the peace. But in dealing with each of these successive crises, we have also had to take care to deal with them with a prudence and a caution so that issues which in the nineteenth century could have thrown the entire world into the explosion of a general war can somehow be handled in a way that permits the human race to survive in the presence of modern weapons. And so we did not throw mass divisions in to relieve the Berlin Blockade. We used an airlift to probe for a peaceful settlement.

There were some who, in the Cuban missile crisis, wanted to go in with full bombing weight just as soon as the missiles were discovered. But President Kennedy decided that although it was necessary to make it very clear to the other side that the missiles must go, it was important to provide an opportunity for them to go by peaceful means. We did not open up a nuclear war because of Korea. Therefore, we have tried to show restraint and we have found on occasion, that the other side, at least some on the other side, understand the importance of restraint.

Now I suppose, Senator, if I could illustrate the point with a rather extreme illustration, no one, I think, believes that a nuclear exchange is a rational act of policy. But if two sides came to a table, each utterly convinced that under no circumstances would the other fight a nuclear war, then that could create a very dangerous situation. And we are not talking about nuclear business in South Vietnam question at all, at all. It has not come up. We have not considered this matter. This is certainly not in the picture.

What I am saying is that if one side only worries about escalation, then you can have a big war. The other side must also think about this question. The other side must realize that this is a dangerous and reckless thing for them to contemplate. The other side must understand, just as we, that if they knew their own interests, they don't want a larger war any more than we do. Of course we are concerned about where this will go. Of course. And the other side is concerned, and we would hope that, as has happened in other crises in this postwar period, that there will come a point when these concerns will lead to peace, where the cost of what they are trying to accomplish is too much for them. Maybe they were somewhat surprised that we were willing and able to do as much as we have done to stand in their way.

Now when they discover that they are not going to have an easy military victory in the South, and when they discover that the South Vietnamese are not going to just disintegrate and lie down in front of them, when they discover that international opinion is not going to build up in such a way as to force the United States to change its policy, and when they discover that internal differences in the United States is not going to pull us out of South Vietnam and let them have the country, then perhaps they will start looking towards the conference table and start giving us some peace. . . .

SENATOR CHURCH: . . . I think that the purpose of these hearings is to inquire both behind and beyond Vietnam, to try to determine where we are, how we got there and where we are going. In that connection, you said this morning, Mr. Secretary, that we do not want U.S. bases in Southeast Asia, that we do not desire to retain U.S. troops in South Vietnam, and I am completely in agreement with this, and I think it is very important that it be emphasized. But in a way, Mr. Secretary, it has a certain familiar ring that does disturb me. I have here a copy of the Committee print of the Senate Foreign Relations Committee back in 1951 which was compiled by General of the Army Omar N. Bradley, who was at that time Chairman of the Joint Chiefs of Staff. From notes kept by the conferees at the time of President Truman's meeting with General MacArthur, in Wake Island; this Committee print was published and made public. . . .

On page one of the print, referring to conversations between President Truman and General MacArthur, I read the following, which purports to be the position taken by General MacArthur. He is purported to have stressed to the President as follows:

"I hope the United Nations will hold elections by the first of the year. Nothing is to be gained by military occupation. All occupations are failures." (I read, the President nodded agreement. Then it goes on, presumably MacArthur continuing:)

"After elections are held, ten divisions with our equip-

ment supplemented by a small but competent air force
and also by a small but competent navy. If we do that,
it will not only secure Korea but it will be a tremendous
deterrent to the Chinese Communists moving south.
Again I emphasize the fact that the military should get
out the minute the guns stop shooting and the civilians
take over."

Now here it is 1966. As I recall your testimony two
weeks ago, Communist China withdrew Chinese troops
from North Korea about ten years ago, and there is not
and has not been a guerrilla war in South Korea. We have
in the meantime built up a very moderate and effective
Korean defense force, yet fifty-five thousand American
troops appear to be permanently stationed in Korea. In
the face of this, it seems to me, we didn't follow General
MacArthur's advice. Is that not true?

RUSK: That is correct. . . .

CHURCH: . . . Is it not also true that China is now developing a nuclear capacity, that is she has already deto-
nated two atomic bombs.

RUSK: That is correct, sir.

CHURCH: Is it your surmise that China is engaged upon
a serious effort to develop a nuclear capacity of its own
. . . and a modern delivery system of its own?

RUSK: That is correct, sir.

CHURCH: Would you say then, looking ahead perhaps
ten years, that China may have achieved the formation
of a formidable nuclear arsenal and perhaps a modern
delivery system including intercontinental ballistic missiles?

RUSK: In a continuous span, I think that is entirely possible.

CHURCH: Then, isn't it also possible that at such a
time . . . China may turn to us, assuming that we still
retain military bases in South Korea, and say, "Get out;
we don't think you belong here on the mainland of Asia
with military bases so close to China," as we said to
Khrushchev, when he attempted to establish Russian

military bases in Cuba, "Get out; you don't belong here so close to the boundaries of the United States and we will not permit it"?

I am trying, Mr. Secretary, to look ahead, based upon what we have done and how we feel, and vivid is the memory of that crisis in 1962 which took the world to the brink of nuclear war. I thought then that the American position was absolutely valid. I am wondering how the Chinese may view American military bases so close to China once they have developed a nuclear capacity of the kind that would give them some semblance of power commensurate with that of the United States.

RUSK: Well, Senator, it is true that we have retained fifty-five thousand men in the Republic of Korea. This is our principal ground force in Northeast Asia directly revelant not only to our interest in the security of Korea but also in the security of Japan and indeed the total strategic situation in the northern Pacific. I do not believe that this is a guideline for Southeast Asia. Indeed, we have already demonstrated in the case of Laos that if there is a peaceful situation, that we are prepared to withdraw our forces and would expect others to withdraw their forces.

After the agreement on Laos in 1962 we had several hundred military men in Laos. We took them out, we took them out. So as far as Southeast Asia is concerned, what I would say to the other side is, "If you don't believe us, come and test it, come to the conference table. Work out these agreements. We will tell you that if peace is assured, American military forces will depart from Southeast Asia."

CHURCH: I, Mr. Secretary, am in full accord with that.

RUSK: We will write that into it. In other words, there is no need for the other side to say, "Well they still have them in Korea, they have them in South Vietnam. Let them come and test so far as Southeast Asia is concerned."

Now the other question on what might happen ten

years from now: a great deal depends upon Peking's attitude toward peace and toward the right of smaller nations to live next door to them without being molested, and what use Peking might expect to make of the power which they may at that time have. . . .

CHURCH: Because in that connection it was stressed this morning that Peking is presently regarded even by some Communist governments as the principal threat to world peace because it has not embraced the doctrine of coexistence. . . . I think you emphasized that.

RUSK: Yes, sir, that is correct.

CHURCH: That raised in my mind some questions relative to Vietnam, because I think there is a tendency in our discussion of Vietnam to intermingle China and North Vietnam together, and interchange them as though there were no real distinction. Do you feel that what we face in Vietnam in a case of Chinese aggression, or is it a case of North Vietnamese aggression? Is there a distinction between the two, and does it matter?

RUSK: The instrument of aggression, that is the active agency of the aggression, is Hanoi. The doctrine which is used to support this aggression is from Peking, and there is indication that Peking even more than Hanoi has blocked the path toward a conference table.

CHURCH: Do you regard Ho Chi Minh then as the mere agent of Mao Tse-tung?

RUSK: Not entirely, not entirely. I think there are elements of freedom of action, and we would hope that a situation could be found in which he could exercise that freedom of action and come to the conference table even though Peking might object. . . .

SENATOR SYMINGTON: Now, there is a great deal of criticism of your policies and the present policies of the Administration by a certain group who, in my opinion, are predominantly interested in the problems of Europe, and they talk a good deal about spheres of influence. In the

world today, where you can go around it in eighty minutes—and especially considering missiles launched from
submarines, either surface or Polaris, nearly every town
in the world will have a warning of at best under ten
minutes—do you think that spheres of influence have
gotten to a point now where any particular part of the
world is a great deal more important than any other
particular part when it comes to facing up to aggression? . . .

RUSK: There is the general question of spheres of influence, and the other is of whether some areas are more
important than others. I do believe that those who say
that Southeast Asia or Korea are in a natural sphere of
influence of Peiping have an obligation to develop that
in some detail as a concept for the organization for the
political structure of the world. They should determine,
they should advise us who, in their judgment, are supposed to be these master races. Who are the great powers
who are supposed to have these dominant spheres of influence. How many of them are there? The United States,
Peiping, Soviet Union, anybody else? If so, we ought to
identify who these people are.

They ought to make clear what they have in mind,
then, is that everybody else is subject to such a sphere of
influence, not with the independence of Mexico and
Canada, our own nearest neighbors, but somehow subject to the domination of these nearby great powers.
Then they ought to address themselves to the further
question as to what happens if these identified great
powers, three, four, five, whoever they are, then engage
in a struggle among themselves for spheres of influence.
There is where the great danger lies. . . .

It seems to me when we were thinking long and hard
about these questions at the end of World War Two, we
did in fact come up with the wisest answer, and that is
large and small nations have a right to live without being
molested by their neighbors, and that a small nation has

a right to live in peace and without domination by somebody else if—than if it is within the reach of some great
power. So I must say, I am very much concerned about
substituting the idea of spheres of influence among a few
great powers for the structure of international life laid
out in the United Nations Charter.

Now, on the matter of whether some areas are more
important than others. It is true that on some basic cri-
teria of strategic position or industrial power or the qualities of population and so forth, in terms of education, that
there are certain areas that are of the most vital importance. Western Europe, for example, the great Japanese industrial structure, are of the greatest possible importance from the point of view of the United States. But
even those areas, Senator, can only be secure if the
commitment of the United States is considered to be
valid. Therefore, when we turn ourselves to the question,
can we afford to be negligent about our pledge in this
area, because we do not think that area is very important,
and I happen to think Southeast Asia is very important,
but if we are negligent about that, this bounces back into
an undermining of the validity of our pledges to those
areas which are of transcendent importance, and so I am
fearful if these solemn alliances, which we have undertaken, are not supported, that we would be faced with
a situation where no one would be sure about any of
our alliances.

How could we persuade somebody else, "Now we were
not very strong over there, but don't worry, we will be
all right if you get in trouble"—how are we going to persuade them to rely upon that, and more particularly, how
are we going to persuade the Communist capitals that
although we might have appeared not to have meant business here, we will in fact mean business over there? That
is very dangerous business. That is very dangerous business. So I would think that we need to think about the
structure of the peace for the support of which we went

into these alliances, and to consider the effect upon the possibility of peace if it should prove that our commitments are not reliable. . . .

FULBRIGHT: . . . This morning Senator Carlson raised the question about the failure of SEATO allies to support us. It prompted me to make a few observations of my own. I think this question of failure to support of the SEATO, to furnish men, and I think the figures show about fifteen hundred, primarily consisting of Australians, and about a hundred or a hundred and fifty New Zealanders, and then the others are extremely small as he mentioned. We have none, as I understand it, from Pakistan, from the Philippines, from Thailand . . . and the U.K. and France. The U.K., I believe, is seventeen or something, a very small amount. From India, Indonesia and Japan, which are the nearest major countries, there are none. It seems to me that this is explained by their not sharing your view as to the nature of this war, which, as I understand it, and you feel, is a clear case of international Communist aggression. I think they feel rather that it is a civil war in which outside parties have become involved. I can see no other logical reason why these people, who on the one hand are members of SEATO and on the other hand are nearby, that they would be subject to attack much more quickly I would think, they are more exposed than we are, if this was truly an example of international Communist aggression.

In short, I do not think that they believe that their security is at stake or that the SEATO Treaty requires their participation. We have discussed that at length as to whether it requires it or simply entitles us to it. I don't wish to pursue that aspect of it. But even if they do feel that their security is at stake as in the case of New Zealand and Australia, I think they do, even in that case, they send only token forces. And I suppose in this case they feel that the United States will carry the whole load, and that our men will do the dying and that we will pay the bill. Otherwise, I don't know why they don't send more than a token force.

Now, in the case of Europe and NATO, we did have and we do have collective security in which all members have shared, and when you said several times just a moment ago, How do we organize peace?, I thought that as a general proposition at least that we should use the United Nations, or as we like to refer to it as collective security insofar as possible, and that our policy generally was not to arrogate to ourselves the role of policeman. I think this makes a great difference, too. . . .

[Senator Morse] particularly for a very long time has insisted upon this approach. If one reviews the development, of this war, it clearly began in my opinion as a war of liberation from French colonial rule. That goes back to the time we mentioned this morning, by indigenous Vietnamese nationalists, who, most unfortunately, from our point of view, were led by Communists, and especially by Ho Chi Minh. These nationalists, Communists were twice betrayed, once by the French in '46 after they thought they had made an agreement, and later in '56 by President Diem with the support of the Americans.

Now, after 1956, the struggle then became a civil war between the Diem government and the Viet Cong, who were the nationalist Communists remaining in South Vietnam and who believed they were cheated by the Diem government in 1956. I think this is important and does explain the apathy, if I may use that word, or the indifference, of these friends and allies, that is allies under treaties and friends in other respects. The U.S. participation and the North Vietnam participation was slight until 1960, except for large amounts of money to Diem by the United States. I believe that is fair statement of your own testimony.

Now, after 1960, the character of the war changed, with increased participation by the North Vietnamese and by the United States, and apparently each time one has increased, the other has responded by a similar increase, to where we are now in very large numbers on both sides. In short, I think it is an oversimplification merely to say that this is a clear-cut aggression by North Vietnam Communists against a free independent nation, a neighbor. If that were so, I believe many of these people I have mentioned would be participating. I can see no reason why they won't. It is this point that I believe is responsible primarily if not entirely for the lack of support we have among our friends and also I may say for a good deal of the concern in this Committee.

As to our efforts to negotiate, the real trouble, it seems to me, is uncertainty as to our terms for peace, not merely the procedure for negotiation. We have a lot of talk very involved and complicated about four points and about fourteen points and about the significance of the third point and where they will meet and who will be there. But I do not recall . . . that our government has ever made it crystal clear that we will accept an election supervised by an appropriate international body, and that we will accept the results of that election, regardless of how it turns out.

It is also not clear at all that we are willing to allow any participation of the National Liberation Front either in a provisional government at any time, and, therefore, there is no alternative for them but surrender or annihilation.

With such a prospect, there can be nothing to negotiate about, if this is true, and it seems to me that that is one of the reasons that you keep saying they cannot, they will not, negotiate unless we assume utterly without reason and have no desire even to live, because in my opinion there is no question but that we can kill them all if we wish to put the people over there. There must be some reason that explains this attitude.

There is the further point about our intention regarding leaving at any time. You have repeated time and again that we are ready to leave. But I think few people in Vietnam, and I believe in other places, can quite understand why we are building such extensive, elaborate, and extremely costly, and very large permanent-type bases, harbors, airfields, military housing, and so on, if we have any intention of leaving in the foreseeable future. In short, I don't think they believe us when we say we will get out. As has already been stated here, we haven't gotten out of Korea and the Dominican Republic, and, of course, I don't mean these are analogous in any way, but we do happen to have more troops spread around the world in bases than any other country today.

Finally, in spite of this statement, the policy seems to be unconditional surrender of the National Liberation Front, or to put it in another way, that this not a limited war, that we intend to pursue it to victory even though that may result in bringing in the Chinese, and possibly even the Russians, which would force World War Three.

Frankly, Mr. Secretary, we are very much more deeply involved in Vietnam, far more than I ever imagined possible, and we are worried—I am very worried about the future commitments, as for example in Thailand, without full discussion and consultation, and I hope approval by this Congress.

I have already stated that I regret that I did not discharge what in my opinion I now believe to have been my duty, to have full discussion of the 1964 resolution. I think I made a mistake, at least as one Senator and Chairman of this Committee, in not accepting the amendment offered on the floor by Mr. Nelson, and all of that has just been put in the record by [Senator Gore]. But I hope that any future commitments that might bring this country into a war will not be made by unilateral declarations or agreements between ministers, but should be made by treaties submitted to the Senate. This apprehension on my part has been greatly increased by unilateral intervention in the Dominican Republic only last year, and in my opinion a clear violation of our solemn treaty obligations in that instance.

So, all of this—I have tried to sum up here why I think there is this sort of uncompromising attitude on the part of people who I assume are capable of reason, that is our enemies, and also doubts in this Committee. . . .

I am frank to say it puzzles me when I hear you present it, why do not people be more reasonable, more rational under these circumstances. There must be some explanation, unless we just assume that the world has gone completely mad. . . .

RUSK: Mr. Chairman, I wonder if I might ask you to amplify your statement in one respect. What do you want Hanoi to do in this circumstances?

FULBRIGHT: What I want them to do, both Hanoi and the Viet Cong, is to come to a conference with you and the Russians and the Chinese, everyone who has a legitimate interest, roughly the same people who participated either in Geneva or Laos—I do not care whether it is the Laotian or the Geneva Conference. They are the people with the primary . . . historical reasons or geographical reasons—and to have a conference. I do not think you can have a conference out of thin air, unless you, someone representing this government, go to the parties who were involved and give them some assurance that we mean what we say in public. I am not trying to say that you are trying to deceive anybody, but our actions, which I know you do not control, in my view are not consistent with our words, and I do not blame you for that. You do not build the bases. You do not control the military activities and many other things. You make the best case you can, and very ably made. But I think there is great doubt on the part of certainly these other people. I have no other way to explain why such people as the Japanese, the Indians—I do not wish to repeat what I have said—they will not come in and sacrifice their men in this struggle. Therefore, I do not believe they accept your thesis. . . . That is why I want to go to a conference.

Now I think you would have to assure them as to what

kind of a settlement you will accept. I get the impression, not only from your statement as much as General Taylor's, that we are in an unlimited war, and the only kind of settlement is unconditional surrender. Therefore, there is nothing to negotiate about. . . . But you deny this and I think so did . . . [Secretary McNamara].

RUSK: But unconditional surrender of what?

FULBRIGHT: That they give up and they come to the conference at your mercy and we have total victory. I see no occasion of any disposition to compromise. Now we are the strongest nation in the world. We can probably impose our will. I am saying that this is not wise in the long run even though we have the power. I know we have the power. I think I know it, if I believe, and I do believe you and the Secretary of Defense. But I think this is not the lasting way to do it. This is the way great empires have done it in the past, and it has usually not been very lasting. It has not brought about a stable peace.

I am just saying that I think a compromise, in which, as I stated here, and I have stated it before, you are willing and you assure them in some way that is persuasive to them this time, because once before we did not go through with it, that if an election is held in Vietnam, that we will abide by it, regardless of the outcome. And I do not think that has ever been said in any convincing way by this Administration, and I do not know whether you are prepared to say it.

RUSK: The only convincing way in which you could say that to the other side apparently is to let them have the government to start with that would conduct the elections.

FULBRIGHT: I do not believe that is the only way at all.

RUSK: I am saying what they themselves are saying.

FULBRIGHT: Well, they have not said it to me or in any way that I know of. This is our disadvantage. They may have said this to you. It has not been my impression that they have said, "You have got to turn it over to us and therefore we are going to run it completely without any

interference at all"; or as you say, I have never had the
impression that they require of you that we get out and
turn it over to them without any election or anything to
do about it. It is not clear to me, and I do not think that
there is any good evidence to that effect.

RUSK: Senator, do you have any doubts about the good
faith and the credibility of the other side here in this
situation? . . .

FULBRIGHT: I have no doubts that they are a very cruel,
ruthless, and mean people, as has been expressed here
often. They have engaged in all kinds of terrorism. What
they say in public is very often, and I think generally,
propaganda designed for public consumption. I do not
know what they say in private. We have had these insinu-
ations or even statements that you others have been approached through U Thant and so on. There has been
great mystery about most of these. I am not aware of what
has gone on in the orthodox diplomatic circles. What is
said on these great expeditions of sending people all over
the world and making statements that we are for peace I
do not think are relevant to what I am trying to get at.
To say, We like peace, we are peace-loving people, does
not seem to me to mean much. It is what you say privately
to the people concerned, and how persuasive you are as
to what you are willing to agree to in case you had a negotiation that I am not aware of. . . .

RUSK: Mr. Chairman, on the matter of persuading the
other side, back in 1961 Mr. Khrushchev and Mr. Kennedy
agreed that everybody ought to leave Laos alone, get their
forces out, let these people look after their own affairs. We
went to the Laotian Conference in Geneva. Ambassador
Harriman first, and then I came over for the closing stages.
I was there at the opening. Those were long and complicated negotiations. We accepted the Communist nominee
to be Prime Minister of Laos, the present Prime Minister,
Souvanna Phouma. When the agreements were signed we
took our military people out of Laos. They left several
thousand, Hanoi did, several thousand of their armed

forces in Laos specifically contrary to the agreement. Not for a day did they stop using Laos as a route of infiltration from North Vietnam into South Vietnam, specifically contrary to agreement, and they used a veto to paralyze the ability of the International Control Commission to go anywhere in Laos to look at the possibilities of infringements. . . .

FULBRIGHT: Mr. Secretary, I believe all that. Are you not still glad that you had that, even with all its defects, rather than a world war, or even a major war in that area, with all the difficulties you have cited? . . . You settled it in a way that was unsatisfactory, but nevertheless, it is better than—

RUSK: No, but it is not settled, Mr. Chairman. . . .

FULBRIGHT: It is not settled, but it is not escalating into a war of major proportions.

RUSK: Well, the major North Vietnamese effort is channeling south into South Vietnam. We have no present reason to believe that they have accepted the basic agreement in 1962 as a permanent structure of Laos. . . . They are not permitting the government to function on that basis. They are not permitting the ICC to visit around the country. They are putting more people into Laos.

FULBRIGHT: Do you not think it is influenced to a great extent by the Vietnamese thing?

RUSK: Well, I have no doubt from the point of view of the other side they violated the Laotian agreement because it was convenient to them in order to pursue their enterprise against South Vietnam, but that is no defense. . . . There was no provision in the Laos accord, though of course you can go ahead and use this if you really are going after South Vietnam, just use the infiltration. They were supposed to stop it. . . . For this reason this was supposed to be one of the significant steps towards peace in Southeast Asia. The Vietnam problem would be a quite different problem if Laos were not open to this infiltration from North Vietnam to South Vietnam.

Now we tested the matter of good faith on both sides

in Southeast Asia there. I must say I am not at all—well, let me say this, Mr. Chairman: I suppose that the other side may have some doubts, if they wish to entertain them, that we will draw our troops out of there. All they have got to do is to come and test it. . . .

FULBRIGHT: You cannot test that. I mean if you do not do it, how do you test it?

RUSK: Because arrangements can be made under which our troops will come out, arrangements at the table, the nature of the settlement, the provisions for the withdrawal of forces on both sides. The arrangements can be made. There is no need for us to be obscure about that point. I would be a little disturbed if, say, members of this Committee were to express doubt about our intentions in that respect merely because we are building some facilities there to take care of the forces that we have there in South Vietnam. We have built and abandoned many facilities in the course of the last thirty years, forty years, in many places. This has nothing to do with good faith. This is a matter of meeting our present military requirements which we will be prepared to abandon if the other side makes peace. These things can be easily tested.

I find it hard to get the other side to come in with anything that would show their interest in peace or their good faith with respect to the 1954 and 1962 agreements. And so I find it difficult to be—for people to press saying, "Oh, but you have not convinced them. You have got to give them something else." We have given them practically everything but South Vietnam in terms of trying to find a basis for peace in Southeast Asia. Now, I cannot believe that we are expected to give them South Vietnam. In terms of elections, sure. . . .

GORE: What do you mean by that?

RUSK: Elections as you and I would mean them.

GORE: Are you saying now if a free election was held, the United States Government would stand by it?

RUSK: Yes.

GORE: Accept it?

RUSK: Yes.

GORE: That is a great step.

RUSK: But, Senator, it is a step we took a year ago. That is not a new step. . . .

MORSE: We did not say it in [1956]. . . . In '56 the problem there was elections throughout Vietnam on the issue of unification. . . . The situation developed in such a way that it was quite clear that North Vietnam was not going to have free elections. They will not have them today. . . . The other side has said North Vietnam is a member of the socialist world, "And you can forget it. We are not going to be talking about North Vietnam. What we are going to be talking about is South Vietnam."

Now, they made it very clear that there are going to be no free elections up there, so that they with some seventeen million people up there, with seventeen million votes in their pockets, then wanting some elections in the South so that the numbers would clearly mean that they then would take over South Vietnam through that process. Now, there were violations of various sorts in those days, including the terrorists that were left behind to make those elections more difficult, and to insure their effect in the South. But what we are saying, Senator, is that if that is the issue, let us have the elections. . . . Let the South Vietnamese decide.

Now, we have not qualified that, Mr. Chairman. What I have said is that I do not myself believe that the South Vietnamese people in genuinely free elections would be the first people in history voluntarily to elect a Communist regime to power. I have said that, and therefore that is in turn interpreted by some as, "Oh well, then you do not mean elections." Well, of course we mean elections, but let the South Vietnamese decide these questions for themselves.

FULBRIGHT: I do not wish to impose on the time, but has it not been quite clear that you have coupled this with the idea that no matter what happens, there is no possibility of any participation by the National Liberation

Front, and therefore they have no alternative but to fight on? Has that not been pretty clear from what you have said and others in the Administration have said?

RUSK: Well, Senator, it has not been said in those terms, but they do have an alternative.

FULBRIGHT: To give up.

RUSK: They do have an alternative. They are the front of Hanoi. They do have an alternative of quitting, stopping this effort of being an agent of Hanoi for the purpose of receiving men and arms from the North for the purpose of taking over South Vietnam.

FULBRIGHT: That particular question is disputed by some people who know much more about it than I do, that South Vietnam, while they are allies with them and supported by them, that they have an identity of their own. They have representatives abroad of their own. They treat with people—that is, they have representatives in various countries, not this one. . . .

I have my doubts, if I may say, about our knowledge generally of this whole area, as well as China and South Vietnam, as to what the actual facts are, the actual relations between the National Liberation Front and the people. I do not really know. I doubt that anybody knows very well except the people within their own organization. But all I am really trying to say is I do not think that this dispute here is worthy of an escalation that would result in a confrontation with China in a world war. I do not believe that there is much evidence that this is the kind of a test that if we should make a compromise, that then all the world will collapse because we have been defeated. This country is much too strong, in my opinion, that it would suffer any great setback. We are much stronger than Russia was when she withdrew from Cuba. Within a week, maybe, people said she had had a rebuff and within a month everyone was complimenting them for having contributed to the maintenance of peace. We are certainly strong enough and decent enough and good enough in every respect to withstand any kind of a compromise that is at all reasonable.

RUSK: Yes. I do not understand though, Mr. Chairman, just what the substance of the compromise would be. . . . I mean some of the things you said suggested that we should abandon the effort in South Vietnam.

FULBRIGHT: No. I am suggesting that we should not abandon it, but we should have a conference, and I do not think you will get it until you propose reasonable terms that would allow at least the Vietnamese, even the Liberation Front, to have an opportunity to participate in an election. After all, Vietnam is their country. It is not our country. We do not even have the right that the French did. We have no historical right. We are obviously intruders, from their point of view. We represent the old Western imperialism in their eyes. I am not questioning your motives. I think our motives are very good, as has been testified on numerous occasions. But I still think from their point of view it is their country, and however bad the people have acted, other countries have had civil wars, we had one. In my part of the country we resented it for a long time. So did yours. You can remember the feelings that were there. These are very unfortunate controversies. But what bothers me, and I know a number here, that this is in one sense a relatively minor matter. In another sense it seems to be the trigger that may result in a world war, and I do not want that to happen, and that is what we are really concerned with.

RUSK: And none of us want it to happen, Mr. Chairman, but when you say this is their country—

FULBRIGHT: It is their country, with all its difficulties, even if they want to be Communists. . . . Just like the Yugoslavs. I do not know why we should object to it.

RUSK: We are making a distinction though, that is that South Vietnam is not Hanoi's country.

FULBRIGHT: It is not our country. It used to be one country.

RUSK: But there was a settlement, Mr. Chairman, on the basis of the 17th Parallel. There were some differences about various aspects of that.

FULBRIGHT: What kind of settlement was it? I think it would be fine if you would make it very precise. Did it divide it into two separate nations?

RUSK: It did not establish it as two separate nations, but it provided some procedures by which this could occur if that is what the people wanted. And then it worked out so that North Vietnam was not interested at all in holding anything like genuinely free elections. It was perfectly clear that North Vietnam was marking time for the time when it could seize South Vietnam regardless of the views of the South Vietnamese.

FULBRIGHT: I have no doubt they expected to win that election. They thought they had won the war at Dienbienphu, didn't they?

RUSK: I suppose they did.

FULBRIGHT: And didn't the Viet Minh occupy a great deal of South Vietnam, which is now South Vietnam, and withdrew in response to that settlement, cease-fire?

RUSK: They withdrew in part. . . . They left substantial numbers behind.

FULBRIGHT: Many South Vietnamese thought they had been cheated by the Geneva Accord, didn't they?

RUSK: You mean the North Vietnamese?

FULBRIGHT: The South Vietnamese did, too. They thought they had been sold out by the North because they did have to withdraw, but they were persuaded by the Russians and I think ourselves and the French that we had better have a cease-fire, this was leading to a terrible situation so they agreed to a cease-fire anyway. Isn't that about true?

RUSK: I think the people in Hanoi undoubtedly felt that they had been let down by the agreements in 1964, and they immediately rolled up their sleeves to go after it again.

FULBRIGHT: And the only reason they accepted it, the

best that I can read, is that they thought this would be an election and undoubtedly they thought they were going to win, and General Eisenhower, I think, thought they would, too. He indicated that in his book.

RUSK: He indicated that in terms of the period of the fighting, not in terms of the period of the—

FULBRIGHT: Well, he referred about it.

RUSK: Yes.

FULBRIGHT: One of our protégés, of course, throughout Bao Dai, shortly thereafter. It was really the French's responsibility to guarantee the elections, wasn't it? They signed the cease-fire. They are the only two. The only people who signed the Geneva Agreement were the Viet Minh and the French.

RUSK: That point was a little confusing because the French were not in a position to hold elections.

FULBRIGHT: They retired.

RUSK: The responsibility was turned over to the South Vietnamese and the South Vietnamese government did not sign the agreement.

FULBRIGHT: No. There wasn't any South Vietnamese government at that time. That was constituted subsequently. It was only the Viet Minh who were the Communist national—

RUSK: The French military command signed the agreement with the Viet Minh.

FULBRIGHT: That is right. There were only two signatures and that was the cease-fire. These other so-called declarations, nobody signed them. They just accepted them . . . as a kind of a procedure?

RUSK: That is right.

FULBRIGHT: The French responsibility was to see that it was carried out.

MORSE: It was voted by voice vote.

FULBRIGHT: They didn't sign that?

MORSE: They voted.

FULBRIGHT: But the French retired and gave up their responsibility to hold the election. We didn't sign it. I will grant it wasn't ours. Our participation was by proxy through Diem. I apologize. I don't wish to take all the time. . . .

RUSK: Mr. Chairman, I would comment that that is not or need not be the obstacle today, because there can be elections in which the South Vietnamese people can make their own decisions about these matters. But the Liberation Front or at least Ho Chi Minh in his message to the heads of government, particularly to President Radhakrishnan, recently says, "If we really want a peaceful settlement, we must accept the four-point stand of the North Vietnamese government and prove this by actual deeds. We must end unconditionally and for good all bombing raids and other acts against the DRV," with no reference whatever to any of the acts of war that they are committing and that, "We must recognize the Liberation Front as the sole genuine representative of the people of South Vietnam and engage in negotiations with it."

FULBRIGHT: Mr. Secretary I know they have said that. We say things. You, this morning, I think I gathered that our statements at Honolulu, part of that was sort of for public consumption and try to bolster their morale. This is what I call a form of propaganda. I think you can find both sides have said things that are designed to help morale. I don't think they are final at all. The National Liberation Front itself has said on numerous times they call for free elections. Now, I don't think this can be settled in public declarations by one propaganda agency or another. I am suggesting that it has been, it has to be done in the old-fashioned way of going to these people privately and trying to assure them if you can't make them believe that we would agree to the kind of program that I mentioned of genuine free elections.

I think it would be a major undertaking to convince them that we would live up to that, in view of their past experience, not just because of ourselves and particularly the French, and in 1956. I am not saying you or this country is responsible for all that. I don't think we are.

But there have been some very, very difficult historical facts here that are hard to overcome and make people believe and have any confidence in a conference. But all I am pleading with you for and have been very awkwardly, I think, is, this isn't the kind of conflict that warrants a vast escalation, a vast expenditure of money and many thousands of deaths. I think it is not that kind of a vital interest, as I can cite many other instances. And I also think that the great countries, especially this country, is quite strong enough to engage in a compromise without losing its standing in the world, without losing its prestige as a great nation. On the contrary, I think it would be one of the greatest victories for us in our prestige if we could be ingenious enough and magnanimous enough to bring about some kind of a settlement of this particular struggle. . . . That is all I am trying to get at. I don't want you to give up and curtail or do anything disgraceful.

RUSK: Mr. Chairman, we wouldn't have much of a debate between us on the question of compromising and a settlement, but we can't get anybody into the discussions for the purpose of talking about it.

FULBRIGHT: I think there is something wrong with our approach, because, let's assume that these people are utter idiots. There must be something wrong with our diplomacy.

RUSK: Senator, is it just possible that there is something wrong with them?

FULBRIGHT: Yes, there is a lot wrong with them. They are very primative, difficult, poor people that have been fighting for twenty years and I don't understand myself why they can continue to fight, but they do.

RUSK: And they want to take over South Vietnam by force.

FULBRIGHT: It is said the Liberation Front would like to take it over by election. That is what they say.

RUSK: They are requiring us to accept the Liberation Front as the sole genuine representative of the people of

South Vietnam. Now, that is what we have heard privately. We are not hearing a lot of things privately that you don't get publicly. . . .

SYMINGTON: . . . Do you believe that the fear of Red China reacting to some action that we took in protecting our interests under these treaties and agreements [with] South Vietnam should be decisive with respect to the decisions we make about our foreign policy around the world?

RUSK: No, sir, because if we do not meet those responsibilities, we shall find a Red China much more voracious and much more dangerous, if they should discover that this technique of aggression is successful.

SYMINGTON: Do you believe the President is doing everything that he can to obtain a just peace, but with honor?

RUSK: Everything that we can possibly think of, and he spends an enormous amount of time analyzing the situation and trying to find out whether there are others who might do more or whether we could do more in this direction, to probe for the possibilities of peace.

SYMINGTON: He is spending more time on this than anything else, in your opinion?

RUSK: I would think this is the overriding problem. There are many other matters around the world to which he has to give attention, but this is a matter which naturally engages his deepest interest in the maintenance of peace here, and so he spends a great deal of time on it.

SYMINGTON: I understand we have about forty treaties with other countries, and that we base the peace of the world upon these agreements. Is that right?

RUSK: These are the alliances that we have involving just over forty countries.

SYMINGTON: Perhaps the person high in government best able to comment on this . . . told me that if we recognize the National Liberation Front, that any Saigon government would promptly fall, and in addition to that, he said in his opinion within a relatively short time there would be riots in West Berlin. Would you comment on that?

RUSK: I think that is possible. I do very much have the impression that if we were to recognize the Liberation Front as the sole representative of the South Vietnamese people, and try to impose them on the South Vietnamese people in the way that the Front wants us to, that we would have to turn our soldiers around in order to impose them on the South Vietnamese people, because I am absolutely convinced that the South Vietnamese people don't want any part of them, and that if we have any respect at all for what these people in South Vietnam want, we cannot recognize the Viet Cong as their spokesman. . . .

SYMINGTON: . . . I have one more question, if I may. That is, from what I gather in these hearings, nearly everybody thinks you are doing good but not doing good enough. What else is it that you can do? I am sure you have thought of everything that you could do and I am sure you want to see a peace, but I am sure you want to see a peace without sacrificing the honor of the United States because of what it entails based on what you have said in the last three or four minutes. What else is there you can do in this really now-desperate effort subject to the heavy criticism that you are getting from the Congress and from the Senate? What else can you do in order to get us a peace, a viable peace and a peace with a reasonable amount of honor in it so that we don't go around with our heads down?

RUSK: Senator, I do not believe that there are procedures or forums or diplomatic channels that are available or that could be created that have not been used. I do not think that we are in a situation where a procedural invention is going to deal with the situation. I think that while we keep all these channels open, and we keep the discussions going among governments and across the curtains with governments in the Communist world, that we have got to meet the central Four Points on which Hanoi seems to have been living. First, their hope for military victory in the South. It must be made clear that they are not going to get that. Secondly, that there will be an internal collapse in the South. I do not believe they are going to get that, and their hopes for that must be disappointed, and I think those are being steadily disappointed.

SYMINGTON: Unless we run out on the South Vietnamese?

RUSK: That is right. Third, that international opinion might build up to force us to change our commitments. That is not going to happen, but Hanoi must be persuaded. And fourth, that internal divisions in this country might cause us to change our commitment, and they must be persuaded that that is not going to happen. Then I think they will be ready to realize that they are off on a futile track, and that it will be well then for them to start exploring the possibilities of peace on a more serious basis. . . .

PELL: Mr. Secretary, having sat here now for four days in these hearings, [and having heard] two witnesses with somewhat different views than yours—you and General Taylor presenting the Administration's view—I am struck by the fact, when you dig into what each of you have said, the points of similarity are much stronger than the points of difference. It seemed to me that there is a great area of agreement, which is that we must keep the military presence there as long as is necessary. The question really is . . . whether we should increase that presence or not, and I am wondering if you would bear with me that we have to keep our eventual objective in mind. The only leader in the world today that I know of who seems to have a grand design is President de Gaulle. He has his design; we do not have to agree with it, but I think he has a picture of the kind of globe he would like to see. I am wondering if we could visualize our globe that we would like to see, would it not basically be a world where nuclear weapons are under national control; and also, do we not accept the fact that with the passage of time the militancy, the drive, and the virulence of Communism, which is an utterly unnatural and cruel and impossible system, will wear itself out? What we need, looking for the long goal, is the passage of time without plunging into a general war. Would that be a correct statement?

RUSK: I think we need the passage of time. I think this country does have some great designs of its own in terms of the general structure of the world community. I think you would be one of the best witnesses to describe the world community that we saw in the United Nations Charter at the end of World War Two, because those general propositions there represent a pretty good statement of the long-term policies of the American people toward the rest of the world. So I think we have some good ideas about the structure of the world community.

President Johnson has been trying to support that structure in every way possible in the economic and social, educational, health field as well as in these security matters that are so troublesome. Senator, the question of time is important. We do not know, for example, what the next generation of Chinese leaders will look like. We have some impressions of, shall we say, the second generation of leaders in the Soviet Union. But we do not have much of an impression of the next group in Peiping. But . . . we cannot buy time at the expense of a successful aggression against smaller countries. And this is the problem. We need to stabilize that postwar settlement. We need to stabilize that international community as sketched out in the UN Charter, and then let time try to heal some of the memories, and let time give us a chance to deal with some of the specific questions that need solution.

In our own dealings with Peiping—we have had a hundred and twenty-eight discussions with them now in the last ten years—everything turns on Formosa. We try to talk about disarmament, we try to talk about Southeast

Asia, we try to talk about the exchange of newsmen or the exchange of doctors. They always keep coming back to the point, "Well, are you going to surrender Formosa?" because they say that if we do not do that there is nothing to talk about. Well, maybe time will get over that. As you know, the Eisenhower Administration attempted to get agreements from Peiping to renounce force in the Formosa Straits. Well, they have never been willing to do that.

So, gentlemen, time may help, but we cannot let time get away from us by having it used by the other side to develop a momentum and an appetite and a danger that will be increasingly difficult to bring under control.

PELL: I guess the differences between some of us as I see our role and my role is that of trying to hold the thing down and work for time. I think there are others, yourself and others, who would believe that we could achieve these goals perhaps more quickly. This is what has come through in these four days of hearings.

RUSK: Well, Senator, let me say that as far as South Vietnam is concerned, the United States has not been rushing into this matter in order to achieve a quick solution regardless of cost. The time factors and the rate of escalation have been determined really by the action of the other side.

PELL: I realize that, but the thing that concerns me and concerns the people in my own state is the thought that, as Senator Russell pointed out, or Senator Stennis, the present planning is for an expansion in the order of another two hundred thousand by the end of this calendar year, and a further commitment of the same number next year. In my own view, if that could be held down to last over a five-year period, if necessary, we would be better off. I gather your view is we ought to move.

RUSK: I think the planning has to be on the basis of leaving to the Commander-in-Chief, as he consults with others who are constitutionally responsible, such as the Congress and the congressional leadership, to give him the chance to have choices when the necessity for choices occur. Now, if we did not have those bases, for example, in process of construction, and it became necessary some time later to use them, you couldn't do it if they were not there. But, on the other hand, if Hanoi were to start moving toward peace, by the first of March, then that would turn the situation around.

In other words, we are not on track here where everything is frozen on both sides. We don't know what the other side is going to do in this situation. We do know that they must face the fact that they are not going to have a military success in the South, and we hope that will mean then that they will start moving toward peace, and we move down these commitments, and that is where de-escalation can come.

But I do believe, Senator Pell, that there is more agreement than some of the conversations these past few weeks would indicate, particularly when one takes into consideration the necessity for choosing among real alternatives. Now, there is the major alternative of abandoning South Vietnam. There seems to be very little interest and support in that point of view. There is another major alternative of rushing into a general war or a larger war, get it over with as quickly as possible, regardless of cost, without a sense of the prudence and care that one must use in these matters in the modern world. I think that there is relatively little to support generally from that point of view.

Now, that leaves the center position. That leaves the position of firmness coupled with prudence and some care in the way this matter is handled. That has about it certain dissatisfactions. It has about it certain concerns, because we can't know for certain exactly what the future will hold. But I think that it is always useful in thinking of these matters to try to put the question to oneself whether a private citizen or official, in terms of what would I do about this if I were in fact the President of the United States, to try to reach the way toward the point of view which is nailed with responsibility rather than simply discuss it—and I am not suggesting we have been doing that—simply discuss it in terms of opinion or in terms of not having to live with the results, because it is the President who must guide us in choosing among the real alternatives.

I think, myself, without any doubt that the country understands that he has approached this matter with the greatest solemnity, that he has tried to act with the firmness necessary to organize the peace, but to act also with the prudence which is necessary to prevent events from moving out of control, and that as we move ahead here, every chance to bring this to a peaceful settlement will be explored. But that unless we make it clear to the other side that they will not succeed, there is no avenue to a peaceful settlement that has any chance of producing the peace that we are after. . . .

VINTAGE POLITICAL SCIENCE
AND SOCIAL CRITICISM

VINTAGE HISTORY—AMERICAN

VINTAGE HISTORY EUROPEAN

VINTAGE RUSSIAN LIBRARY

VINTAGE FICTION, POETRY, AND PLAYS

VINTAGE WORKS OF SCIENCE
AND PSYCHOLOGY